THE
WORLD ATLAS OF
SKIING

THE
WORLD ATLAS OF
SKIING

Stephen Pooley

HAMLYN

ACKNOWLEDGMENTS

I would like to give special thanks to Rosemary Burns and her colleagues at the Ski Club of Great Britain and the Directors and staff of national, regional and local tourist offices.

The Publishers would like to thank the following contributors to the book:
Roger Bray, Minty Clinch, Linda Crammond, Felice Eyston, Peter Hardy, Elisabeth Hussey, Felicity Johnson, Stephen Lee, Pixie Maynard, Julia Snell, and Arnie Wilson.

The Publishers would like to thank the following artists who painted the trail maps: Nick Skelton, Kevin Dean, Richard Bonson, Jamie Andrews and Chris Forsey.

Published in 1990 by
The Hamlyn Publishing Group Limited
a division of The Octopus Publishing Group,
Michelin House, 81 Fulham Road, London SW3 6RB

ISBN 0 600 57062 2

Produced by Mandarin Offset
Printed in Hong Kong

Page 1 *Michaela Gerg of West Germany*

Page 3 *Ski acrobatics in the French Alps*

CONTENTS

INTRODUCTION   7

———————— EUROPE   9 ————————

———————— THE AMERICAS   127 ————————

———————— THE REST OF THE WORLD   181 ————————

———————— INDEX   190 ————————

INTRODUCTION

Aspen, Chamonix, St Moritz and Zermatt all have world-wide renown – they are perenially fashionable among good skiers and the jet set glitterati alike. Yet there are, quite literally, thousands of ski resorts around the world and choosing where to ski is difficult. Sure, the dedicated ski bum will spend the winter flitting between the great alpine centres in Europe and those of the rockies in North America but the recreational skier, who has just a couple of weeks skiing each winter finds the choice bewildering. *The World Atlas of Skiing* introduces you to the top resorts around the globe, whether you are looking for constant challenges on deep powder bowls, high-speed on-piste cruising where daily mileage is the order of the day, gentle meandering slopes for a family holiday, or just want to admire the skiing areas used by the professional skiiers on the World Cup circuit.

EUROPE

Whatever the claims of North America, the Alps remain at the heart of the downhill skiing. Estimates vary, but there are, quite literally, thousands of ski resorts in Europe. There are hundreds of tiny hamlets in Austria and Switzerland, boasting no more than a couple of T-bars, and there are the resorts favoured by the international jet-set: Gstaad, Davos, Klosters and St Moritz regularly feature as often in gossip columns as they do on the sports and travel pages of national newspapers, yet each should be visited by good skiers as they provide a lot more than the opportunity to share a chair-lift with stars of movie screens and sports arenas.

Recreational skiing in Europe was established by adventuring Edwardian gentlemen early in this century and their legacy has been the development of the sport into a world-wide pursuit – witness the cacophony of Swedish, Japanese, German, Italian and American voices on the early-morning cable cars at St Anton or Zermatt. They trek, pilgrim like, to Austria and Switzerland not just for some of the best skiing in the world but also for old-world alpine charm.

On the other hand, many skiiers prefer ultra-convenient centres such as Les Arcs and Tignes in France or the spectacular scenery and laid-back attitude of the locals in the Italian Dolomites. Don't forget the Scandanavian countries – Norway, in particular, is making big efforts to promote its excellent downhill skiing and to prove that it is more than Mecca to crosscountry enthusiasts. For the adventurous there is skiing in the USSR and, for the hardy. In Scotland. Whatever you want, there genuinely is something for everyone, non-skiers included, in Europe.

ISCHGL AND THE PAZNAUN VALLEY

Ischgl is the largest and liveliest of the four ski resorts in the Paznaun valley. Kappl and See are two tiny ski stations and Galtur, at the head of the valley, is a delightful little village, well worth a couple of days' exploration. Ischgl's skiing also connects with that of Samnaun, over the Swiss border, so that good skiers should take full advantage of the Silvretta lift pass which gives access to all five skiing areas.

The village was originally known as 'Yscla', the valley's first inhabitants having tramped over the Silvretta mountains from Swiss Engadine where the language was Romansh. Today, the locals speak the Tyrolean dialect tinged with an accent so thick that visitors from Landeck, down in the Inn valley, have difficulty in understanding them—it is completely beyond the Germans, who constitute the Paznaun valley's biggest market.

Ischgl is regarded as one of the smarter ski resorts in the Tyrol and is able to command relatively high prices in hotels and restaurants. That is not to say that visitors do not get value for money—service is of the highest order and visitors feel like honoured guests. The tourist office provides an excellent booklet, 'What, When, Where and How in Ischgl', printed in English every week giving details of special events, as well as regular activities, at the excellent sports hall plus entertainment scheduled at the three nightclubs. It also provides full details of every shop in the village. Ischgl remains one of the best places for an all-round winter holiday with plenty of non-ski and *après-ski* options, good restaurants and friendly bars and cafés, plus genuinely

The Paznaun Valley has some spectacular off-piste skiing, notably on Ischgl's Holltal and Vesil sections. High-alpine touring is popular in Galtur.

good skiing for all aspirations and abilities.

Skiing, of course, is the big draw in winter and Ischgl's investment in lifts has resulted in three gondolas rising from the centre of the village, two of them converging on the Idalp plateau (2311m/7582ft). This plateau is the hub of Ischgl's

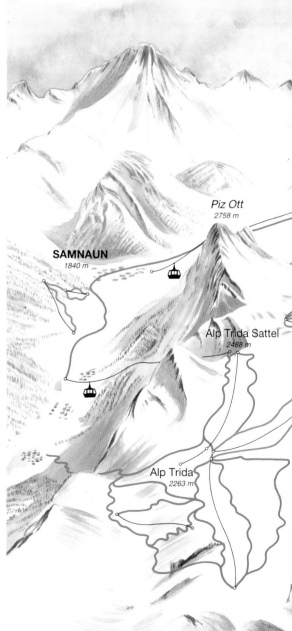

Piz Ott
2758 m

SAMNAUN
1840 m

Alp Trida Sattel
2488 m

Alp Trida
2263 m

skiing with lifts fanning in all directions. It is also the meeting place for the ski school so that beginners immediately feel the thrill of being high in the mountains. At the end of the day they can ride the gondola back to town and, as they progress, feel some real achievement by skiing all the way down to the valley on a choice of tree-lined trails. They should also take care as too many good skiers fly down these runs as if they were on a downhill course, with no regard for fellow skiers.

Expert skiers head immediately for the Palinkopf (2864m/9396ft), especially after a heavy snowfall, for wonderful off-piste skiing on the Holltal and Vesil areas. The lower sections run through woodlands to Taja Alp and Bodenalp, a little mountain hamlet where many skiers choose to stay to be sure of the best early-morning skiing. The runs down from the Pardatschgrat (2624m/8609ft) also provide good off-piste work while those on Idalp itself are long and undemanding, as is the run down from Idjoch to Alp Trida, over the Swiss border. Although the trail map shows all the runs on this section to be in the easy-to-medium category, there is good off-piste skiing below the Visnitzkopf and Alp Bella.

The cable-car from Samnaun deposits skiers at Alp Trida Sattel, where there is an excellent self-service restaurant, but to ski down to Samnaun itself it is necessary to take the long medium-grade run from Inneres Viderjoch or Palinkopf, at the far end of the lift system. There is a run down to Compatsch on the Swiss side, but the long walk to the Raveisch cable-car makes it an unattractive proposition. The village of Samnaun, due to its remote situation,

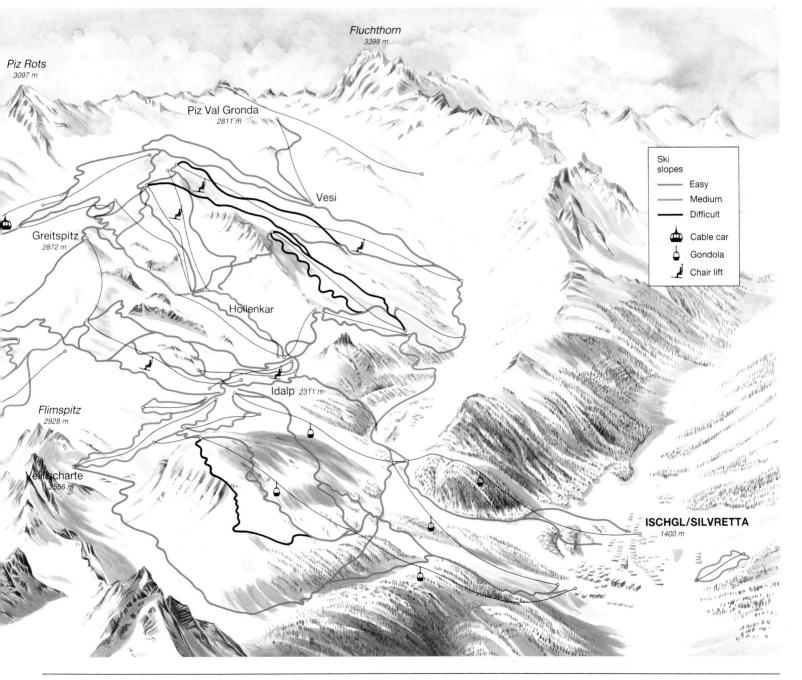

has enjoyed duty-free status for years—rather like Livigno in Italy—and is a popular destination for a change of scene and for shopping. Remember to take your passport and, if you wear a backpack, be prepared to be searched at the customs post on returning to the Austrian side.

Ischgl is well endowed with mountain restaurants and those around Paznauner Taya and Bodenalp are the most atmos-

pheric. They are not cheap, however, and are even more expensive on the Swiss side where, if you pay in Austrian schillings, be prepared for a poor exchange rate. The local bus service runs to Kappl and See, back down the Paznaun valley, and on to Galtur, tucked in below the Fluchthorn (3398m/11148ft). Even good skiers should visit Kappl and See, perhaps splitting a day between the two, as they are

charming little places and if the skiing is limited, both provide at least half-a-day's amusement.

Galtur is a very different proposition. It was Ernest Hemingway's mountain retreat for walking, climbing and writing. The locals say that Galtur isn't the end of the world, but that you can see it from there! It certainly is in a remote situation, with hardly a tree in sight, but the

Above: *Alp Trida forms a part of the border between Austria and Switzerland and is the dispersal point for skiers looking for steep powder bowls and beginners for gentle slopes close to hand.*

Left: *An excellent snow record ensures the Paznaun Valley's continuing popularity: The beauty of the mountains, charm of the villages and friendliness of the locals.*

villagers are extraordinarily friendly and hospitable. Each of them seems to have several jobs and it is quite usual to see someone from the tourist office spinning discs in a bar in the evening and to encounter your ski instructor serving drinks. For such a tiny place the hotels are excellent. There are two noisy late-night discos and the sports centre has an incredible variety of activities with swim-ming, tennis, squash, table tennis and skittles plus a bar and restaurant. The village priest delights in showing visitors the church and explaining that it has had to be rebuilt on several occasions over the years as a result of warfare with the Engadine Swiss — he is equally pleased to tell you that the local lads would cross the border and wreck the Swiss churches in retaliation!

Galtur is a long-established base for high alpine touring with a guide. Other than one lift serving a nursery area, most of the skiing is a little out of town at Wirl, served by a regular, free bus service and at the end of the day it is possible to ski alongside the road all the way back to the village. There is some good off-piste skiing but most of the marked runs are easy — Galtur takes pride in its ski school and has a good reputation for teaching children. Immediately after skiing, tea dances at the Hotel Wirlerhof are an institution and the rest of the evening is usually spent bar-hopping and dancing in an informal and relaxed atmosphere.

Ischgl's *après-ski* scene is more energetic with bars such as the Club Après, Christine and Taja being lively venues for quaffing sessions. Tyrolean evenings are held regularly at the Silvretta Centre, sleigh rides to Mathon are popular, and, in addition to several disco bars, there are three nightclubs with live bands. The Silvretta Centre also provides skittles, swimming, steam room, sauna and massage facilities while other non-ski and *après-ski* options include tobogganing at Kappl, cross-country skiing, visits to the lovely folk museum at Mathon and walking in the foothills, all the time marvelling at the beauty and grandeur of the Silvretta mountains.

SAALBACH-HINTERGLEMM

Chosen to host the 1991 World Championships, Saalbach and Hinterglemm are two separate villages which have gradually stretched out along the Glemm valley to meet each other. They form the centre of a 160km (100 mile) pisted circuit, skiable in either direction and known as the Ski Circus. In all, there are some 295km (185 miles) of marked trails plus another 72km (45 miles) at Leogang whose lifts connect with those of Saalbach-Hinterglemm via the Asitz peak (1914m/6280ft).

This is the most popular resort in Austria among Austrians. Guests hoping for a twee little alpine settlement will be disappointed, and those looking for an inexpensive, gentle winter holiday will be aghast, as Saalbach-Hinterglemm is both bustling and pricey. While it appeals to good skiers who want to take advantage of

its brilliant choice of marked runs and off-piste diversions, many well-heeled visitors simply come to parade their top-of-the-range ski wear outside ice bars and in mountain restaurants. But good skiers should not be deterred as the skiing range is enough for anyone in a two-week stay—they must simply be prepared to pay for the best. Yet there is a choice. In addition to some very smart hotels, complete with all the facilities anyone could ask for, there are plenty of modest guesthouses and, as well as elegant restaurants with fine wine lists, there are dozens of little cafés for a simple meal at more affordable prices.

Saalbach-Hinterglemm is also a good destination for mixed-ability groups as there are nursery slopes right by the centre of both villages and plenty of easy trails in the mountains aloft. Thanks to

Saalbach, like its neighbour Hinterglemm, has nursery slopes by the village centre. Saalbach really comes alive immediately after skiing.

the design of the lift system, it is easy to meet for lunch and for a gentle cruise home at the end of the day. There is a good selection of mountain huts and restaurants for a quick drink or lunch.

If you try to ski the vast circus at full tilt every day you will have no time to enjoy the beautiful views, notably across the Kitzbuheler Alps from above Hinterglemm. It is far better to select a different itinerary each day, leaving enough time to make a re-run of any trails which have been particularly interesting—this is easily facilitated by the 'Ski Circus Information A la Carte' booklet which is available, in English, from the Tourist Office

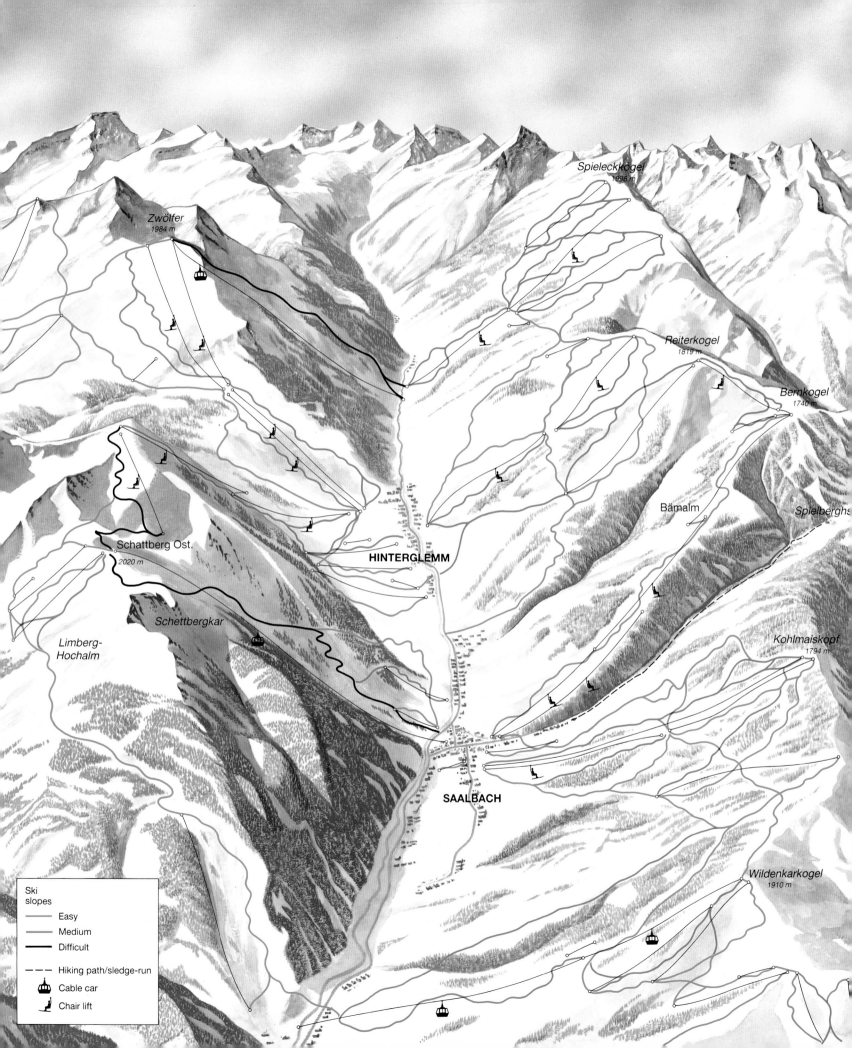

Spieleckkogel
1936 m

Zwölfer
1984 m

Reiterkogel
1819 m

Bernkogel
1740 m

Bämalm

Spielberghs

Schattberg Ost.
2020 m

Schettbergkar

Limberg-
Hochalm

Kohlmaiskopf
1794 m

HINTERGLEMM

SAALBACH

Wildenkarkogel
1910 m

Ski
slopes

⎯⎯ Easy
⎯⎯ Medium
⎯⎯ Difficult
‐ ‐ ‐ Hiking path/sledge-run
🚡 Cable car
🚡 Chair lift

Above: *A 100-mile ski circuit, skiable in either direction, makes Saalbach-Hinterglemm ideal for recreational skiers eager to rack up daily mileage.*

Left: *A well-integrated lift system helps skiers move about the mountainsides with minimal delay; Lofer, a separate resort, is covered by the same lift pass.*

and most hotels. Its centre pages are devoted to a panoramic map showing the entire network (other than the Leogang section) and indicates the areas with artificial snow-making facilities. The rest of the booklet gives comprehensive details of services available (more of which later), lift ticket prices, the capacity and journey length of every lift plus four sub-divisions of the piste map, each one worth at least a day's attention, and each the size of a medium-grade resort in its own right.

Dealing with these areas in turn, the Schattberg Ost, Schattberg West and Zwolferkogel are grouped together and provide the biggest challenge for experts who can test themselves down the new World Championship downhill course and several other demanding trails. The two main north-facing Schattberg runs, of which the Nord trail beneath the cable-car (the longest in Austria) is the more difficult, are not too demanding if taken

carefully but the lower section of the unpisted ski route from the Zwolferkogel is of frightening demeanour and is strictly for stout-hearted skiers with excellent technique. Otherwise, there is some good intermediate skiing over the ridge beyond the top station of the Schattberg cable-car (2097m/6877ft) and a long 7km (4½ mile) intermediate run to Jausernalm. There is also some good off-piste skiing in this area on unmarked and unpatrolled terrain although the reward at the bottom is a long, boring run-out to the foot of the Jausernalm lift.

This point is, however, an integral part of the Ski Circus with the Vorderglemm gondola station across the road (crossed via a tunnel) and the mid-station has a large restaurant with a south-facing terrace which for some represents the last of the day's skiing. Those with more resolve head up to Wildenkarkogel Hutte from where they can opt for an excursion to Leogang or continue the Circus back to Saalbach along a variety of easy or intermediate trails, some of them rolling through woodlands and others wide open and perfect for bombers. The 1991 World Championship slalom courses are here.

The Bernkogel triple chair-lift rises from the opposite side of Saalbach. At the top there are several unpisted ski routes leading back to the valley providing a variety of descents. Otherwise, continue

up to Reiterkogel at 1819m (5968ft) for skiing down to Hinterglemm or to Sport-alm to ride up to Hasenauerkopfl. This is yet another link in the Circus which, at this point, is an easy trail along a ridge before dropping to Sonnhof, the mid-station of the Spieleckkogel (1998m/6555ft) and Reichendlkopf (1942m/6371ft) lifts. This is a glorious intermediate domain with a good choice of fast, wide trails—ideal for practising technique—and the Circus is completed at the base of the lift system by taking the 12-person gondola to the Zwolferkogel.

Don't ignore Leogang, too often considered to be Saalbach-Hinterglemm's poor relation in the next valley. Leogang is a pleasant little village with lower prices—other than in a couple of magnificent hotels, notably the Krallerhof which boasts quite remarkable health and fitness facilities and top-class dining—and is popular with families who enjoy curling, sleigh rides and skating. Visitors can also choose between the local Leogang lift pass or a ticket which gives access to Saalbach-Hinterglemm's vast skiing.

Back in Saalbach-Hinterglemm, each morning sees hordes of sleepy skiers, testament to its vibrant nightlife. Traditional alpine pursuits such as sleigh rides, tobogganing and skating are available along with squash and indoor tennis. No fewer than 25 hotels have their own swimming pools and nearly all of the rest have sauna and Jacuzzi—each village also has its own public indoor pool complete with sauna and Jacuzzi.

With 60 lifts serving 185 miles of skiing, Saalbach-Hinterglemm's skiing statistics are impressive enough. Off the slopes they are similarly formidable with 40 mountain huts and restaurants scattered about the hillsides, eight restaurants with live music for dancing after dinner, five discotheques, several places with tea dances at five o'clock and countless bars and cafés which turn the twin villages into a vast debating theatre with the chatter continuing well into the night. One popular evening diversion is to walk for about an hour from the centre of Saalbach up to the Spielberghaus for a merry supper with the return home either by ratrac or toboggan on a long course alongside the frozen river.

KITZBUHEL

Like St Anton, Kitzbuhel has become synonymous with Austrian skiing and has an international cachet which draws skiers from around the world like a giant snowy magnet. Kitzbuhel is also well known to TV audiences who sit agog as they watch the most fearsome race on the World Cup downhill programme—the Hahnenkamm race down the Streif course above Kitzbuhel. The little Tyrolean town buzzes with activity and the race attracts a ghoulish crowd which congregates to watch the inevitable high-speed falls. It also attracts the real fans who come to cheer their death-defying heroes who hurtle down the Hahnenkamm, seemingly without regard for life, limb or even the laws of gravity. The supreme master of the Hahnenkamm was the 'Kaiser', Franz Klammer. Austria's greatest skier and downhill racer took the crown on four occasions, including two spectacular victories during his run of nine consecutive downhill wins in the mid-seventies.

But there is a lot more to Kitzbuhel than the greatest ski race in the world. There is also some of the best and most extensive recreational skiing in the Alps,

The Ski Safari affords seemingly endless opportunities for fast on-piste cruising, steep mogul runs and off-piste forays in an area which has world-renown.

and there is a lovely town where the jagged outline of the rooftops in the medieval centre echo the soaring peaks of the Wilderkaiser mountains behind. The only problem is that Kitzbuhel is too popular for its own good. The early-morning wait for a place on the Hahnenkamm cable-car can be horrendous and, even if you use the (very efficient) free bus service to the Fleckalmbahn gondola, the situation is frequently no better. Pushing and shoving in lift lines seems to be the local sport. The smart move is to take the bus to Jochberg or Pass Thurn where there is little congestion but this does mean that the first 20 minutes of the skiing day are spent cramped up with dozens of fellow skiers spilling skis and sticks all over the place. Still, Kitzbuhel's devotees argue that all the hassles are worth it because, once you are up above the valley, there is lots of brilliant skiing all around and lift lines on the upper reaches are rare.

Gr. Rettenstein
2363 m

Ski
slopes
——— Easy
——— Medium
——— Difficult
○—○ Ski lift

Pengelstein

Steinbergkögel

Ehrenbachöhe

Aschau

Hahnenkamm

Obergaisberg

Kirchberg

Even though it is not the best place for beginners or families, the great Toni Sailer, triple gold medallist at the 1956 Olympics, is head of the children's ski school and the instructors attached to the main ski school—known as the Red Devils—maintain its reputation for being one of the finest in the Alps. Nursery slopes are conveniently placed on an apron at the bottom of the Hahnenkamm downhill course so that first-timers can truthfully say that they have skied this great run, albeit the last 50 yards!

The rest of the skiing is in six sections, some of them interlinking. The south-facing slopes of the Kitzbuhelerhorn (1996m/6549ft) provide undemanding intermediate trails, similar in scope to those of adjacent Aurach. The big advantages are that congestion in these two areas is rare and that the views from the summit of the Kitzbuhelerhorn seem to span the entire range of the Alps. The Raintal bowl catches the early-morning sun and provides the most interesting skiing—the two trails back to the valley become tedious once you have skied them a couple of times. The lifts around Trattalm (just below the Hornkopfl) lead to trails ideal for novices and improving intermediates.

Kitzbuhel's Ski Safari consists of three of the other four areas although it can only be skied in one direction. The runs in the fourth area, above Aschau, are, again, best for intermediates although skiing through the trees is popular after a snowfall. Kirchberg, the starting point of the Ski Safari, is a ski resort in its own right, and has a small separate area, the Gaisberg, in addition to the lifts and pistes which connect with Kitzbuhel; it is also a cheaper place to stay.

The lifts immediately outside Kirchberg rise to meet the Fleckalmbahn gondola at Ehrenbachhohe which is set at 1800m (5906ft) and is the junction for skiing all the way down to Kitzbuhel or continuing the Ski Safari to Jochberg via the Steinbergerkogel and Pengelstein. Many good skiers prefer to stay in the immediate vicinity, however, as there is some very challenging work to be found, on and off-piste, including unmarked routes down to Aschau. Intermediates can quite happily spend the entire day, or

Franz Klammer tackling the Hahnenkamm course at Kitzbuhel. Austria's greatest hero won this Blue Riband event four times, including three consecutive victories between 1975–77.

even a week in this area, choosing long runs down to Kirchberg or Kitzbuhel unless they opt for the Kaser trail which is sometimes perfectly groomed for high speed. Better skiers tend to dip through the little tunnel for access to Fleckhochalm where there is a near-300m (1000ft) vertical drop designed to sort out technicians from stylists. Alternatively, there is a more modest descent down to Klausern on a wide cruising run and there are plenty of off-piste diversions through trees. Be careful here, as far too many people gaily follow tracks only to find that they, and their predecessors down the mountain, are lost and have a long walk to a lift. Everyone, of course, wants to ski the Streif—the Hahnenkamm downhill racing track—but few are sufficiently competent to do so in complete control at speed on the top section. Many stop through sheer fear, others fall, and so even the best of skiers should take care, not for themselves but for the tumbling, exhausted and frightened skiers all around.

The Steinbergerkogel provides the best off-piste and mogul skiing in the region as well as being the next link in the Ski Safari (which is indicated by an elephant insignia along the way). Be prepared for a five-minute walk along the last part of the run to Jochberg.

Both Jochberg and Pass Thurn are sizeable ski resorts in their own right, parts of the latter being in Salzburgerland, over the border from the Tyrol. Their lifts are interconnected and, as previously indicated, provide the chance to beat the crowds in the morning. Most of the on-piste skiing, other than around the Zweitausender, is best for intermediates but after a snowfall the woodlands are alive with the happy chatter of powder hounds exploring unmarked runs.

Eating out in Kitzbuhel is a treat and a full range of culinary delights is available with traditional Tyrolean fare, Chinese specialities at the Peking China Restaurant and French cuisine all to be found

—there is even a branch of McDonalds in the town centre. Tea rooms such as Kortschak and Praxmair serve excellent cakes and pastries and hotels such as the Tiefenbrunner house several restaurants including a residents' dining room, the elaborate Rossheimmel for a grand dinner and the Sitz, a little restaurant trading in local specialities and ideal for a quick bite. Elsewhere, the Schloss Lebenberg, just out of town, offers *nouvelle cuisine* while a

taxi ride to the wooden chalet-style Saukaser Stuben, 10 minutes out of town, is worth while for a plate of *Pressknodel* (potato, cheese and onion dumplings fried with sage and parsley and served in a beef broth) or *Blutwurstgrostl*, a tasty combination of black pudding, onions and potatoes, fried and served in an earthen-ware pan.

The Londoner bar is a Kitzbuhel institution and a favourite meeting place immediately after skiing. Later on there are queues to get in and the atmosphere is rarely less than rowdy with the biggest challenge being the downing of a two-litre boot-shaped *stein* of beer. In sedate contrast, there is a trio of bars which share an entrance in Vorderstadt, opposite the Tenne (which regularly hosts Tyrolean evenings as well as cabaret acts and dancing). The Slicht is the quietest while both the Kaiserkeller and Nachtschwar-

mer stay open very late and are the most promising boy-meets-girl places in town. The Goldene Gams, next door to the Tiefenbrunner, appeals to an older set which enjoys dancing to live music in a relaxed atmosphere. The Adam Bar, the Drop-In and Toni's are other popular Kitzbuhel night spots. Gamblers can play roulette, baccarat, blackjack and slot machines at the Casino where admittance is denied to men not wearing jacket and

tie — a passport is another necessary appendage. Sleigh rides to the Schloss Munichau at Reith afford a pleasant evening away from the hubbub.

Kitzbuhel also offers the entire range of accommodation with centuries-old hotels, apartments, rustic chalets, simple but charming little guesthouses and farmhouses, and even a camp site for motor homes. Take care when booking, as much of the accommodation is well away from both ski lifts and bus stops. Most of the best hotels are in the town centre, however, and that means that they are a short walk from the Hahnenkamm cable-car and railway station whose car park doubles as a bus station for services to the

Fleckalmbahn, Jochberg and Pass Thurn. The Tiefenbrunner is at the bottom of the main street and, in addition to its three restaurants and a convivial bar, has a swimming pool, sauna and Jacuzzi — facilities which are also to be found at the Goldener Greif which nestles into the 12th-century city walls and is bedecked with panelled walls and antique furniture. The Greif Keller, downstairs, provides traditional Tyrolean entertainment and the Casino is next door. The Tenne is also in the main street, across from the Tiefenbrunner, and has a cosy dining room and a large café for passers-by to drop in for a coffee and watch the world go by.

As well as holding Tyrolean evenings,

For all its reputation for being a severe testing ground for ambitious skiers, Kitzbuhel provides good care and tuition for beginners thanks to the ski school's 'Red Devils'.

the Tenne is the scene of the regular Friday evening party given by the Red Devils of the ski school, for anyone who has been taking lessons during the week, and for anyone else who cares to drop in. The Sporthotel Reisch, close by the tourist office, the Maria Theresa and the Schweizerhof are also among the best places in town to stay.

Many visitors to Kitzbuhel have no interest in skiing and they find plenty to

Kitzbuhel's medieval centre is home to dozens of excellent hotels and restaurants, plenty of friendly bars and cafes to fuel the thirst and appetite of avid apres-skiers as well as very good sports facilities.

do, from shopping for Sportalm sportswear and Rattenberg glass crystal products, curling on a little natural rink in the main street, swimming at the Aquarena, playing tennis or squash on indoor courts, to skittles evenings at the ancient Gasthof Untern Rain in Kirchberg with tots of schnapps the inevitable prizes. Kitzbuhel is on the railway line which runs between Innsbruck and Saltzburg and people find that wandering in their twisting alleys,

pausing for a cup of hot chocolate, is a rewarding day's excursion; day trips by coach are also available.

The Kitzbuheler Alps are strewn with ski resorts and it is worth mentioning some of them because although only Kirchberg, which connects with Kitzbuhel in any case, is covered by the same lift pass, many can be reached directly by rail and provide a contrast to Kitzbuhel's challenging skiing and sophisticated nightlife.

The Wilderkaiser Grossraum constitutes Austria's largest interlinked skiing area and is served by seven villages, two of them — Brixen and Hopfgarten — being on the railway line between Kitzbuhel and

Worgl. Itter, Soll, Scheffau, Ellmau and Going complete the septet. The Grossraum provides a vast playground for intermediates with apparently endless permutations when choosing an itinerary for the day. Soll is particularly popular among young British skiers, especially first-timers, as its reputation for providing cheap and very cheerful ski holidays is fully justified. Westendorf, also served by the railway and covered by the Grossraum pass (although its lifts do not connect with the others), another popular place for beginners as the exquisite little village is complemented by high alpine nursery slopes with wonderful views across to the Hohe Salve (1828m/6001ft) and the Kitzbuhelerhorn (1966m/6549ft).

In the opposite direction from Brixen, Westendorf and Hopfgarten, the railway runs to St Johann in Tirol, a jolly little town set around a twin-towered baroque church. Its skiing is on the north side of the Kitzbuhelerhorn which, combined with artificial snow-making equipment, has ensured decent skiing in even the mildest of winters. Indeed, there have been many occasions when people staying in Kitzbuhel have opted to spend the day at St Johann as, even if the skiing is less extensive, it is usually far more reliable. St Johann's other bonus is 17 restaurants dotted about the mountainsides. Nightlife is informal here and can take the form of a couple of beers in the bar above the brewery prior to a supper of traditional regional specialities before dancing in any one of half-a-dozen disco bars.

The railway continues to Fieberbrunn, known as the *schnee winkl* (snow pocket) thanks to its consistently favourable snow conditions. The village straggles along the valley and gives access to some lovely rolling runs through trees, making it highly popular with families. Kitzbuhel, however, is not generally an ideal family resort as its ski terrain is too daunting for little ones and the nightlife is wasted on them. It is a far better bet for groups of keen young skiers who have the energy to ski all day and carouse all night. It is also perfect for anyone looking for an all-round winter holiday with excellent skiing as the focal point amidst a kaleidoscope of other activities.

LECH AND ZURS

From a distance Zurs looks like a tiny farming settlement. Closer inspection of the faithfully preserved village centre reveals sumptuous hotels and a glittering clientele. Lech is also a very smart little town. Along with St Anton, Lech and Zurs are the foremost resorts in the Arlberg region, which straddles the border between the Tyrol and the Vorarlberg, and if neither provides the sheer size of St Anton, they do offer great variety for all grades of skier although they may be a bit too expensive for beginners.

Zurs is the most centrally positioned of the Arlberg network, which also includes St Christoph and Stuben, but the lift system is not completely interlinked. It is possible to ski to Zurs from St Anton via the back of the Valluga (2811m/9222ft) on a long and, in parts, very difficult off-piste high alpine route in the company of a guide. Without doubt this is the most terrifying experience for most skiers as they undertake it but once completed, it is the most satisfying. You can take a 10-minute ride on the Post Bus to Rauz from where the lifts connect with those of St Anton and there is a pleasant run down to Stuben, a sweet little village too often ignored by visitors in their rush to ski at the Arlberg's better-known centres.

In the immediate vicinity, Zurs has runs on both sides of the valley and, on a sunny day, there is glorious skiing on wide pistes and in secluded bowls for everyone. But

On first impression, Zurs looks like a remote, rustic farming settlement – closer inspection reveals some of the grandest hotels and smartest guests in the Alps.

Trittkopf
3722 m

Ski
slopes

⎯⎯ Easy

⎯⎯ Medium

⎯⎯ Difficult

🚠 Cable car

🚡 Chair lift

⛷ Drag lift

Patteriol
3056 m

Muggengrat
2450 m

Stuben
1407 m

Seekopf
2208 m

Madloch
2432 m

ZÜRS
1720 m

Rüfikopf
2350 m

Zug
1511 m

Kriegerhorn
2178 m

Mohnenfluh
2457 m

LECH
1445 m

Oberlech
1730 m

this is a very remote corner of the Alps, with hardly a tree in sight and, when the weather closes in, visibility can be reduced to zero and there is no protection from cold winds. Lech's topography and the presence of a few wooded glades gives rather more protection if it is snowing.

The areas below Hexenboden, on the eastern side of the valley, provide some easier skiing but the adjacent section below the Trittkopf is far more demanding. Given the right conditions, it is possible to ski on unpisted runs all the way to Stuben, crossing the Flexen Pass. Even beginners are able to ride all the way

up to the top of the Muggengrat chair-lift for long, easy runs at high altitude while piste-bashers tend to head for the Madloch, from where there are several medium-to-difficult runs connecting with the circuit which links Zürs and Lech. The first port of call is a charming little hamlet called Zug, not a resort in its own right but an integral part of Lech's lift system and the destination for evening sleigh rides as well as being home to an alpine institution, the Rote Wand restaurant and nightclub.

From Zug, the circuit continues up to the Kriegerhorn which is linked to the

Zuger Hochlicht by a cable-car. These twin peaks provide plenty of skiing without the need to ski the circuit, the toughest marked trails being the Osthang and Sudhang runs from the Kriegerhorn, while the Zuger Hochlicht is the starting point for the longest off-piste trails. Both provide plenty of gentle runs, either all the way to Lech or to Oberlech, a little satellite village perched above the valley and one of the most popular areas for a lunchtime break at its numerous restaurants and bars, many of them attracting a crowd more keen on cutting a dash than carving a turn. The Goldener Berg is

lunchtime heralds the end of the skiing day for many visitors.

Although there are a few inexpensive places to eat in Lech, most dining is confined to hotels, of which the Gasthof Post, Arlberg and Almhof Schneider in Lech and the Alpenrose-Post, Haus Mathies and Zurserhof in Zurs are generally considered the best places to stay, and for dinner. Again, most of the nightlife is confined to the hotels with traditional Austrian evenings as popular as modern disco nights. Zurs tends to be more sedate than Lech although unruly behaviour is virtually unknown in either—high prices in the resorts serve as a deterrent to the rowdy brigade.

Both Lech and Zurs attract a regular crowd of European royalty and international stars from the worlds of film and sport. Needless to say, they in turn attract hordes of hangers-on. Yet, somehow, both villages remain unpretentious—maybe it is simply because they and their visitors are genuinely stylish and have no need to prove anything to the rest of the world. The glitterati who choose this valley as their winter playground tend to do so year after year, safe in the knowledge that they will be in the company of other celebrities and will not be the only objects of curiosity on the slopes and restaurant terraces.

If all this makes Lech and Zurs sound like the mountain retreats of smart people for whom skiing holds no real attraction, this is not the case as most of them are good skiers. There is, however, a smug satisfaction in skiing over to Zurs via the Valluga from St Anton in the knowledge that no matter how competent the poseurs in the expensive suits may be, they won't have skied anything half as difficult as that run during the morning.

best for a civilized lunch, the outdoor bar at the Burghotel for people-watching.

Lolling on terraces has been elevated to art-form status in both Lech and Zurs although it must be said that many of the beautiful people are very good skiers. And they have to be to return to Lech from the Rufikopf instead of continuing the circuit to Zurs. From the top of the cable-car, the choice is between continuing to Zurs on manageable trails or dropping back down to Lech on unprepared and unpatrolled trails, all of which are precipitous in parts and some of which can only be skied with a guide. Were it not for this section, the

circuit could be skied in either direction by any competent intermediate; as it is, most skiers are happy to ski clockwise, happy in the knowledge that as well as access points from close to the centre of both villages, there are plenty of escape routes back to the valley if the going gets too tough. The circuit has several alternative descents at most points.

The only snag is that there are few mountain restaurants along the way other than at Oberlech. Most visitors seem happy to ski back to the valley where the bars and cafés in the villages positively bubble with excited chatter—indeed,

SCHLADMING

A merry little town in Styria, just over an hour's drive from Salzburg airport, Schladming is one of the best resorts in Austria for groups of mixed ability looking for an unpretentious and lively ski holiday. Schladming was largely unknown outside Austria until it shot to prominence when hosting the 1981 World Championships. That was when Harti Weirather won the Men's Downhill in thrilling fashion to the acclaim of his countrymen and put the little market town on the international skiing map. Schladming is now a regular fixture on the World Cup circuit and the Planai downhill course the fastest of them all. Likewise, neighbouring Haus in Ennstal (home of the great Austrian racer Helmut Hoeflehner) held the Ladies' events in 1981 and continues to host international competitions.

The local lift pass covers both Schladming and Haus, as well as Rohrmoos and Reiteralm, both within easy reach by the local bus service, and all four are covered by the Top Tauern Skischeck which is a regional pass giving access to a score of resorts in Styria and Salzburgerland— Obertauern, St Johann im Pongau, Wagrain, Kleinarl, St Michael am Katschberg and Filzmoos are among the options for a day's skiing. Many visitors like to stay in Schladming for two weeks, skiing in the immediate vicinity for the first week and then branching out into the rest of the Tauern Alps for the second. A car is essential to make full use of the Top Tauern Skischeck.

Artificial snowmaking equipment has played a big part in Schladming's success in attracting both international racers and recreational skiers over the years and this facility continues to be the resort's major asset. It does not rank alongside St Anton or Kitzbuhel in size or scope but for most intermediate skiers it is an excellent choice, particularly if they visit Haus, Rohrmoos and Reiteralm during their stay as each provides lovely tree-lined runs which are ideal for improving technique and, when the mood is right, skiing at high speed in safety.

Beginners will enjoy Schladming as the nursery slopes are high above the valley so that they feel an immediate sense of achievement. Novices are not advised to ski all the way back to town, however, as although the top section of the Planai downhill course is wide and not too steep, the lower reaches are precipitous and invariably mogul-infested. The gondola provides a more gentle descent for the faint-hearted. Most of the skiing is on north-facing slopes although the east-facing runs immediately below the top station (1894m/6214ft) are popular as

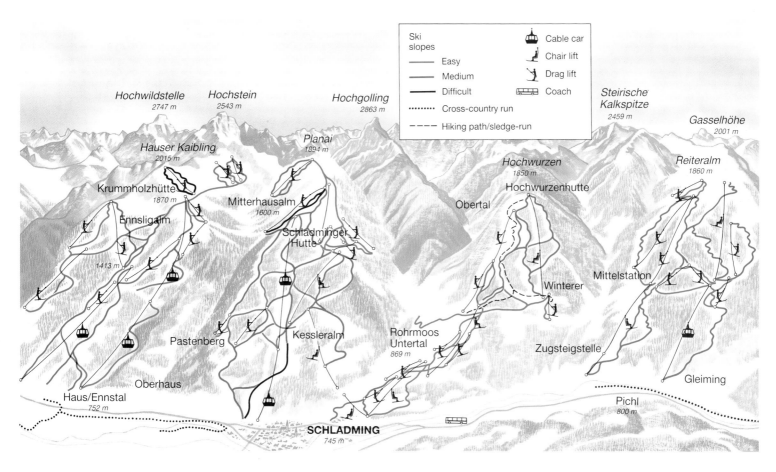

Ski slopes
Easy
Medium
Difficult
Cross-country run
Hiking path/sledge-run

Cable car
Chair lift
Drag lift
Coach

Hochwildstelle
2747 m

Hochstein
2543 m

Hochgolling
2863 m

Steirische Kalkspitze
2459 m

Gasselhöhe
2001 m

Hauser Kaibling
2015 m

Planai
1894 m

Hochwurzen
1850 m

Reiteralm
1860 m

Krummholzhütte
1870 m

Hochwurzenhutte

Ennsligalm

Obertal

Mitterhausalm
1600 m

Schladminger Hütte

1413 m

Winterer

Mittelstation

Pastenberg

Kessleralm

Rohrmoos
Untertal
869 m

Zugsteigstelle

Gleiming

Oberhaus

Haus/Ennstal
752 m

Pichl
800 m

SCHLADMING
745 m

Left: *Schladming boasts the fastest downhill course on the World Cup circuit. The Austrian Harti Weirather took gold here in the 1982 World Championships.*

Below: *Schladming, Haus, Reiteralm and Rohrmoos are all covered by the local ski pass and are among the score of resorts available on the Top Tauern Skischeck.*

they are wide open and provide many optional routes down. There are also a couple of friendly restaurants for lunch in this area, notably the Sepp Walcher Hutte, named after Schladming's World Cup racer who tragically died in a skiing accident.

Down in the valley, Schladming is a busy if not particularly pretty little town, dominated by the Catholic and Protestant churches. The Igloo Bar is a popular meeting place although most visitors prefer the ancient Talbachschenke ('The Valley Brook Inn'), a cavernous place which is just right for a relaxed supper and a few drinks in the company of fellow skiers and the locals. Accommodation can either be in a quiet little guesthouse or one of the many comfortable hotels. The Sporthotel Royer is very modern and has health and fitness facilities as well as an enormous indoor swimming pool, a friendly bar and a choice of four dining rooms. In complete contrast, the Hotel Alte Poste, in the centre of town, is a traditional Austrian hostelry full of charm and hustle and bustle.

ST ANTON

St Anton is at the heart of the Arlberg and, to the *cognoscenti*, that means the heart of Austrian skiing. The Arlberg is the name given to the region straddling the border between the Tyrol and Vorarlberg—St Anton and near-neighbour St Christoph are in the former while Stuben, Lech and Zurs comprise the Vorarlberg contingent, making up one of the world's greatest ski centres. Hannes Schneider first gave ski lessons here in 1912 and, since then, St Anton has been high on the shopping list of keen skiers from around the world—witness the merry cacophony of Japanese, German, Dutch and English in the early-morning cable-cars.

St Anton and the Kandahar Ski Club are synonymous. The club was founded in 1911 and took its name from Field Marshal Earl Roberts of Kandahar—curious, as he didn't ski! Members of the Kandahar, which had developed from the Public Schools Alpine Sports Club, were visiting St Anton in 1927 and introduced slalom racing to the locals, awarding a cup to the winner and providing another for downhill races in future years. Thus the Arlberg-Kandahar races, the oldest open events in the world, were born.

The racing tradition has lived on and, in recent years, St Anton has been an occasional venue on the World Cup circuit. In 1968 Karl Schranz, who ran the St Anton ski school, and Heini Messner, now in charge of race-training camps at Steinach, took the first two places in the downhill to the delight of the whole of Austria.

St Anton's development has been carefully managed so that despite its size it retains its old alpine atmosphere. The centre is traffic-free and many visitors choose to arrive by rail and use the Post Bus service for visiting neighbouring resorts. The Zurich—Innsbruck railway line runs through St Anton and the town's station houses one of the great alpine institutions—a café which is a ski bum's paradise. Tales of derring-do are swapped and job prospects are discussed. Café owners and hoteliers know that the station is the hunting ground for cheap

labour. But, for most visitors, the slopes beneath the Valluga outcrop are the compelling factor, glistening in readiness for seemingly limitless adventure and apparently capable of devouring a cowering novice in one gulp.

Indeed, St Anton is not for beginners. Sure, there are plenty of easy runs, particularly around the Rendl area but most novices are daunted by both the sheer size of the area and the top-class skiers who congregate there year after

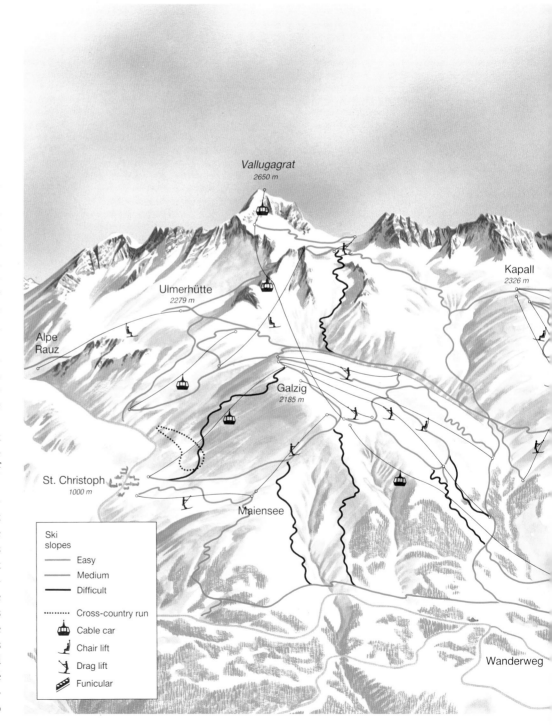

Vallugagrat
2650 m

Kapall
2326 m

Ulmerhütte
2279 m

Alpe
Rauz

Galzig
2185 m

St. Christoph
1000 m

Maiensee

Wanderweg

Ski slopes

——— Easy

——— Medium

——— Difficult

·········· Cross-country run

🚠 Cable car

🚡 Chair lift

🎿 Drag lift

🚟 Funicular

Fortunately, there is plenty of respite from St Anton's wealth of difficult terrain. The tranquillity of some of the more remote trails and paths is in sharp contrast to the buzz of activity in the town centre.

Hoher Riffler
3168 m

Eisenspitze
2854 m

2645 m

Rendl
2100 m

Gampen
1850 m

St. Jakob

ST. ANTON
1304 m

Oberdorf

The British introduced racing to the Arlberg region. Here is the British Ski Team of 1931 with Peter Lunn, of the great skiing family, on the right.

year. Good skiers want to test themselves on the Osthang bumps run below the Galzig cable-car or the tortuous descents beneath the Valluga. For the ultimate thrill, go with a guide to ski the region's 'missing link', the run from the top of the last section of the Valluga cable-car for the off-piste run to Zurs. This section is not for the faint-hearted. After inching along a narrow ridge with no apparent exit below, the guide leaps down and encourages his charges to do likewise. At this point he'll be grinning in anticipation while the rest tremble in trepidation, wondering how to negotiate what seems like a sheer drop with no exit. In negotiating the first wind-blown section, man's frailty becomes obvious.

The fact that the top classes of St Anton's ski school are full of Austrians who have been on skis since they were tiny tots is an indication of the esteem in which the traditional teaching methods are held. Indeed, instructors from other

resorts frequently enrol in classes. The teaching of skiing is taken seriously and pupils are expected to want to learn to ski rather than just have some fun cavorting about in the snow. The conscientious attitude of the instructors ensures that beginners and experts alike benefit from being pushed to what they had previously thought to be beyond their limits, either negotiating debutant snowplough turns or being given a rigorous examination of off-piste technique. Far too often, good recreational skiers want to get on with skiing rather than be strapped into the requirements of a class but the St Anton ski school is genuinely one of the best and instructors combine tuition with guiding of the vast area so that many miles are covered during a day in the top classes.

There are four major interconnected skiing areas, plus the Rendl section, a three-minute (free) bus ride from the centre of town, and Stuben, a separate resort covered by the Arlberg lift pass and easily reached on skis by all but the complete novice. The Arlberg pass also covers Lech and Zurs (q.v.).

The first morning of a visit to St Anton should be spent finding one's ski legs with a meander down to St Christoph on gentle runs from the top of the Galzig cable-car. Off-piste skiers can investigate the alternative descent into St Christoph—straight down gullies from the Galzig. St Christoph is a sweet little village on a mountain pass and is home to one of the great alpine hotels, the opulent Arlberg Hospiz. It is also home to the government-run ski school for instructors and one of the thrills of a visit is to see platoons of instructors following their leader down mountainsides, at terrifying speeds in perfect formation. There are several cafés overlooking the slopes at the foot of the lift system providing a cheaper alternative for lunch than the Arlberg Hospiz. The little 15-person cable-car runs back to the Galzig summit and there is a network of T-bars running to just below.

The Galzig section provides several options. The easiest route back to town is the wide, swooping run leading to the Steissbachtal ('Happy Valley'). There are plenty of good intermediate pistes, there is the old Kandahar downhill course and the Osthang bumps. The bumps are a thorough examination of your knee ligaments and nerves alike and provide a relentless ride down the moguls. There are two restaurants at the top of the Galzig cable-car (2075m/6809ft), one of them cheap and cheerful and the other just as cheerful but not so cheap, while the journey back to St Anton can be broken at the famed Krazy Kangaruh bar where it seems *de rigueur* for young Swedes to attempt ski-jumping from the roof after a tot of schnapps too many.

A three-section cable-car rises from the Galzig summit (2185m/7169ft) to the Valluga (2811m/9222ft) for some of the Arlberg's most testing skiing, on and off-piste. Timid skiers should stay away because although several runs have easy sections, none is easy all the way down, most are consistently treacherous for the unwary, and all are treacherous for the incompetent. There are three main sectors, wide bumpy bowls whose challenge is relentless, and several challenging and tricky gullies. (Note, however, that this is designated an off-piste area and is, therefore, unpatrolled.) An alternative route to the top of the Vallugagrat is via the Arlenmahder and Schindlergrat chair-lifts from the outskirts of St Christoph—they help avoid the occasional congestion for the cable-cars on which it is necessary, at peak times, to reserve a place in advance. The third section of the cable-car is open only to skiers accompanied by a qualified guide.

The run to Zurs is splendid and is only really difficult on the upper reaches. Thereafter, the glorious unpisted run is within the scope of most good skiers but the top section can only be contemplated in the company of a guide whose snow

craft, rather than his ability to instruct in technique, is of vital importance as the wind-blown crust can be metres deep at the start and reduce to a few millimetres around the corner. One way to avoid this difficult terrain, and the cost of a guide, is to climb the near-vertical bank outside the lift station for the last stage, cutting footholds in the snow. This provides the opportunity to enjoy the high-alpine route down to Zurs, too high for animal tracks, without danger.

St Anton's cable-cars give access to some of the region's toughest off-piste descents, notably the run from the Valluga all the way to Zurs.

There is more than enough challenge below the Vallugagrat, however, on the Mattunjoch and Schindlerkar bowls which both eventually connect with Happy Valley for the run back to town. The other route from the Vallugagrat is on the other side of the Schindlergrat and provides an easier descent past Ulmer Hutte and thence to Rauz. Here it is necessary to remove skis to cross the road for a gentle run down to Stuben, a delightful little chocolate-box village. At first sight, Stuben appears to be strictly for intermediates and they certainly have a wonderful time cruising the many fast slopes. However, Stuben offers expert skiers some extraordinary off-piste skiing,

notably down to Langen from the Albona Grat (2340m/7874ft) and on the route behind the Maroj-Sattel. Both require an uphill trek at the start but the rewards are worth the physical effort and the Maroj-Sattel route provides a beautiful, tranquil and remote run to St Christoph, off-piste all the way.

The upper sections of Stuben's on-piste skiing are not especially demanding but, by opting for one of the unmarked ski routes, there is plenty of challenge for experts, particularly after a heavy snowfall. Timid intermediates should not be deterred, however, as they can take a moderate red run at their own pace to the mid-mountain restaurant, pause for a bowl of *Leberknodlsuppe* (liver dumpling in broth) and a glass of wine, and continue back to Rauz on an easy blue trail. From Rauz, a chair-lift rises to the Ulmer Hutte (2279m/7477ft) and the run back to St Anton is gentle—take care in Happy Valley late in the day, however, as far too many skiers treat this run as a downhill course in their rush to be quaffing at the Krazy Kangaruh.

The Gampen-Kapall section is the most accessible from the centre of St Anton and is an intermediate's dream. Proficient skiers can take several difficult diversions from the pistes which provide challenge without terror, and one of the joys is to test your skill on the new Kandahar downhill course which starts just below Kapall (2333m/7654ft). On a sunny day, with the piste groomed, wide swooping turns flatter the ego but this section is open to the elements and when the wind blows, it blows hard.

Rather than taking the Kandahar run all the way down, most skiers prefer to stay on the upper section because the lifts which start in town are unable to cope with peak-season demand, particularly in the morning. A cable-car and a cable-railway, which run parallel, rise from just behind the railway station and the latter has more capacity. The Galzig cable-car also suffers from long queues in the morning in the height of the season and the only ways to beat the rush are to take the bus to St Christoph, which gives access to all the main areas, or to Rendl, which does not.

Rendl is, however, a good place to start

the day simply to allow the early-morning crowds to disperse elsewhere. Because it does not connect with the rest of St Anton's vast area, good skiers ignore it to their loss. Again, first appearances are deceptive. The gondola car terminates at the Brankreuz mid-station (2100m/6890ft) and the area below consists of friendly blue runs with a couple of undemanding reds. Above, a single T-bar serving two fast red runs rises to 2407m (7897ft). What is not immediately apparent is that this T-bar also serves two

St Anton is on the railway line between Zurich and Innsbruck, giving easy access. The village centre is traffic-free and despite its popularity it remains unspoilt.

excellent ski routes which provide a couple of hours' fun for good skiers while they wait for the main lifts to become less congested. The Rendl area is best for beginners as they are not overawed by its sheer size and can make the graduation from gentle blue trails to marginally difficult reds without too many tears. For

the first few days, beginners take the gondola back to the valley and, as they progress, are able to ski all the way back down.

Incidentally, St Anton's piste markings are designated by Austrian skiing standards. A black run is for an expert Austrian and a red for an intermediate Austrian — an intermediate Austrian skier tends to be an expert by most other standards!

St Anton children's ski school was criticized during recent years but the deficiencies have now been rectified and the school is once again highly regarded. The Jugendcenter, catering for three to 14-year-olds, is open all day and provides lunch for children in classes as well as care for those who are not.

Eating on the slopes can be a bit of a bun-fight as the better establishments tend to be overcrowded. In addition to the restaurants at the Galzig top station,

The Arlberg attracts keen skiers from around the world for a great combination of fast on-piste cruising, tough mogul fields and forays into the deep stuff.

the Ulmer Hutte is an institution — an old mountain hut converted into a fine eatery with a smoky atmosphere on cold days and, when the sun shines, scores of happy diners lolling in deckchairs outside or chatting over a drink at the ice bar. The self-service restaurant on the Rendl also has a terrace which styles itself as the Rendl Beach. Otherwise, there are several inexpensive places at the foot of the lifts in St Christoph and more a short walk up the road.

Back in town, immediately after skiing, St Anton hums with excited chatter as tales of the day's activities are exchanged in the hotel bars and main street cafés. Plates of pastries are guzzled and glasses

of *schnapps* and beer gulped down as a prelude to the evening's activities which can be as sedate or rowdy as the mood takes you. Several of the larger hotels have fully fledged nightclubs where discos blare at full throttle until the early hours. Others feature traditional Tyrolean bands and as well as a few grand restaurants — mostly in the larger hotels — St Anton boasts many small, friendly and inexpensive cafés.

One misconception is that with its status as one of the world's great ski centres, St Anton is desperately expensive. Certainly, should you opt to stay at the St Antoner Hof, the Schwarzer Adler or the Alte Post, you need to be on a big budget. If, like the Prince of Wales, the Arlberg Hospiz is your choice, your budget needs to be enormous. But there is plenty of modest accommodation and a wide variety of unpretentious night spots.

THE MONTAFON

The Montafon is not a ski resort but five separate areas, two of which are interconnected, set around a gorgeous valley in Austria's Vorarlberg region. Each has its own character and, combined, they provide skiing to suit all requirements. The free ski bus system is highly efficient although the Montafon mostly appeals to the self-drive market. The discerning Swiss favour the Montafon, appreciating its high standards of comfort and cooking in the hotels and, in particular, lower prices than at home. That is only to say that the Montafon is cheap by Swiss standards—it is one of Austria's more expensive skiing destinations and this, combined with the fact that Zurich and Munich airports are several hours away, has kept the mass-market tour operators away.

There is an atmosphere of quiet sophistication throughout the valley, redolent of the days when families came to enjoy an all-round winter holiday, not just to clock up ski miles each day. The Montafon doesn't rank alongside Kitzbuhel or St Anton among the great resorts, but it

doesn't try to. Instead, the region is perfect for families and excellent for couples who want a romantic interlude from the rigours of city life.

Schruns is the busiest and most elegant of the five resorts with a pedestrian shopping centre, tranquil cafés for enjoying a mug of hot chocolate as well as several discos. The railway from Bludenz terminates here so that Schruns is a favourite among visitors flying into Zurich and transferring by rail while a combination of indoor tennis and swimming, sleigh rides, skating and curling makes it popular with non-skiers. The skiing is on two sides of the Hochjoch; much of it is tree-lined and there is an 11km (7 mile) run from just below the Kreuzjoch outcrop (2335m/7661ft) right down to the valley via the Kappell mid-station where there is a large, rustic restaurant. The slopes above Kappell are wide open and generally easy.

Tschagguns is separated from Schruns by the river and has south-facing fast slopes which are perfect for improving intermediates. Tschagguns occasionally

Above: *Too many visitors to the Montafon Valley confine their activities to the piste which is a shame as the region provides some excellent off-piste work.*

Right: *The Montafon's Anita Wachter took gold in the Calgary Olympics and was third overall in the 1987–88 World Cup. Four villages claim her as their own!*

hosts World Cup Ladies' Downhill races, as befits the village which claims double Olympic medallist Anita Wachter as its own—three other villages in the vicinity also claim her! The skiing is a little out of town and is reached by the free bus service. The charming village boasts a couple of good hotels although most of the accommodation is on a self-catering or bed-and-breakfast basis.

St Gallenkirch is the most central of the Montafon resorts and its skiing connects with that of Gaschurn. Combined, they form the most extensive skiing area in the valley and each claims to have a top station at 2200m (7218ft). The two systems, served by gondolas, converge at

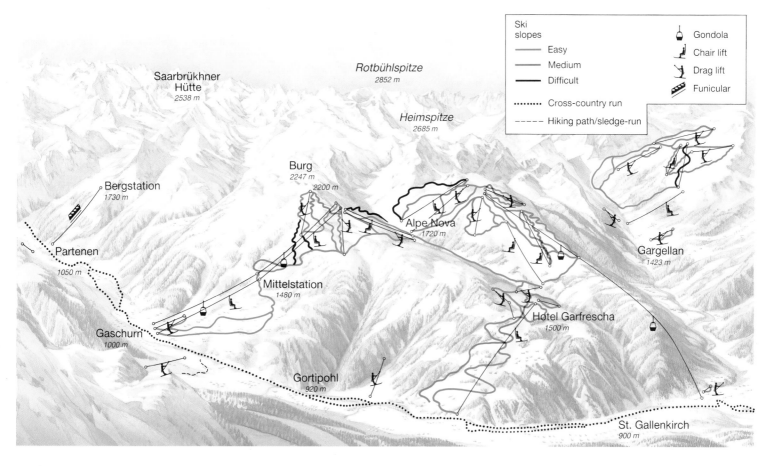

Ski slopes

——	Easy
——	Medium
——	Difficult
········	Cross-country run
------	Hiking path/sledge-run

Gondola
Chair lift
Drag lift
Funicular

Saarbrükhner Hütte
2538 m

Rotbühlspitze
2852 m

Heimspitze
2685 m

Burg
2247 m
2200 m

Bergstation
1730 m

Alpe Nova
1720 m

Gargellan
1423 m

Partenen
1050 m

Mittelstation
1480 m

Hotel Garfrescha
1500 m

Gaschurn
1000 m

Gortipohl
920 m

St. Gallenkirch
900 m

Alpe Nova (1720m/5643ft) where the skiing can be as easy or as hard as you like, being on wide bowls. Lower down, the runs are tree-lined. St Gallenkirch and Gaschurn are friendly and informal.

Fifteen minutes up the valley is Gargellen, a hamlet with a population of exactly 100, a figure which is, unaccountably, perennial! Though tiny, it attracts visitors from throughout the region for its restaurants and a couple of fine hotels, notably the Madrisa which is right next to the slopes. The only thrill for experts is to cross the Swiss border to ski down to Klosters but Gargellen, like Montafon, does not base its publicity on tough skiing but on old-fashioned hospitality.

The Montafon's residents speak a dialect heavily influenced by the ancient Romansh language and St Gallenkirch's church was founded in 1254 by the Celtic monks who introduced Christianity to the region. Farming and ironworks were the mainstays of the valley's economy for centuries but today tourism is the economic base—visitors are assured of a warm welcome.

ALPE D'HUEZ

Like many of its French counterparts, Alpe d'Huez is a modern development where convenience has taken precedence over creating an attractive environment. It is one of the few major resorts to have remained a preserve of the French — although several British tour operators are making inroads, to the delight of their clients, and a few British property developers are realizing the potential of the area by selling apartments at Oz en Oisans, down the valley and connecting with the main lift network.

The skiing is ranged in a semi-circle around the rather dispersed village, and every part is served by lifts at which queues are rare. Beginners have their own slopes close to the village, and the Baby Club looks after little ones, while intermediates and experts have no end of challenge high above the resort.

The skiing is ranged around three sep-

Good skiers are attracted to Alpe d'Huez for the tricky descents from the Pic Blanc – beginners should not be deterred as there is plenty of undemanding terrain immediately above the village.

arate, but interlinking, areas and the most demanding terrain is to be found on the runs immediately beneath the Pic Blanc which, at 3350m (10991ft), is the highest point and the one to which good skiers are inexorably drawn. This section is known as the Grandes Rousses and is reached by a two-stage gondola and a cable-car. The choice is between the Tunnel run, which takes its name from the little tunnel which provides some shelter for skiers before the shock of what they see below, or the Serrenne trail which is an estimable 16km (10 miles) long. Although being

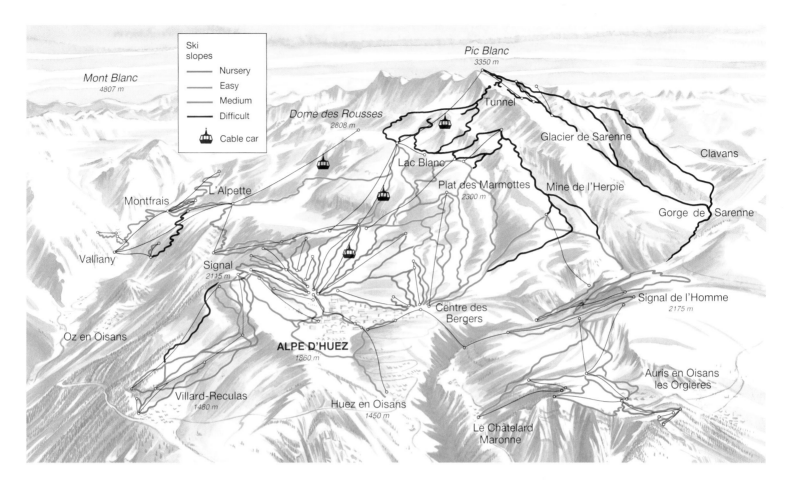

Ski slopes
— Nursery
— Easy
— Medium
— Difficult
🚠 Cable car

Mont Blanc
4807 m

Pic Blanc
3350 m

Dome des Rousses
2808 m

Tunnel

Glacier de Sarenne

Clavans

Lac Blanc

Plat des Marmottes
2300 m

Mine de l'Herpie

L'Alpette

Montfrais

Gorge de Sarenne

Valliany

Signal
2115 m

Signal de l'Homme
2175 m

Centre des Bergers

Oz en Oisans

ALPE D'HUEZ
1860 m

Auris en Oisans les Orgieres

Villard-Reculas
1480 m

Huez en Oisans
1450 m

Le Châtelard Maronne

designated 'black', this ends in a scenic but undemanding run-out back to the resort; it is, however, steep and narrow on the top section. In addition to these two marked trails, there are several off-piste itineraries from the Pic Blanc which should only be attempted in the company of a guide.

Intermediates will want to test themselves on these difficult runs but they will find more pleasure on the Signal runs immediately to the west of Alpe d'Huez, and on the north-facing Signal de l'Homme trails, of which the trail down to Foret de Maronne is the most challenging and interesting. The constant installation of new lifts has helped Alpe d'Huez muscle into the top league of French resorts. While it lacks the sheer size of the Trois Vallees network or Val d'Isere and Tignes, it has plenty of variety.

Off the slopes, most of the accommodation in Alpe d'Huez is in apartments with a smattering of hotels and some staffed chalets run by British tour operators. The resort is blessed with some excellent restaurants, plus dozens of small

Alpe d'Huez is a sprawling village, lacking in alpine charm. The compensation is in good skiing for everyone plus an excellent choice of bars, cafes and discos.

cafés, pizzerias and the like (some open well into the night), and has several bars and discos where the atmosphere is essentially French, particularly at peak holiday times and at weekends.

Alpe d'Huez is not the best place for an all-round winter holiday although there are some good cross-country routes, an outdoor heated swimming pool, an ice rink for skating and curling, hang-gliding and cleared paths for walking. Indoor activities include squash and tennis. It is, primarily, a ski resort and boasts 81 lifts serving 221km (138 miles) of marked trails plus many off-piste variations. The Grande Galaxie lift pass allows a day in each of Alpe d'Huez, Les Deux Alpes (which is also accessible via a helicopter service), Serre Chevalier, Puy-St-Vincent, Bardonecchia and other Italian resorts across the border—perfect for the self-drive holiday.

PORTES DU SOLEIL

likely to feel like beggars at the banquet when they listen to tales of derring-do from their more accomplished friends in the evening. That being said, for all the vast expanse of the interlinking lift systems, several resorts can be regarded in their own right—both La Chapelle d'Abondance and St Jean d'Aulps are excellent places for learners while Torgon is ideal for improving intermediates.

The contrast between high-tech French Avoriaz and sleepy, rural Planachaux, over the Swiss border, is stunning. And if you have skied down the notorious 'Swiss Wall' you are likely to feel stunned after negotiating a precipitous mogul field.

The Portes du Soleil is full of such contrasts. Visitors have the option of staying in vibrant Avoriaz, purpose-built in an architectural style sympathetic with the surrounding mountains and with all the buzz of an ultra-modern French ski station; they can choose Morzine or Chatel, both stone-built Savoyard villages with a merry and unpretentious nightlife; or they can opt to stay on the Swiss side of this massive network of 12 resorts, enjoying traditional hospitality in Champery or a modern hotel right next to the slopes at Les Crosets.

Les Crosets is the destination for skiers attempting the 'Swiss Wall'. The skiing in the immediate vicinity holds few terrors, however, and is perfect for intermediates.

Let your own mood dictate your agenda. If you crave adventure, try the endless mogul fields above Avoriaz on the Col du Fornet and Les Hauts Forts sections; if gentle meandering on wide, tree-lined runs is the order of the day, cruise around between Les Gets and Morzine; if daily mileage is the essential ingredient, start at Chatel, for example, and ski over the Swiss border to Morgins and thence Champoussin, Les Crosets and Planachaux before recrossing the French border for the mouthwatering return home, via Avoriaz.

There is something for everyone in the Portes du Soleil although beginners are

Thanks to an unusual agreement that overcame local and national political rivalries, a single lift pass covers all 12 resorts in the Portes du Soleil, although they do not share a single lift system. The circuit comprises Chatel and Avoriaz on the French side and Swiss centres Morgins, Champoussin, Les Crosets, Champery and Planachaux. There are two major diversions: Torgon is reached from Chatel and connects with La Chapelle d'Abondance while it is often possible in good snow conditions to ski all the way from Avoriaz to Morzine from where the

lifts run to Les Gets. Apart from the sheer size of the skiable terrain – 220 lifts serve 600km (375 miles) of marked trails and scores of off-piste gullies and powder bowls – the main attraction is being able to criss-cross the Franco-Swiss border at will and sample the completely different atmosphere of each village.

As the most central of the villages the futuristic Avoriaz is the hub of the Portes du Soleil. More attractive than most French purpose-built ski stations, there are several good hotels and masses of tiny self-catering apartments. Alternatively,

there is a Club Mediterranee where the volatile mixture of *joie de vivre* and *esprit de corps* combine to provide a heady atmosphere, day and night, despite the club's stark exterior and spartan interior design. Club Med is certainly not for those whose idea of a merry night is curling up with a good book.

The mountains around Avoriaz soar high and, if the village centre lacks rustic alpine charm, it is certainly impressive and blends perfectly with the stern peaks all around – the jagged outline of the rooftops is in harmony with the stark,

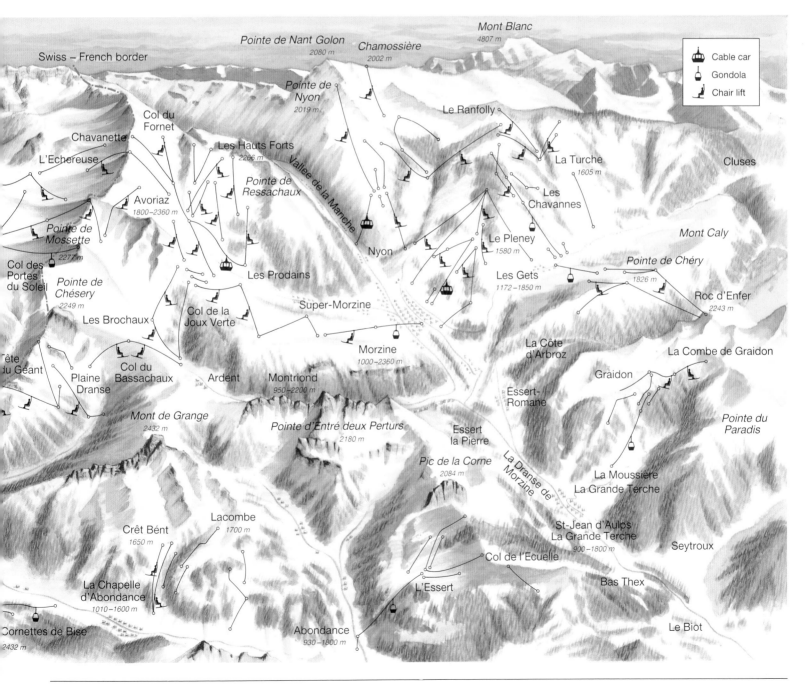

treeless mountainsides as all of the buildings have been completed in a wood cladding. Avoriaz is traffic-free and transport from the outlying car park is by ratrac or horse-drawn sleigh. There is a collection of apartment and hotel complexes and it is possible to ski right to the door of most of them. This is very convenient but beware of skiers zipping by your doorstep when you step outside – there may be no motor traffic, but the ski-borne variety can be just as lethal.

Nightlife in Avoriaz is very lively. It has to be, as even the closest of friendships are strained by being cooped up in tiny apartments and it is far preferable to cruise the cafés, bars and discos than to sit all evening in a claustrophobic heap. You can eat reasonably cheaply, if content with a *croque-monsieur* (toasted cheese and ham sandwich), but the better restaurants are pricey while the discos are exorbitant. A problem for the wobbly imbiber is that there are no covered walkways and the journey home can be hazardous. Other non-ski activities include visits to the cinema (films in French), shopping, dance and aerobics classes plus swimming in a heated outdoor pool.

Avoriaz offers the most varied skiing in the Portes du Soleil. The nursery slopes on Le Plateau are easily reached from anywhere in the village, there are plenty of gentle runs for improving intermediates and some frighteningly difficult runs for experts only. The Village des Enfants has a good reputation for providing children with an enjoyable introduction to skiing. Mono-ski and surf-ski, the big French fads, are highly popular and there is a festival at the end of the season which includes participation in these activities as well as parascending and speed skiing.

The excellent lift system is imaginatively designed so that more time is spent coming down the mountains than riding up. Lift queues are rare thanks to the installation of high-speed three and four-person chair-lifts. Good skiers tend to find that the mogul fields below the Hauts Forts have an adherent quality while there is plenty of good off-piste work from this section down through the trees to Les Prodains, in the direction of Morzine. The most notorious run is the Chavanette: its nickname, the Swiss Wall, is appropriate as it seems to drop vertically down over the Swiss border. Late in the season it is manageable as the moguls are big enough to break a fall and the snow is soft by mid-morning. But in the depths of winter it can be windswept and icy with no room for error!

Many visitors staying in self-catering apartments choose to return for lunch, and all runs and lifts connect with the village centre where there are plenty of cafés and restaurants, and so Avoriaz has few mountain restaurants. One lunchtime treat is to ski over to Les Lindarets, an old goatherd's settlement which houses some of the best restaurants in the region—prices are reasonable and portions gargantuan, designed to replace calories burnt away during the mornings' exertions.

Les Lindarets is *en route* to Chatel, a bustling Savoyard stone-built town with a more lived-in atmosphere than Avoriaz. Although a part of the circuit, Chatel's lifts do not provide a complete link and it is necessary to take the free bus service from the base of the La Linga gondola to its counterpart at the other end of the village. The installation of 10-person gondolas has helped to make this connection relatively painless but do be aware that Chatel is the most accessible resort in the Portes du Soleil from Geneva and is a popular starting point for locals at weekends. From Chatel you can ski back to Avoriaz, continue the circuit to Morgins or meander around the Super Chatel section. The skiing is on rather dull open slopes, although there is a link with Torgon which provides more variety.

Chatel's *après-ski* scene is more informal and cheaper than in Avoriaz and it is a good base for non-skiers, particularly those with a car, as visits to Geneva, Montreux, the Chateau de Chillon and dozens of little French and Swiss villages ranged around Lake Geneva are fascinating excursions. Spa towns such as Evian and Thonon are close by and a visit to

Chapels such as this, above Les Crosets on the Swiss side of the Portes du Soleil, with the Dents du Midi in the background, are dotted about the mountainsides.

Yvoire, a gorgeous medieval village, provides a tranquil antidote to the hectic Portes du Soleil scene.

Morgins has had a long-standing relationship with British skiers. The albums of the White Bear Club in the tourist office show pictures of adventuring Britons who visited the region early this century for winter sports holidays which encompassed skating and tobogganing as well as skiing. If you wanted to ski down a mountain in those days, you had to walk up—the albums show just how cosseted

Chatel is on the French side of the Portes du Soleil network, connecting with Avoriaz and, over the Swiss border, Morgins. It is the most accessible from Geneva.

we are today. The atmosphere here is very different from its French neighbour Chatel and visitors come for the charm of Morgins, not for a vibrant nightlife. Most of the skiing in the vicinity is tree-lined, very different from the stark landscape around Avoriaz, but there is little to interest experts.

The circuit continues from Morgins to Champoussin and provides yet another contrast. This purpose-built Swiss settlement, with its apartment blocks looking like outsize chalets, is a perfect location for families looking for a self-catering holiday. The little nightlife available is merry and unpretentious with dancing in a couple of hotels. The skiing around Champoussin is, in the main, easy but the runs down to Les Crosets are more demanding and from there a couple of lifts take skiers up to the French border

for the testing descent of the 'Wall'.

Les Crosets is a rambling modern ski-station, lacking in charm but the locals are hospitable and the lifts disperse from a central point outside the Hotel de la Telecabine. There you can continue the circuit back into France for a variety of runs to Avoriaz or branch off to Planachaux, a little farming settlement on a plateau above Champery. It is tempting to linger on a restaurant terrace and spend the rest of the day wondering at the jaw-dropping aspect of the Dents du Midi and Dents Blanches ranges across the valley. Champery itself is a lovely traditional Swiss village which was an established ski resort long before the Portes du Soleil was constituted. A new cable-car has speeded the progress of skiers up from the valley but to return on skis entails

Above: *Futuristic Avoriaz is at the centre of the Portes du Soleil network and has been designed to merge with the surrounding landscape.*

Right: *Snow surfing is one of the great French fads, having outstripped mono-skiing in popularity, and is taught in most ski schools.*

difficult descents through the trees or a long, at times almost flat, run home via Grand Paradis. Most skiers spend the day around Planachaux and Les Crosets and take the cable-car back in the evening.

Back on the French side, given the right conditions, it is possible to ski from Avoriaz to Morzine. Like Chatel, Morzine is stone-built and is a jolly, bustling little town with links on skis to Les Gets, a

quiet village ideal for a secluded holiday. The Princess Royal is a fan of Morzine but experts will prefer the terrain around Avoriaz. A new lift system now links the two, meaning that good skiers who prefer the traditional Savoyard atmosphere can stay in Morzine and join the circuit at Avoriaz each morning, and get the best of both worlds. Morzine is one of several diversions from the Portes du Soleil circuit and, combined with Les Gets, provides plenty of opportunities for intermediates. Indeed, every resort has its own character and each is worth exploration in a fortnight's stay.

La Chapelle d'Abondance is probably the best bet for beginners and has one gorgeous easy run all the way from the top of Lacombe through a wildlife park where chamois, marmottes and wild goats

are to be seen cavorting among rocks and through the woods. The village is a farming community renowned for gourmet food in practically every hotel. Certainly not very lively at night, the stone and wooden-built settlement exudes a very friendly atmosphere as well as pervasive farmyard smells and the welcome is genuine, born of old-fashioned alpine courtesy, not a money-grabbing veneer of hospitality. Children are invariably happy in Chapelle and the instructors are very caring. Many speak good English and others are learning fast in an attempt to court the British market. In addition to its own downhill skiing, and its links with Chatel, Chapelle has a 38km (24-mile) cross-country circuit.

Purpose-built Torgon is 4km (2½ miles) from the old village, perched on a cliff with views all the way to Lake Geneva. The resort has triangular-shaped apartments with discos and restaurants while the skiing is very good for improving intermediates. Apartments in Switzerland are invariably more comfortable than their French counterparts – there are no hotels in the old village.

St Jean d'Aulps is another small purpose-built family resort, on the French side of the border, with small apartments and several hotels. The nearby old village is another farming community, complete with an ancient abbey. The skiing links with Belleveaux, where, as it is not a part of the Portes du Soleil system, a small supplement is payable. The skiing is more extensive than indicated on the piste map with plenty of off-piste opportunities and fast easy-to-medium pisted runs. Finally, Abondance is an unspoilt Savoyard town with an abbey and skiing for beginners and intermediates. None of the hotels is remotely grand and one can relax thanks to the informality of the locals.

If the Portes du Soleil sounds unmanageable due to its sheer size, the annual Raid des Portes du Soleil provides families and groups of friends the chance to explore the region in teams of four. The *rallye* includes parallel slalom events, powder skiing and orienteering between the resorts. It is designed to help recreational skiers familiarize themselves with all 12 resorts and takes place over a week in March every year.

CHAMONIX AND ARGENTIERE

Frivolity seems misplaced in Chamonix, an elegant little town tucked in beneath Mont Blanc. Its first tourists were serious rock climbers and mountaineers; today they are serious skiers, intent on conquering the off-piste descents around Argentiere and, later in the season, skiing the Vallee Blanche—a 22km (14 mile) high altitude winter wonderland of twisted glacial monoliths and deathly quiet gullies.

As a venue for competitive winter sports, Chamonix hosted the Olympics in 1924 (before Alpine skiing was included) and the World Championships in 1937 and 1962. The latter year was the scene of a near-clean sweep of gold medals by the Austrians—between them, Schranz, Zimmerman, Haas and Jahn took five of the six gold medals.

Skiers arrive in Chamonix as if it were Mecca, contemplating their pilgrimage to some of the most awesome skiing in the Alps. Even combined, Chamonix and Argentiere cannot compare with Val d'Isere and Tignes, or the Trois Vallees resorts, in either scale or convenience.

Le Brevent is the closest of the valley's ski areas to the centre of Chamonix. It has good intermediate terrain plus a few interesting sections for good skiers.

Helbronner
3466 m

Les Grands Montets
3275 m

Croix de Lognan
1965 m

Mont Blanc
4807 m

Aig. du Midi
3842 m

Prarion
1966 m

Le Brévent
2525 m

Les Houches

Col Cornu

CHAMONIX
1035 m

La Flégère
1894 m

Argentiere

Ski
slopes

——— Nursery

——— Easy

——— Medium

——— Difficult

Cable car

Gondola

Chair lift

Indeed, with skiing on six different areas, none of which connect, and only one of them within walking distance of the centre of Chamonix, you need to be a keen skier to endure the daily ritual of walking and riding on crowded buses. The free ski bus service is, however, highly efficient although a car is a definite asset, particularly if you want to make full use of the Mont Blanc lift pass which covers 13 resorts in the region including Les Contamines, Megeve and St Gervais. Mere inconveniences such as tramping through town carrying skis and waiting for a bus and, quite often, queuing for a cable-car, matter little to the avid powder hounds and fans of steep, hazardous skiing who head for Les Grands Montets each morning. They would be uncomfortable in an ultra-modern purpose-built resort where daily mileage is the order of the day.

Of the six areas, Le Brevent is closest to the centre of Chamonix (where most visitors to the valley stay) and has some extremely difficult skiing, especially from the top station (2525m/8284ft) from where there are several alternative descents: one is a pisted black trail and the rest are off-piste *couloir* runs which should only be contemplated in the company of a guide as avalanches are a frequent hazard. There is a little bar at the top to help fortify one's courage and a pleasant restaurant at the Planpraz mid-station to recover from the morning's trials. The skiing around Planpraz is mostly easy but the route down to the valley is strictly for good, and very fit, skiers.

La Flegere is adjacent to Le Brevent and is reached by a cable-car from Les Praz, on the outskirts of Chamonix. This is the best sector for intermediates, particularly those who enjoy fast on-piste skiing down long, rolling runs. There are several quite easy off-piste diversions along the way and, given the right conditions, a very interesting and at times difficult run all the way back to the valley. Check that there is snow cover all the way down before starting as, otherwise, it is a long walk.

Close to the Swiss border, beyond Argentiere, Le Tour is the best area in the valley for beginners with long, gentle trails and lovely views. It is neglected by

the good skiers who look for action elsewhere and lift queues are rare. Le Tour is also the starting point for an off-piste touring route, which requires a little climbing at the start, down to Chatelard via the Col de Balme in Switzerland; return to both Argentiere and Chamonix by rail. Incidentally, the rail journey, which originates in Martigny, is a gorgeous mountain experience in its own right, perfect for non-skiers in the party, and provides the ideal transfer if spending a week in Verbier or Zermatt, for example, before sampling the delights of Chamonix.

Like Le Tour, Les Houches is neglected by good skiers and is grand for families as its wooded slopes provide good shelter. In the right conditions, it is possible to ski down to St Gervais and return to Prarion (1966m/6450ft) by mountain railway (check train times first). Access to Les Houches is by cable-car and gondola, from either end of the village, and in addition to several trails for beginners there are a few for fast intermediates. The downhill course, despite being marked as for experts on the piste map, is within the scope of any competent intermediate.

Le Brevent, La Flegere, Le Tour and Les Houches are merely the supporting cast for the valley's star attractions, Les

Above: *Chamonix hosted the 1962 World Championships. Marianne Jahn, on the left, took gold in the slalom and giant slalom and her fellow Austrian, Crystal Haas, won the downhill.*

Right: *The glaciers below the Grands Montets provide an unbeatable combination of spectacular skiing and even more spectacular scenery.*

Grand Montets and the Vallee Blanche. For all the good skiing on Le Brevent, and despite the fact that the gondola rises from near the centre of Chamonix, it simply does not compare with Les Grand Montets and is usually ignored by keen skiers anxious to attack unmarked trails across glaciers, impossibly narrow *couloirs* and deep powder bowls, supplemented by on-piste skiing which seems to consist entirely of never-ending mogul fields.

The late Patrick Vallencent chose Argentiere as his base for *Ski Extréme* skiing and he was frequently to be seen leading groups of very advanced skiers down near-vertical descents beneath Les Grand Montets. With a top station at 3275m (10745ft), this section is the target for every ambitious skier. Again, do not even consider the off-piste terrain unless accompanied by a guide as both

the weather and glacial conditions can change by the hour. So eager are people to be first to break fresh powder after a heavy snowfall that it is not unknown for fist fights to break out as jostling for a place on the first cable-car of the day turns into bedlam. The mid-station at Croix de Lognan (1965m/6447ft) is reached by a single cable-car from the valley and has been supplemented by a chair-lift to Plan-Joran, a good place for lunch as most visitors confine themselves to the terrain above. The final stage of the cable-car to Les Grand Montets is not covered by the lift pass and requires a separate payment—places can be booked in advance. From the top, the choice is between tortuous mogul fields or near-impossible off-piste routes. The pisted runs below Bochard are fast and ideal for speed-conscious intermediates.

One alpine myth is that the Vallee Blanche is only to be attempted by experts. Not so. Rather than being an examination of technique, it is a glorious high-altitude run through a winter wonderland of magnificent glacial monoliths and serene valleys, with breathtaking views all around.

The starting point is at the top of the Aiguille du Midi (3842m/12605ft) which is reached by cable-car; many visitors like to take this ride simply for the thrill of rising from the valley floor as if in an elevator and for the staggering views at the top, with Chamonix like a little toy town straight down below. After edging along a narrow ledge, a new world opens up and the *cognoscenti* take a back pack containing a picnic on a fine day. Although the Vallee Blanche can be skied in a couple of hours, it would be a shame to race all the way down without stopping to gaze at, and to photograph, the amazing seracs spread about this extraordinary wilderness.

While it is justly renowned for its magnificent and mostly difficult skiing, Chamonix is one of the best resorts in France for an all-round winter holiday. There is a casino, many sophisticated restaurants as well as plenty of cheerful cafés, an Alpine Museum, sightseeing from the top stations of several cable-cars and day trips to Annecy and Megeve as well as the railway over the Swiss border.

TROIS VALLEES

The Portes du Soleil resorts which straddle the border between France and Switzerland dispute the claim of the Trois Vallees to be *le plus grand domaine skiable du monde* but there is no doubt that this network of lifts spanning three valleys, and served by four major ski resorts in the French Savoie, is one of the largest interconnected skiing areas in the world. It is also one of the best, with extensive skiing for everyone.

By continually updating the lift system and putting the needs of skiers first, the Trois Vallees continue to attract keen skiers from around the world, some to attempt to conquer the *couloirs* above Courchevel and others to enjoy life in a staffed chalet in Meribel-les-Allues, which is something of a British enclave these days. Meribel-les-Allues consists in the main of chalets and hotels while Meribel-Mottaret, further up the valley, is an attractive collection of apartment blocks speckled with a few hotels. 'Attractive' is not a word that is ever applied to either Les Menuires or Val Thorens, however, and these two purpose-built settlements sell themselves on convenience for the slopes, high-altitude skiing and the presence of a glacier above Val Thorens.

Although Meribel is the most central of the quartet, making it ideal for skiers who want to fan out in a different direction each day, Courchevel is without doubt the best for both skiing and range of accommodation. There are four villages, each taking its name from its altitude (1300m, 1550m, 1650m and 1850m) and it is rare to be staying more than a couple of minutes from either a lift or a piste.

Fur-coated Parisians, often in the company of a fur-coated toy dog, enjoy disporting themselves on restaurant terraces during the day as a prelude to dancing in some very expensive discotheques in the evening. Keen skiers are too absorbed in their sport to stop even for a quick snack at lunchtime and are far too tired to contemplate dancing the night away. The only real problem confronting good skiers is that after a few

days they start to fret, worried that they will never ski everything on offer – nor will they! No one can hope thoroughly to explore the region, even in a month.

The hub of Courchevel's activities, on and off-piste, is 1850, with skiing above

and below. Beginners have their own slopes immediately above the resort and are able to graduate to a couple of long, wide trails after a couple of days. Experts head up to La Saulire, usually ignoring a couple of difficult runs all the way down

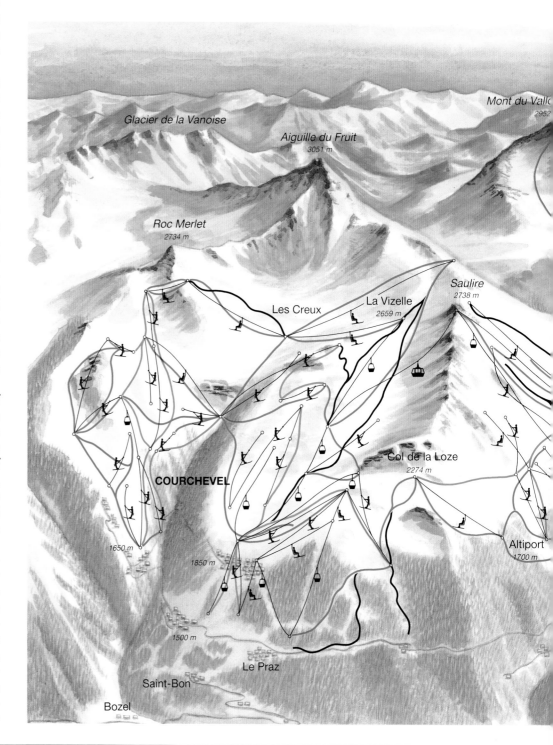

Courchevel 1850 is the largest of the quartet of purpose-built villages which attract keen, and smart, skiers from around the world for brilliant skiing and a vibrant nightlife.

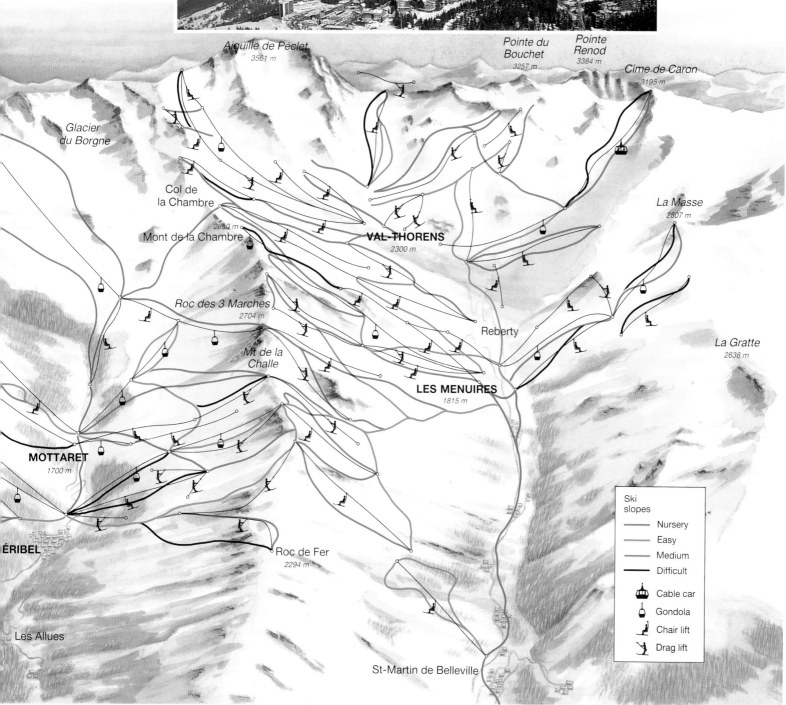

Aiguille de Péclet
3561 m

Pointe du Bouchet
3257 m

Pointe Renod
3384 m

Cime de Caron
3195 m

Glacier du Borgne

Col de la Chambre
2850 m

Mont de la Chambre

VAL-THORENS
2300 m

La Masse
2807 m

Roc des 3 Marches
2704 m

Reberty

La Gratte
2638 m

Mt de la Challe

LES MENUIRES
1815 m

MOTTARET
1700 m

ÉRIBEL

Roc de Fer
2294 m

Les Allues

St-Martin de Belleville

Ski slopes
— Nursery
— Easy
— Medium
— Difficult

▯ Cable car
▯ Gondola
▯ Chair lift
▯ Drag lift

to 1300 via 1550, and use the 160-person cable-car for access to the three *couloirs* which have, over the years, dented the egos of countless skiers. La Saulire is the main connecting point for skiing the rest of the Trois Vallees network from Courchevel; it also provides intermediates with a long roller-coaster run back through a pretty valley to Prameruel which forms one of the junctions between 1850 and 1650. La Saulire and its neighbour, Vizelle, give access to all sorts of trails, several quite gentle and others designed to test the fittest mogul freak.

Most of the skiing around 1650 is north-facing, undemanding and popular with families. The exceptions are the marked pistes and unmarked trails from Col de Chanrossa (2544m/8346ft) leading down to Les Creux. To the west of 1850, lifts rise to La Loze from where there are easy runs back down, some interesting and difficult descents through trees to 1300 and 1550 plus another connection with Meribel. The Jockeys and Jean Blanc black trails are especially testing.

Most of Meribel's skiing is broken into two sections, east and west, by the valley and there is a third section to the south which forms the link with Les Menuires. The eastern side connects with Courchevel, via La Loze direct to 1850 or by way of La Saulire for the runs on the upper reaches. The easiest run to Meribel from La Saulire, the Biche, is simple enough, no more than a traverse in parts, and is in strict contrast to the Couloir Tournier which requires a bit of a hike at the top and a lot of technique on the way down. La Saulire is at 2708m (8885ft) and Meribel-Mottaret at 1681m (5515ft) so that whichever route you take down, there is a total vertical drop of 1027m (3370ft), meaning that many miles can be

Above: *Meribel Mottaret has a vast array of lifts to take skiers to the top of Saulire for access to Courchevel, or in the opposite direction for Les Menuires and thence Val Thorens.*

Left: *With Meribel Les Allues in the background, a skier thrills to the vast expanse of the Trois Vallees network.*

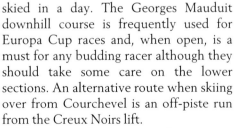

skied in a day. The Georges Mauduit downhill course is frequently used for Europa Cup races and, when open, is a must for any budding racer although they should take some care on the lower sections. An alternative route when skiing over from Courchevel is an off-piste run from the Creux Noirs lift.

There is artificial snow-making equipment around both Meribel-Mottaret and Meribel-les-Allues and each village has its own nursery slopes—there is a particularly pleasant wooded area for beginners close to the Altiport. Courchevel, too, has an Altiport and on sunny days lunching skiers watch from restaurant terraces as the glitterati arrive in private planes.

The western side of Meribel's skiing area is most popular in the morning, when it gets whatever sunshine is going, and as well as connecting with Les Menuires has excellent off-piste skiing below a range of formidable outcrops which combine to form a ridge of stern impressiveness. There are *couloirs* and powder bowls, wide pisted runs above the tree-line, several tough mogul fields and some delightful trails for intermediates. There are even a few gentle runs for novices, particularly on the lower reaches. It is possible to ski on an almost-flat *autoroute* piste from Meribel-Mottaret to Meribel-les-Allues, but not vice versa.

St Martin de Belleville is not a ski resort in its own right but is a worthwhile excursion from Meribel or Les Menuires for its off-piste runs—perfect for improving intermediates—and some long, easy pistes for novices and timid intermediates. Les Menuires is, however, a proper ski resort and one which has been constructed purely with the skier in mind, with no attempt to merge with the surrounding countryside resulting in a real eyesore. Still, some people like it, probably because prices are lower than in Meribel and Courchevel. There is a network of lifts rising from Les Menuires itself, and from its satellite settlement, Les Menuires Reberty, to the eastern slopes in the direction of Col de la Chambre (2750m/9022ft). This is intermediate territory—the nursery slopes are down by the village centre—and it can become very congested, particularly at the end of the day. The challenge for experts and strong intermediates is on the other side of the valley where there are bowls and narrow trails, gullies and fast pisted runs. Behind La Masse there are a few very special off-piste descents, which should be skied with a guide, as well as the lovely run down to St Martin de Belleville. There is another interesting off-piste itinerary off the back of the

Pointe de la Masse (2804m/9199ft) through a valley running by the Lac du Lou.

Val Thorens is just up the valley from Les Menuires and presents a marginally less miserable first impression; the second impression, of the village, reveals a thoughtfully designed centre and the third impression, of the surrounding mountains, has skiers jumping up and down in excitement. Again, there is something for everyone with nursery slopes immediately above the village centre and the runs below Col de Thorens (3115m/10 220ft), the Glacier de Gebroulaz (3301m/10 830ft) and Col Montee du Fond (3200m/10499ft) are ideal for cruising with some steeper sections for experts. The run from the chair-lift above the gondola drops 1104m (3622ft) to just below Val Thorens; some skiers like to spend all day repeating the exercise over and over again.

Strictly with a guide, it is possible to ski from the glacier to Meribel-Mottaret although most people make the connection via the quad-chair to Mont Peclet at 2952m (9439ft). None of this really compares with the runs below Cime de Caron, served by a 150-person cable-car to the highest point of the Tr̂ois Vallees circuit. The views from the top of the cable-car are breathtaking, as is the altitude – the Cime de Caron is set at 3200m (10499ft) – and there is no end to the skiing possibilities for good skiers. There is a steep fall-line run immediately beneath the cable-car, brilliant powder skiing after a heavy snowfall and very arduous mogul fields when there has been no snow for a few days. There are a couple of points where a traverse is necessary to find good skiing on unmarked trails and the reward is a collection of powder bowls which inevitably have American visitors whoopin' and hollerin' in delight.

Courchevel, Meribel, Les Menuires and Val Thorens are all sizeable resorts in their own right. Courchevel has 66 lifts serving 184km (115 miles) of marked trails, Meribel 43 serving 190km (119 miles), Les Menuires 53 serving 101km (63 miles) and Val Thorens boasts a further 36 lifts and 120km (75 miles) of pistes, adding up to an almost incredible network of 198 lifts and 595km (372

miles) of marked trails. And these formidable statistics take no account of the inestimable unmarked ski routes, powder bowls and off-piste drops down *couloirs*. There is almost too much skiing and visitors inevitably return home frustrated that they have barely scratched the surface of this huge area. If you are staying in Meribel, the most centrally located, it is easy to branch out in a different direction every day but if your accommodation is in one of the other three, a day's itinerary covering the whole circuit will, at least, give some idea of what you are missing in and around the other valleys.

Many British tour operators have ski leaders who take parties around the circuit; otherwise it is necessary to either hire a guide or be a competent piste-map reader. It is also necessary to be able to tell the time because a taxi ride from, say, Val Thorens to Courchevel is an expensive exercise if you have missed the last lift connection. Novices should forget the idea of a visit altogether, as although there are plenty of variations along the way, some testing skiing is on the menu somewhere *en route*.

With a good deal of self-catering accommodation in the three valleys, many skiers return to their apartments for lunch. Yet the mountain restaurants are frequently congested and the scene of much shoving and elbowing. Each of the

Left: *Either way, there's great skiing ahead. Both Courchevel and Meribel have their die-hard fans but each offers fabulous skiing served by a sophisticated lift system.*

Right: *Without being remotely pretty, Les Menuires sells itself on convenience for the slopes, good hotel restaurants, pleasant little cafes and a good range of non-ski activities.*

resorts has plenty of less frenetic places to eat in relative calm. One advantage to this is that, with the French taking lunch very seriously, the slopes are uncrowded during the middle of the day. So, have a large breakfast and a late lunch.

Dining is an all-preoccupying event in the evening, too, and there are some excellent restaurants, particularly in Courchevel where Le Cabichou has quickly risen high on the list of great alpine eateries. Le Bistro du Praz (at the hamlet of Le Praz, just below 1300) is an institution and is worth a visit from Courchevel for its farmhouse atmosphere and excellent cooking. La Bergerie, Le Bateau Ivre, Le Mangeoire, La Saulire, Le Chouca and La Brasserie de la Patinore have all won plaudits over the last few years for providing good food throughout the price range. Meribel also has a branch of La Bergerie, a little chalet-style place with a rustic atmosphere and a welcoming log fire, and Le Grand Coeur, the modern Mont Vallon and La Petite

Rosiere are among Meribel's best known and most popular restaurants. The tourist office publishes a useful guide to dining and other activities in Courchevel.

Both Les Menuires and Val Thorens have good hotel restaurants with a less exclusive atmosphere, although this is not to say anything against the quality of food and service. By contrast Courchevel and, to a lesser extent, Meribel attract a well-to-do-crowd for whom being seen in expensive restaurants is a big part of a ski holiday. Both the latter resorts, incidentally, have plenty of pleasant little cafés and pizzerias so there is no need to worry too much about your budget.

The breakdown of the rest of the après-ski scene is similar, with Courchevel home to some of the classiest and most expensive nightclubs in the Alps; Meribel is in the middle of the range while both Les Menuires and Val Thorens have carefree, unpretentious night spots. Again, there are a few affordable piano bars and the like in Courchevel and

Meribel meaning that there is something to the liking of most people, and most people's pockets. There is very little for non-skiers although Courchevel is popular with a number of Parisians who are happy to parade about in their finery without even thinking about hitting the slopes. Meribel's staffed-chalet life, with ready-made sociability, is understandably popular among the British. The Trois Vallees resorts are good for families as each tries hard to make ski lessons for children fun—they can also enjoy skating on the rink at Meribel where hockey matches provide good spectator sport.

So, the choice in the Trois Vallees is between smart and chic Courchevel, merry Meribel, functional Les Menuires and the highest resort in Europe, Val Thorens, which at 2320m (7612ft) literally stands high above its alpine rivals. Whatever your choice, there is excellent skiing all around in one of the largest interlinked ski areas in the world—certainly France's biggest and, say its devotees, the best.

FLAINE

Flaine was one of the first of the French purpose-built resorts, an architectural style which has now given way to the aesthetically more pleasing neo-Savoyard, 'nouveau purpose-built' style. But if the somewhat grim concrete apartment blocks leave much to be desired, skiing is Flaine's *raison d'etre*. It has 35 varied pistes served by 30 lifts. That may not sound much for today's piste-basher who has been spoilt by the multi-miled ski circuses and arenas of France and Austria. But Flaine is well linked with neighbouring Samoens, Morillon, and Les Carroz. Together the area has over 100 lifts and an impressive network of runs.

Flaine has a particularly good snow record for a 1600m (5248ft) resort with skiing that goes up to 2500m (8200ft). It holds the snow in its bowl-shaped terrain until late April. It is essentially a family resort and a good, if harsh, place for beginners. The nursery slopes are of a high standard, as are the two ski schools which have a high proportion of fluent English speakers who teach ski surfing as well as mono-ski and hang-gliding. Flaine is one of the few French resorts which teaches *ski évolutif*. Beginners start on one-metre skis and go up 10cm a day until they are able to handle the longer skis by the end of the first week.

The village has been built on three levels. The central level, Forum, the first to be built in 1968, is linked by lift to the higher level of Foret. *Après-ski* queuing between them has been minimized by the introduction of a second lift. The lowest tier is called Front de Neige. All three tiers have direct access to the slopes and are car-free. From Forum swift jumbo gondolas take you up to 2480m (8134ft) and the summit of Les Grandes Platieres from where there is a huge variety of runs to take you back down the side of the bowl into Flaine.

From the Tete Pelouse there are some excellent off-piste runs to be skied with a guide, but only in the best of powder snow conditions. The most difficult skiing lies in the Gers area. It is steep and unpisted, and often closed early in the season. At the other end of the complex, the Aujon ski area close to the vertical cliffs of the 2337m (7665ft) Croix de Fer, provides gentle powder slopes and plenty of easy runs for beginners. It is reached by an extremely steep drag lift which beginners often fall off and then have to choose between skiing down to the bottom off-piste between tightly packed trees or climbing up to the top carrying skis. Apart from that little hiccup, blue or green runs all around provide easy routes for the beginner. The expert can take a nearby red or black run and end up at the same restaurant for lunch.

One of the resort's best-known expert runs is the Diamant Noir, which follows the path of the lift pylons down from Platieres. It is difficult in icy conditions but wonderful in deep new powder. Don't attempt it at all unless you really feel up to it.

Opposite: *Flaine usually enjoys good snow until well into April and provides good English-speaking tuition in* ski evolutif, *mono-ski, ski-surfing and hang-gliding.*

Below: *Flaine's somewhat grim apartment blocks are home to first-class kindergarten and day-care facilities making it a favourite destination for families.*

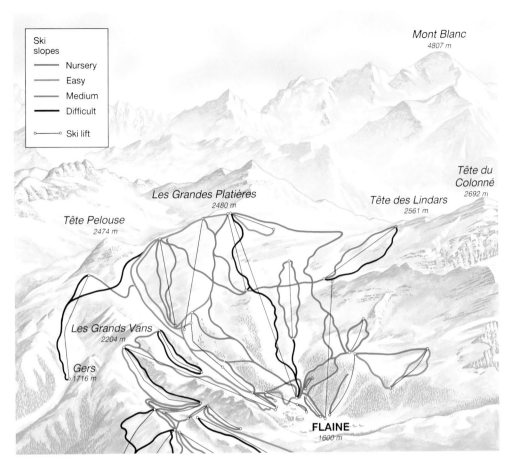

Ski slopes
— Nursery
— Easy
— Medium
— Difficult
○—○ Ski lift

Mont Blanc
4807 m

Tête du
Colonné
2692 m

Tête des Lindars
2561 m

Les Grandes Platières
2480 m

Tête Pelouse
2474 m

Les Grands Vans
2204 m

Gers
1716 m

FLAINE
1600 m

Flaine has some atmospheric mountain restaurants which serve reasonably priced lunches. Meanwhile, back in the resort you have a choice of five hotels, three of which are three-star: the Totem, the Gradins Gris and the Grand Hotel Le Flaine. Of the two two-stars, the Aujon offers an adequate service, though the food is neither sufficient in quantity or quality. The Hotel Les Lindars is well known for its in-house baby-sitting service, nursery and kindergarten.

Flaine is a resort for skiers and has little to offer in the way of nightlife as it is a largely self-catering resort for budget-conscious holidaymakers. The Totem and the Gradins Gris have restaurants worth trying and there are several good pizzerias and creperies. Chez Daniel and La Trattoria are both worth a mention. Much of the *après-ski* revolves around the Snow Bub bar which you will pass on your way back from the piste. The children's play area is opposite, so you can keep an eye on your youngsters from the terrace. The other pub, much loved by Scots, is the White Grouse Pub. There is also a swimming pool and health centre.

FONT ROMEU

The old streets of Font Romeu were familiar to medieval pilgrims. Now that Perpignan airport takes international flights, today's skiing pilgrims can reach the place more easily. The little town has a great deal to offer visitors as well as skiing, so it is a good place to visit for a first ski holiday or for those travelling with non-skiers. The Pyrenees offer a gentle alternative to the Alps. Their mountains are more rounded, their wood-lined slopes more sheltered. English is widely spoken in the ski schools and the prices both in the mountain restaurants and in the villages are lower than those in the Alps.

From Font Romeu a cable-car leads up to Airelles, where skiing really starts. There is a road up there too, and a regular bus service. From Airelles chair-lifts, including a fast four-seater, and teleskis spread out over the east slopes of Col de Pam. From here can be reached the more testing pistes on the Roc de la Calme (2204m)/7229ft and also the purpose-built resort of Pyrenees 2000 in the next valley. The circuit takes in 22 lifts and

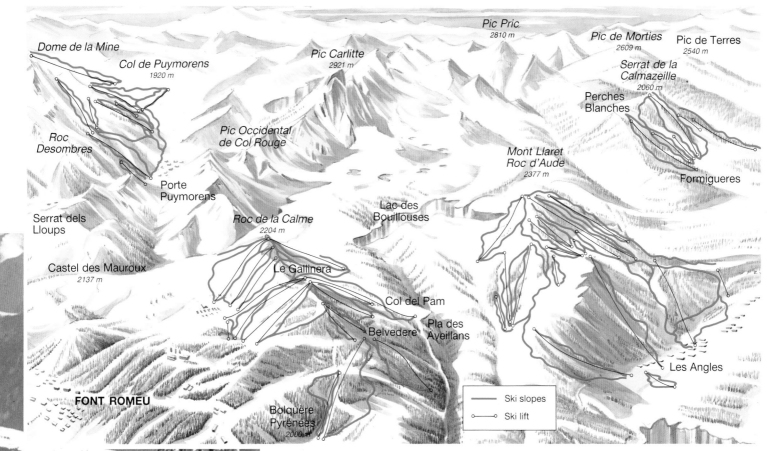

Ski slopes
Ski lift

The Pyrenees has a long-established reputation for being the perfect region for beginners and families thanks to clean air, a sunny climate and good pistes.

42km (26 miles) of piste. Big mountain restaurants save coming back down to Font-Romeu at lunchtime. Snow-making machines ensure that the pistes are well-covered and some of the runs are floodlit at night. The great lamps light up large areas and make night skiing a lot more fun than by the more usual flickering torchlight.

The air is so clear and the sun so warm in this area that it was chosen as the site for the world's most powerful solar research station. Like an immense satellite disc consisting of 20 000 mirrors, it looks curiously out of place at Odeillo on the approach road to Font Romeu. It can be visited any day of the year.

In 1968, when the Summer Olympics were held in Mexico, a high-altitude training centre was built at Font Romeu. It includes an Olympic-sized ice-rink and a big covered pool which skiers use when they come off the slopes. A quite different training centre — for dogs — lies on the slopes above Font Romeu. Siberian Huskies are taught to draw sledges and visitors can learn to drive the teams. It is a great feeling to career along on a sledge behind two or four bounding huskies — a lot more exciting than driving a skidoo.

Cross-country skiing is very well developed in the Pyrenees. From a centre such as Font Romeu trails radiate out and are well marked with distance and standards of difficulty. It is possible to go off for five easy kilometres, or to travel practically the length of the Pyrenees.

The town has a casino with blackjack and roulette, many good bars and restaurants and a night club. With the facilities of the high-altitude training centre as well as covered tennis and squash, there is no lack of things to do. An interesting outing for non-skiers is the little yellow train, built in the early years of the century, which travels to the old towns nearby. A fascinating day's visit is to Villefranche de Conflent with its 11th-century church and fortifications.

ISOLA 2000

There are not many ski resorts within an hour-and-a-half's drive from the sea, and the Mediterranean at that. Isola 2000 benefits in several ways from its position in the Alpes Maritimes above Nice. For one thing, the winds off the Mediterranean drop their moisture as they rise over the mountains and this falls as snow. So Isola's snow record is consistently good. Then there is the caressing warmth of the southern sun, to soften the harshness of the winter landscape. Trees

grow at 2000m (6562ft) here, protecting both pistes and village. Nice is also handy as an international airport and a great shopping town with a fascinating old centre as well as its aristocratic Victorian seafront.

Isola was built by a British company and opened in April 1972, a time when massive architectural blocks were popular in high-altitude resorts. It made sense at 2000m to collect apartments, hotels, shops and restaurants under one roof so

that no one need go out at night and, in the mornings, skis could be put on at the front door. In time, however, this stark architecture lost its appeal and the resort was allowed to run down.

A Lebanese company then bought out the original owners and the resort is now run by Ziad Tadieddine, who was enthusiastic himself about skiing. Regarded by his staff with respect and affection, he is renowned for knowing exactly what is going on in every part of the resort. The

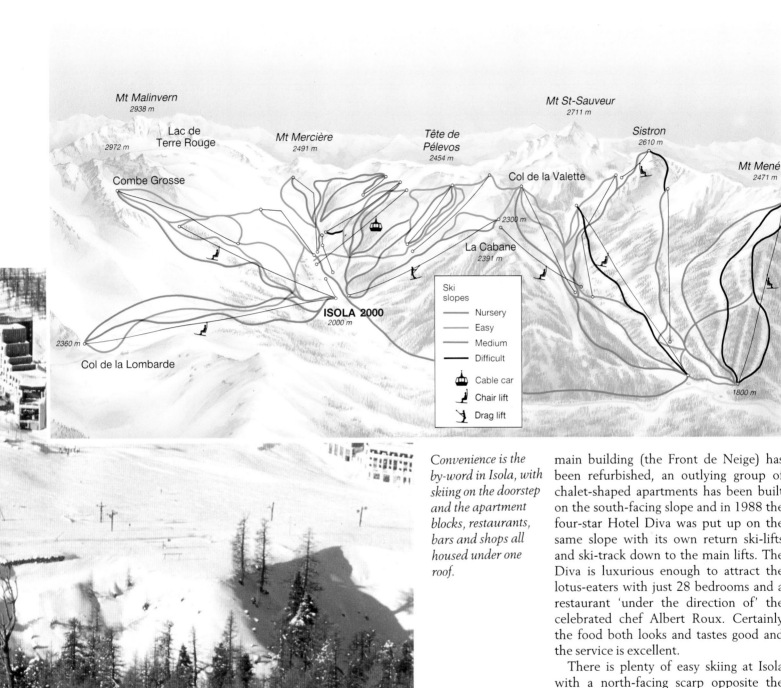

Mt Malinvern
2938 m

Lac de
Terre Rouge

2972 m

Combe Grosse

Mt Mercière
2491 m

Tête de
Pélevos
2454 m

Mt St-Sauveur
2711 m

Sistron
2610 m

Mt Mené
2471 m

Col de la Valette

2300 m

La Cabane
2391 m

ISOLA 2000
2000 m

2360 m

Col de la Lombarde

1800 m

Ski slopes

— Nursery
— Easy
— Medium
— Difficult

🚠 Cable car
🚡 Chair lift
🎿 Drag lift

Convenience is the by-word in Isola, with skiing on the doorstep and the apartment blocks, restaurants, bars and shops all housed under one roof.

main building (the Front de Neige) has been refurbished, an outlying group of chalet-shaped apartments has been built on the south-facing slope and in 1988 the four-star Hotel Diva was put up on the same slope with its own return ski-lifts and ski-track down to the main lifts. The Diva is luxurious enough to attract the lotus-eaters with just 28 bedrooms and a restaurant 'under the direction of' the celebrated chef Albert Roux. Certainly the food both looks and tastes good and the service is excellent.

There is plenty of easy skiing at Isola with a north-facing scarp opposite the Front de Neige. Easy blue and red pistes link up through the larch trees and there are some blacks at the west end stretching down to 1800m (5906ft). Good nursery areas curl round to the east and link with the south-facing slopes. The ski-school at Isola finds plenty to challenge its clientele, who can learn mono-skiing and ski-surfing. The ice-driving circuit and walks up over the col to the Parc du Mercantour to look at chamois and mouflons fill any idle moments.

LA PLAGNE

Half-a-dozen modern, purpose-built ski stations and four old Savoyard farming settlements comprise La Plagne, about four hours from Geneva airport. Nearly all of the purpose-built centres have been designed to merge with the surrounding landscape. The exception is Aime-la-Plagne, which at 2100m (6890ft) is the highest. From a distance the apartment complex looks like an outsize ocean liner. At least the architects have learnt from this mistake: the most recent addition, Belle Plagne, is an attractive mixture of apartments, hotel, shops and restaurants with access to the gondola.

La Plagne's biggest assets are skiing on the doorstep, a wide variety of pistes and a glacier, which assures at least some sort of skiing in even the mildest winters. Throughout the summer months the lower slopes buzz with galloping horses, and there is a full programme of archery, tennis, tuition in boxing, judo or karate, rafting, dance classes, fitness training, hiking, paragliding, mountain biking, fishing, swimming and walking in flower-speckled meadows.

The local lift pass allows a day in each of Tignes, Val d'Isere and Les Arcs although only the last named is within easy reach and is accessible on skis, via Peseix-Nancroix, given the right snow conditions. La Plagne's own skiing is best for intermediates and families although there are a few interesting sections for experts. Each of the six modern complexes has its own ski school plus ski kindergarten and day-care facilities.

Using the thoughtfully designed lift system linking the villages, it is easy to rack up big distances in a day's skiing, either sticking to the central area immediately to the south of Plagne Centre, Plagne Villages, Plagne Bellecote and Belle Plagne, exploring the runs around the Bellecote glacier where the top station is at 3250m (10 663ft) or diverting down to one of the villages in the foothills, where there are more atmospheric places for lunch. The vertical drop from the top of the Bellecote glacier to Montchavin is 2000m (6562ft) during the course of a run of some 15km (9½ miles) and is quite enough to turn anyone's thoughts to refreshment.

A dozen or so pistes run down from Roc de Verdous (2500m/8202ft) and La Grand Rochette (2505m/8219ft), none holding any terrors for half-competent skiers, and this sector is La Plagne's major playground simply because it is the closest to most of the accommodation. This is a shame as if just a little more time is taken, there is such good skiing to be found in the outlying areas. In addition to good trails for beginners and intermediates, the glacier gives access to a couple of steep descents for experts only and a lovely unpisted run which drops 1450m (4757ft) to Les Bouches where a lift transports skiers back up to above Montchavin. With a guide, and given the right

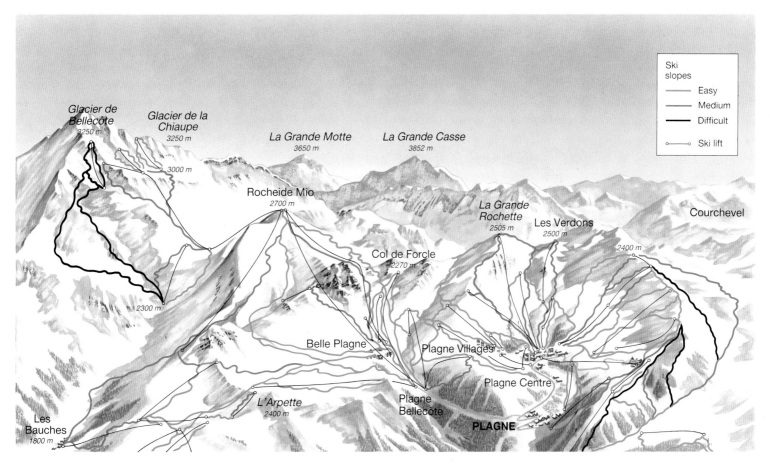

Glacier de
Bellecôte
3250 m

Glacier de la
Chiaupe
3250 m

3000 m

La Grande Motte
3650 m

La Grande Casse
3852 m

Rocheide Mio
2700 m

La Grande
Rochette
2505 m

Les Verdons
2500 m

Courchevel

Col de Forcle
2270 m

2400 m

2300 m

Belle Plagne

Plagne Villages

Plagne Centre

L'Arpette
2400 m

Plagne
Bellecôte
2400 m

PLAGNE

Les
Bauches
1800 m

Ski
slopes

——— Easy

——— Medium

——— Difficult

○—○ Ski lift

conditions, the glacier can be the starting point for the unpatrolled runs down to Peseix-Nancroix and to Champagny-en-Vanoise which is another quiet little traditional Savoyard village.

Anyone used to traditional Austrian or Swiss *après-ski* will find La Plagne, like any other French purpose-built resort, very different. The evening atmosphere is amiable but rarely vibrant, most of the activity being centred around restaurants and a few discos. Most visitors stay in self-catering apartments (which are, in the main, of the standard French shoe box variety) and so there is not the social focus that a hotel bar provides, for example. There is some good cross-country skiing around Montchavin plus tennis and squash at Aime-la-Plagne.

Left: *Mono-ski, ski-surfing and parapente are available in La Plagne where there is skiing year-round on the Bellecote glacier.*

Opposite: *Each of La Plagne's six modern complexes has nursery slopes on the doorstep, its own ski school and ski kindergarten.*

LES DEUX ALPES

Les Deux Alpes is a modern resort but unlike most recent developments in the French Alps it is not purpose-built; the result is a jolly little town which, without being remotely pretty, is one of the better places in France for an all-round winter holiday. It is also one of the best for groups of mixed ability as there are easy slopes high above the valley. After a few days most novices are able to ski for 14km (9 miles) all the way home from the glacier. The town straggles along a main street full of bars and cafés, and accommodation is in hotels, guesthouses and apartments.

Les Deux Alpes is so named for its two skiing areas on either side of town, and most skiers concentrate their attentions on the main section below the Col de Jandri (3200m/10499ft). But it is a

The Diable and Super Diable runs regularly test the nerve, stamina and technique of even the best of skiers. Les Deux Alpes boasts every type of skiing.

shame to ignore the areas to the west of the town as they provide uncrowded skiing on sunny slopes in the morning and give access to a long run down to Bons, a little hamlet which also has some of the best cross-country in the area.

The new Jandri Express 20-person gondola-cum-cable-car has alleviated early morning queues on the main section, to the east, and whisks skiers to the glacier in just 20 minutes. It is also used by skiers who are too tired to ski all the way home at the end of the day. There really is skiing to suit all abilities here and experts particularly enjoy the guided off-piste run

down to La Grave, the Diable and Super Diable bumps runs from Tete Moute (2813m/9229ft) plus a selection of interesting pistes above Lac du Plan. There is good intermediate skiing all over the mountainsides and fast intermediates enjoy testing their technique, stamina and nerve down Descente, the downhill course. Novices have their own nursery slopes adjacent to the main street and quickly graduate to some longer, but undemanding, pistes aloft.

Les Deux Alpes offers 196km (123 miles) of marked trails served by 61 lifts of various descriptions and in addition to standard ski school lessons there is tuition in mono-ski and surf-ski. The Grande Galaxie lift ticket includes Les Deux Alpes as well as Alpe d'Huez, Puy-St-Vincent, Serre Chevalier, and the Milky

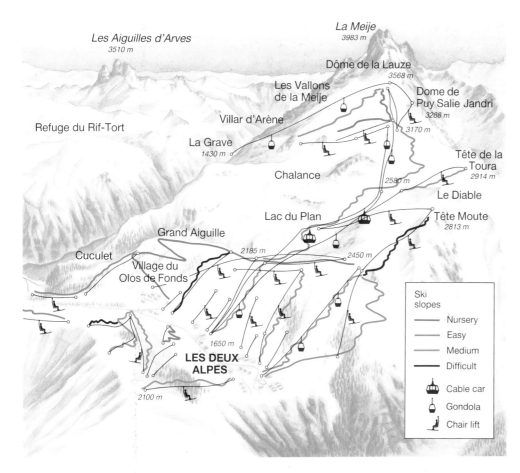

Way resorts which straddle the border between France and Italy plus Italy's Bardonecchia, allowing a day in each — an excellent buy for self-drive skiers. There is a helicopter link between Les Deux Alpes and Alpe d'Huez.

A gondola drops from the south end of Les Deux Alpes down to Venosc, an unspoilt little stone-built hamlet perched above the Veneon valley and worth a visit either for a traditional Dauphiné dinner or simply for a change of pace from the rather frenetic nightlife of Les Deux Alpes. Venosc also gives access to some secluded cross-country skiing.

This resort's nightlife tends to be expensive: bar-hopping is one of the more popular pastimes and there are plenty of very noisy discotheques plus some more sedate piano bars. The public outdoor heated swimming pool is in the same complex as the ice-rink, entry for which is free if you present your lift pass.

The village of Les Deux Alpes straggles along its main street with skiing on both sides of the valley. There is plenty of easy skiing high above the valley.

LES ARCS

Four valleys and three separate purpose-built villages constitute Les Arcs, a modern ski centre which is famous for having an excellent children's ski school, for having developed the *ski évolutif* method (G.L.M. is the American equivalent) and for being the home of the Flying Kilometre. In common with other French resorts, surf-ski and mono-ski are very popular and merit their own classes in ski school. Les Arcs is far removed from the Savoyard stereotype of stone-built farming settlements. Instead, the three villages are modern and exude a vibrant, compelling aura that translates into merriment for all, on and off the slopes. Arc 1600 was the first to be completed, in 1972, and was followed by Arc 1800 and, finally, Arc 2000. Arc 1800 (at 1800 metres) is the largest, busiest and jolliest of the complexes and boasts the best hotel, Le Golf.

The skiing areas served by the three villages converge at several points and are augmented by the slopes above Peseix-Nancroix, a lovely old farming hamlet covered by the same lift pass, and each has nursery slopes right outside. The ski school meeting points positively buzz with excited chatter in the morning and the attitude to teaching is that skiing is meant to be fun—a far cry from the serious approach in many Austrian resorts. The ski school combines this with efficiency and innovation, notably in the development of *ski évolutif*. Children invariably enjoy their classes, which involve lots of games and singing, culminating with the end-of-week test.

At the other end of the scale, the black runs from the ridge below the Aiguille Rouge (3226m/10 584ft) above Arc 2000 are merciless as there are no easy options. The Flying Kilometre course also runs from the ridge and, appropriately, this was the event allocated to Les Arcs for the 1992 Winter Olympics. Arc 2000 is most certainly the best part of the network for good skiers and its terrain can easily be reached from both Arc 1600 and Arc 1800. As well as the off-piste routes down from the Aiguille Rouge, both the Piste du Refuge and Piste des Lanches are tough on-piste trails, strictly for proficient skiers. There is a good variety of red runs for intermediates throughout the valley

Right: *The Flying Kilometre contests below the Aiguille Rouge at Les Arcs sees racers dropping stone-like down the precipitous course at speeds of over 200kph (125mph).*

Left: *Ultra-modern quad chair-lifts have improved the capacity at Les Arcs where the skiing is spread across four valleys served by three purpose-built villages.*

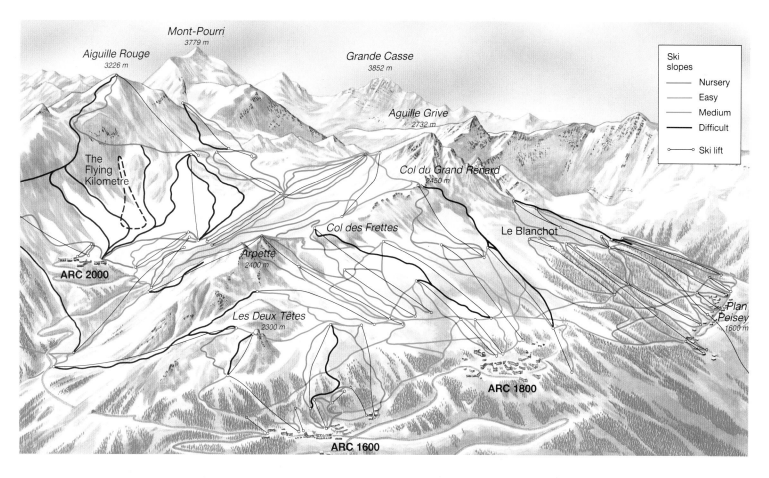

Ski slopes
- Nursery
- Easy
- Medium
- Difficult
- ○——○ Ski lift

Mont-Pourri
3779 m

Aiguille Rouge
3226 m

Grande Casse
3852 m

Aguille Grive
2732 m

The Flying Kilometre

Col du Grand Renard
2450 m

Col des Frettes

Le Blanchot

ARC 2000

Arpette
2400 m

Plan Peisey
1600 m

Les Deux Têtes
2300 m

ARC 1800

ARC 1600

but little for beginners other than a few nursery slopes around the resort complex and the gentle glide down to Pre St Esprit. Although Arc 2000 is easily reached from the other two centres, the queues for lifts back to Arpette (2400m/7874ft) and Les Deux Tetes (2300m/7546ft), which lead back to Arc 1600 and 1800, are often horrendous and it is as well to make a mid-afternoon return to avoid them.

This is not to say that good skiers have to confine their exertions to Arc 2000. The runs from Col du Grand Renard (2450m/8038ft) back to Arc 1800 are challenging all the way and although the routes beneath Arpette and Col des Fretes are marked as red on the piste map, they are frequently mogul-infested and provide many scares for the unwary. One of the prettiest runs in the whole area is the Piste de Malgovert, a delightful little switchback of a trail which twists it way through narrow gaps in the trees. It is worth skiing it several times in succession, first getting to know the course, next to take it full-tilt and, finally, to ski it slowly and marvel at the gorgeous surroundings.

MEGEVE

With its quaint medieval centre, Megeve combines old-world charm with ultra-sophistication. If its own skiing area may not be sufficient for experts, Megeve is one of the resorts covered by the Mont Blanc lift pass which, in all, covers a dozen resorts including Argentiere, Chamonix, Les Contamines and St-Gervais-les-Bains, all within easy reach.

Megeve has been France's most chic resort since the thirties. The combination of an exquisite ancient church, lovingly restored old buildings all around, the absence of modern high-rise concrete, the clip-clop of horse-drawn sleighs plus some gorgeous hotels with fine dining rooms makes it one of the best resorts in

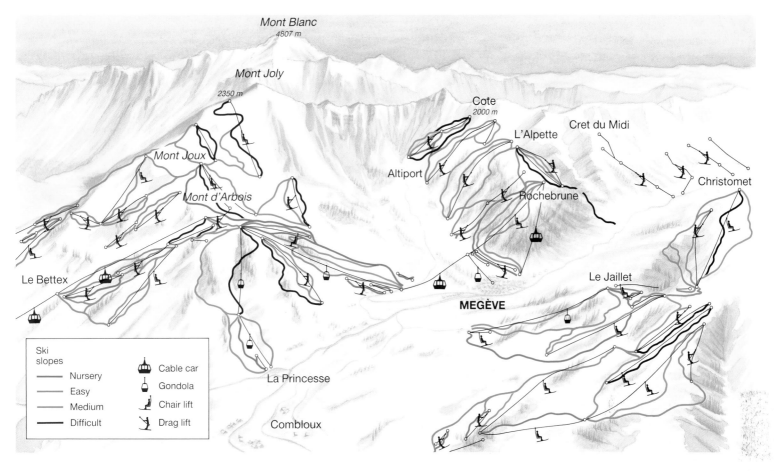

Mont Blanc
4807 m

Mont Joly

2350 m

Cote
2000 m

Mont Joux

L'Alpette

Cret du Midi

Altiport

Mont d'Arbois

Rochebrune

Christomet

Le Bettex

Le Jaillet

MEGÈVE

La Princesse

Ski slopes

Nursery
Easy
Medium
Difficult

Cable car
Gondola
Chair lift
Drag lift

Combloux

Left: *Megeve is so well-served by mountain restaurants that it is easy for lunch, not skiing, to become the focal point of the day. The installation of new lifts hasn't detracted from the traditional ambience.*

the Alps for an all-round winter holiday — in sharp contrast to the better-known French purpose-built centres. Neither does Megeve enjoy the convenience of its modern counterparts as few of the lifts rise from the middle of town. Yet this is a small inconvenience for those who are enthralled by a special ambience which has remained unchanged for half-a-century.

Of the three skiing areas, the main section is Mont d'Arbois, reached by gondola from the outskirts of Megeve and with connections to both St Gervais-les-Bains and St-Nicolas-de-Veroce. This provides beginners with a gentle introduction to skiing, either on wide open slopes or delightful trails cut through trees. There is one long easy trail, Les Mandarines, which gives novices that wonderful feeling of covering some distance on skis rather than spending their

time on the same patch of snow all day. If you have a car, this section can also be reached by gondola from La Demi-Lune, a little out of town, and good skiers find some interesting work down the Princesse run and on the Mont Joux (1962m/ 6437ft) and Mont Joly (2350m/7710ft) areas above Mont d'Arbois — there are some good mogul fields around Mont Joly and off-piste diversions through trees.

The trail map does not show the extent and variety of the runs from Mont Joux down to St-Nicolas-de-Veroce (1200m/ 3937ft). They deserve the attention of expert skiers as in addition to several sweeping runs which can be taken at speed, and a few tough ones that require a degree of caution, the off-piste skiing around here is the best in the vicinity. Good skiers have several options on the Rochebrune section, which has its own lifts from the village and is connected to those serving Mont d'Arbois by a cable-car. Cote 2000 is beyond Rochebrune and, although not a particularly large area, it certainly has a few difficult runs as well as more off-piste opportunities.

Le Jaillet is across the valley, served by a gondola from the outskirts of Megeve, and provides easy skiing. Incidentally, because of Megeve's relatively low altitude (1113m/3652ft) lack of snow can be bothersome but, as most of the skiing is on grassy pastureland, skiing is possible with only minimal snow cover; furthermore, with most trails below the tree-line, visibility is rarely a problem.

Megeve is well served with mountain restaurants and it is easy for lunch, not skiing, to become the main feature of the day. It is also a good place for non-skiers: there is skating on a rink in the village centre, curling, indoor tennis, swimming, plus a casino, or one can simply wander through the pretty streets. Excursions to Annecy or Chamonix using the local bus service each provide an enjoyable day out — Annecy for strolling through little streets and browsing in shops and Chamonix for taking the cable-car up to the Aiguille du Midi to gaze at the Mer de Glace. The *après-ski* scene is smart and is centred around Megeve's stylish cafés, restaurants, nightclubs and casino.

VAL D'ISERE AND TIGNES

Most skiers agree that L'Espace Killy, as Val d'Isere and Tignes style themselves, is the best ski centre in the world. The counter-claims of *aficionados* of French neighbours Courchevel and Meribel, of Zermatt and Verbier in Switzerland and of the top resorts in the Rockies have to concede that for all the plus points of their favourites, the combined attractions of Val d'Isere and Tignes are very hard to beat—they genuinely do have everything. The Trois Vallees network might be larger but neither Courchevel nor Meribel provides sufficient challenge for experts; for all Zermatt's charm its skiing is too dispersed and, like Verbier, its lift system cannot cope with early-morning crowds; there is nowhere in the Rockies to match Val d'Isere and Tignes for variety and sheer size.

Chosen by the peerless Jean-Claude Killy (hence 'L'Espace Killy') as his home, Val d'Isere was originally the hunting lodge for the Dukes of Savoie and today retains some of its traditional Savoyard atmosphere, although purists are disdainful of new developments in the centre. Tignes is purpose-built and, without being remotely pretty, has the guarantee of year-round skiing on the Grande Motte glacier which rises to 3460m (11352ft). In all, 120 lifts serve 276km (173 miles) of marked trails with countless acres of off-piste skiing and no end of *couloirs* to test the technique, and nerve, of the most proficient skier. The whole system is interconnected and Val d'Isere's lifts are served by the highly-efficient Trains Rouges (which are, incongruously, white buses!) while all accommodation in Tignes is only a short walk from a lift.

Despite the area's awesome reputation, L'Espace Killy is a good place to learn to ski and even better for groups of mixed

Despite the stark countryside around Tignes it is a popular year-round sports centre with skiing on the glacier, plus a host of other activities available during the summer.

Pte du Montet
3488 m

Pte des Lessieres

Tete de Solaise
2560 m

Le Fornet
1930 m

VAL D'ISERE
1850 m

ability. The nursery slopes in both resorts are close to the centre and there are plenty of easy runs high above the valley so that novices don't feel like poor relations down in the valley while their more accomplished friends zip about aloft. Moreover, Val d'Isere boasts no less than four ski schools and competition between them ensures a high level of tuition and care.

This competition between the ski schools works to the advantage of good skiers, too. Top Ski, for example, is run by the Zimmer brothers, Jean and Patrick, who followed Killy to Val d'Isere from their native Alsace after a few seasons racing on the World Cup circuit and established their school specialising in off-piste guiding and tuition as well as downhill and slalom racing technique. They also run a heli-skiing programme over the Italian border at Valgrisenche. English is widely spoken in all four ski schools — it has to be as both resorts are very popular among British skiers.

Val d'Isere's skiing is in four sections. Many skiers opt to take the bus to Le Fornet in the morning to avoid the occasional congestion on the Solaise cable-car and chairs, and those rising to Rocher de Bellevarde (2827m/9275ft) across the valley. Le Fornet is a delightful hamlet, noted for a couple of restaurants which serve hearty and inexpensive lunches. Its cable-car rises to the mid-station below which there is a near-vertical bumps run plus an easy, meandering trail winding its way back to the valley. Most skiers prefer to take the gondola from this point, however, and continue up to the Col de l'Iseran where there is the choice of fast freeway skiing in

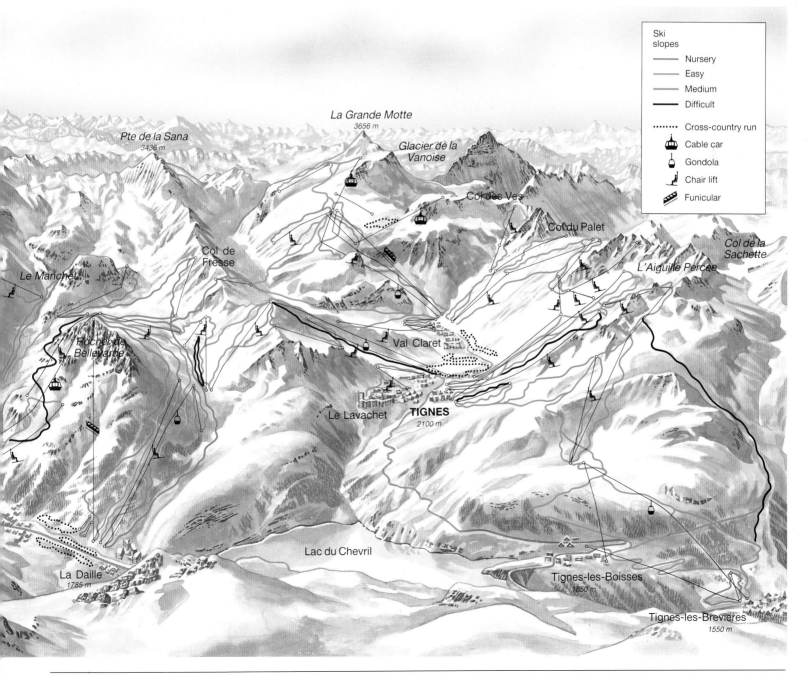

Ski slopes

—— Nursery

—— Easy

—— Medium

—— Difficult

········· Cross-country run

Cable car

Gondola

Chair lift

Funicular

Pte de la Sana
3436 m

La Grande Motte
3656 m

Glacier de la Vanoise

Col des Ves

Col du Palet

Col de la Sachette

L'Aiguille Percée

Le Manchet

Col de Fresse

Rocher de Bellevarde

Val Claret

Le Lavachet   **TIGNES**
2100 m

Lac du Chevril

La Daille
1785 m

Tignes-les-Boisses
1850 m

Tignes-les-Brevières
1550 m

the immediate vicinity, wide open runs on the Pissaillas glacier—which provides skiing throughout the year—or skiing down to the chair-lift which crosses over the Pointe des Lessieres and down to the Solaise section.

The Solaise is deceptive: despite the stern mogul fields which initially confront skiers, there are plenty of gentle trails in the wide bowl above and beginners can take the cable-car home at the end of the day. Better skiers want to test themselves on the world-famous 'bumps', on the off-piste section around Le Manchet, and down the Germain Mattis run to Le Laisinant. This last-named snakes its way through woodlands and is frequently ignored by good skiers who do not want to be stranded in the valley but it really is worth the short wait for a bus back into town.

The cable-car to the Rocher de Belle-varde rises from the same point as that to Solaise and the runs back to town from the top are among the toughest in the region—they are not especially steep but conditions are variable and it is easy to get lost. However, there is an easier but often crowded descent via Rocher du Charvet. On the other side of the summit, life is a lot more comfortable with broad, sweeping red runs and plenty of bland blue trails. There is more off-piste work avail-able on La Spatule than is evident at first and the only drawback to skiing these secluded powder bowls is that it is necessary to ski all the way down to La Daille to return to the top.

La Daille, although a part of Val d'Isere, is a village in its own right and is one of the more attractive French purpose-built settlements. The old gondola cars have been augmented by the 272-person Funival underground railway which whisks its passengers to the top of Rocher de Bellevarde in just four minutes. This is intermediate country, not without challenge, and there are plenty of diversions through trees on the lower sections, most notably down La Piste Perdue which, as its name indicates, isn't easy to find. This should not be attempted at speed as there are obstacles in the form of rocks around every corner, and a corner after every rock. It is very narrow, not steep, and enormous fun.

Right: *The Solaise is home to Val d'Isere's most famous bumps run. Fortunately for timid skiers there is plenty of less-demanding skiing and they can take the cable-car back down.*

Below: *For all their awesome reputation, Val d'Isere and Tignes provide something for everyone.*

The mid-station above La Daille is the starting point for the ascent to La Tor-viere and the drop down to Tignes. The runs on the Val d'Isère side of La Torviere provide endless amusement for all grades of skier but those staying in Val are usually too eager to get to Tignes, and vice versa, to take time to enjoy them. Apart from watching hang-gliders waft into the distance from the ledge at the top of La Torviere, or stopping for lunch at the restaurant, there are plenty of alternatives here. Tignes consists of three main villages and all can be reached from this point on a choice of trails. Novices prefer the gentle run to Val Claret—experts

often follow them to ski fresh powder around La Petite Balme—and there is a long pisted traverse to Tignes Le Lac. Another easy run leads to Le Lavachet while good skiers prefer the moguls beneath the gondola.

The three areas around Tignes all converge on Val Claret and provide such compelling skiing that many visitors ignore the existence of Les Brevieres, down in the valley beyond L'Aiguille Percee. Timid skiers should take care not to veer left on the upper section as the Vallon de la Sache trail is usually very bumpy and is frighteningly steep in parts. The alternative runs down to La Breviere

are more sympathetic and the reward at the bottom is a collection of friendly bars and restaurants with terraces.

The marked runs on the Tignes side of L'Aiguille Percee, and below the adjacent Aiguille du Chardonnet, are of beginner-to-intermediate standard (apart from the steep Oeillet trail) and provide good off-piste work. In fact, this section is often used to teach powder skiing as it is wide, has sufficient steepness to maintain momentum and has no hidden dangers.

The awesome Grande Motte dominates Tignes. The new restaurant at the mid-station (3016m/9895ft) is a pleasant surprise after taking the creaking old gondola

from Val Claret and, on a sunny day, is the perfect spot for sitting on the terrace and gawping at stupendous views all around. As for the skiing, the Grande Motte gives access to the infamous Wall which attracts daredevils from around the world. Local advice must be sought as avalanches are a frequent occurrence in this area; it is best skied with a guide, not just for safety's sake but to find the most interesting descents. Otherwise, there are several tricky intermediate runs, countless off-piste opportunities and some fairly modest runs which enable fairly modest skiers to enjoy the glory of the Grande Motte. One good tip for those staying in

Val d'Isere is to branch off half-way down on to the Dahu or Cairn trails as they lead to the Fresse drag-lifts which ·connect with the Rocher de Bellevarde and La Daille sections.

As well as all this activity in the immediate vicinity, and the connections with Val d'Isere, adventurous souls can hire a guide for the trek to Champagny and Peseix-Nancroix. They are situated between Les Arcs and La Plagne, both of which are covered by the Val d'Isere/ Tignes lift pass. The trip is long but not arduous and homeward transport is arranged.

With its practice areas available year-round on the glacier, Tignes has almost become synonymous with freestyle skiing and regularly holds international events. But the region is best known to television

The great Norwegian Slalom racer Ingemar Stenmark was a regular on the winner's podium at Val d'Isere during his great years. Val d'Isere will hold the Men's Downhill in the 1992 Olympics.

viewers as being host to the first races of the World Cup circuit, at Val d'Isere in mid-December. The problem in recent years is that the race has had to be delayed or cancelled due to poor snow conditions but this didn't affect the decision to award the downhill event to Val d'Isere in the 1992 Albertville Winter Olympic Games. In any case, a new course above the village has been constructed to give the resort two championship courses— the original track above La Daille has seen an inevitable set of victories by those modern giants of the sport: Franz Klam-

mer in the men's downhill, Ingemar Stenmark in the men's slalom and giant slalom and Marie-Therese Nadig who regularly won the women's downhill and giant slalom.

Despite the stark countryside around Tignes, it is a popular year-round sports centre with skiing on the glacier, white-water rafting, golf and tennis during the summer. Yet Tignes should be avoided by anyone looking for a romantic alpine winter holiday and it would be cruel to take a non-skier there in winter. There are activities such as hang-gliding but Tignes is a skier's town first and last. That being said, it is a good choice for self-catering family holidays as there are ski and non-ski kindergartens.

Nightlife in Tignes consists of dining in restaurants or pizzerias lacking in ambience, and dancing in a couple of discos where only the rich can afford more than a round of drinks. If you want the action to continue into the night, Val d'Isere has much more to offer at more affordable prices. Dick's Tea Bar, run by the diminutive Dick Yates-Smith, has become one of the great alpine institutions, demonstrating that the French don't have a monopoly on panache. Most of the clientele is British. The evening begins with quiet music early on, as tales of the day's activities are swapped, and develops into a wild bopping session around midnight with the fun continuing for several hours thereafter. Elsewhere in town there are plenty more typical French night spots such as Bar Jacques (next door to Dick's Tea Bar), Club 21 and Mephisto. Val d'Isere provides a good variety of cafés and restaurants and the range is between simple pizzerias, the cavernous La Taverne d'Alsace and some quite grand dining rooms in the larger hotels.

Val d'Isere is also superior to Tignes for non-ski activities with hang-gliding and parascending, 17km (11 miles) of cross-country trails, skating, cleared paths for walking, and an indoor swimming pool, entrance for which is free with your lift pass. A visit to the ancient church is fascinating although shopping for ski clothing at Jean-Claude Killy's shop in the main square attracts a bigger throng. In summer, in addition to skiing on the glacier, horse riding, golf, mountain biking, fishing and archery are all available. Mountaineering and rock climbing brought many of the first visitors to Val d'Isere and these pursuits retain their popularity.

Val d'Isere offers a wide range of accommodation and has become one of the major resorts among British staffed-chalet operators. Of the 50 hotels, the Sofitel is modern and comfortable with a couple of bars and a 'Therapeos' centre, complete with heated outdoor pool, sauna, massage facilities and gymnasium. The Christiania is like an outsize chalet and provides a tranquil ambience while the refurbished Savoyade also has an exercise room, sauna and whirlpool. Otherwise, the choice is between traditional French establishments such as L'Aiglon or the Bellier, dozens of medium-priced small hotels and *pensions* or self-catering apartments. Chalet hotels are provided by British operators and, in the main, sleep up to 80 guests run along chalet-party lines — they are cheap, usually very cheerful, and invariably provide unlimited wine with dinner.

Most of the accommodation in Tignes is in self-catering apartments, and most of them are tiny. Of the few hotels available, Le Ski d'Or at Val Claret gives quick access to both La Torviere and Grande Motte and is in sharp contrast to the rest of Tignes in that it has been decorated and furnished with meticulous care, is noted for its cuisine and wine list, and exudes the atmosphere of a country hotel — for these delights be prepared to pay. Otherwise, each hotel in Tignes conforms to the same dreary pattern. Unlike Avoriaz, for example, no attempt has been made to blend the architecture with the surrounding landscape although a few have wood cladding which gives them a veneer of attractiveness. The only good news about accommodation in Tignes is that everywhere is close to the lifts and it is possible to ski to the door of many apartment blocks.

Having said all that, let us not forget the advantages of Tignes. On the plus side, skiing is guaranteed on the glacier in even the mildest of winters, there are plenty of English-speaking instructors, the lift system has been cleverly designed for the convenience of skiers — it is constantly being modernized and features many high-speed chairs — and there is plenty of scope for beginners and experts alike. Best of all, its lift system connects with Val d'Isere!

L'Espace Killy boasts a massive lift system which ensures that more time is spent skiing down the mountains than riding up. Bottlenecks are rare.

GARMISCH-PARTENKIRCHEN

Bavaria's biggest and best ski resort is a long-standing favourite among American and British service personnel, and it attracts thousands of skiers from all over Germany, yet it is overlooked by the majority of European skiers who assume that the best alpine skiing in the region is to be found over the border, in Austria. Those who pass it by are missing out.

Garmisch's medieval beginnings are positively modern when compared with those of its neighbour across the Partnach river, Partenkirchen (originally Partanum), which was founded in 15 B.C. as a Roman staging post. Today, both villages retain a Bavarian atmosphere redolent of the mid-18th century although many buildings, complete with gorgeous frescos and intricate galleries, date back much further. The old church in Garmisch was constructed in 1255 (with masonry stolen from a nearby castle!), while the 'new' church was completed in 1733. Inside the hotels, traditional Bavarian hospitality is in keeping with the ornate exteriors and local ordinances dictate that new construction conforms to traditional style.

If all of this makes Garmisch-Partenkirchen sound like a dinky little Bavarian village yet to move into this century, the fact that nearly all of the 55 hotels have saunas and that 18 have their own swimming pools will argue otherwise. Creature comforts are of utmost importance to the visitors who are not only looking for skiing but an all-round winter holiday too.

As befits a resort on the World Cup circuit and one which was the venue for the 1936 Winter Olympics, Garmisch-Partenkirchen boasts some excellent skiing either on the glacier below the Zugspitze (2964m/9724ft), down through glades on the Alpspitz and Hausberg sections, or on mostly uncrowded trails at Eckbauer and Wank, the latter two being neglected by day trippers who tend to head for the tougher work on Hausberg. The Zugspitze is Germany's highest outcrop and forms a part of the border with the Tyrol—good skiers can take the very steep run down to Erwald

on the Austrian side—and provides the guarantee of some sort of skiing, on the glacier, in even the mildest of winters.

Keen skiers like to stay at the Hotel Schneefernerhaus which is tucked in below the Zugspitze at 2650m (8694ft) so that they can be first on to the slopes in the morning without having to endure the rather tedious journey by rail from town via a tunnel cut through the mountain. When snow conditions are good, most visitors prefer to get out half-way down on the return journey and ski back to Grainau from where a free bus service runs into town. On the glacier itself, most of the skiing is for intermediates with just a couple of difficult sections.

The Alpspitz is also good for intermediates and it connects with Hausberg at

Above: *In addition to plenty of gently rolling trails for novices and intermediates, Garmisch-Partenkirchen provides some tough work for experts.*

Right: *Helmut Hoeflehner won the 1985 Men's World Cup downhill at Garmisch-Partenkirchen which was host to the 1936 Winter Olympics.*

Kreuzeck (1650m/5413ft) from where the World Cup downhill course runs back to the valley. After a snowfall there is some delightful off-piste work through the trees. Eckbauer is the best of the five sectors for children as they can ski safely on wide, gently rolling trails while families tend to use the slopes around Wank where one of Garmisch-Partenkirchen's

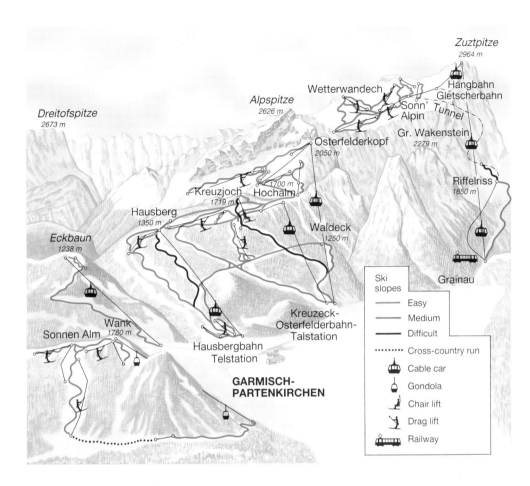

Zuztpitze
2964 m

Hangbahn
Gletscherbahn

Wetterwandech

Alpspitze
2626 m

Sonn'
Alpin

Tunnel

Dreitofspitze
2673 m

Osterfelderkopf
2050 m

Gr. Wakenstein
2279 m

1700 m

Riffelriss
1650 m

Kreuzjoch
1719 m

Hochalm

Hausberg
1350 m

Waldeck
1250 m

Eckbaun
1238 m

Grainau

Wank
1780 m

Sonnen Alm

Kreuzeck-
Osterfelderbahn-
Talstation

Hausbergbahn
Telstation

**GARMISCH-
PARTENKIRCHEN**

Ski slopes

— Easy
— Medium
— Difficult
····· Cross-country run
Cable car
Gondola
Chair lift
Drag lift
Railway

hidden treasures is the farmhouse at Esterbergalm where *Kaiserschmarren* (thick pancakes, cut into pieces and fried with apples) are the speciality.

In addition to being the venue for the 1936 Winter Olympics, Garmisch-Partenkirchen held the 1978 World Championships and is regularly the scene of the German National Championships as well as being the site of one of the 'Four Hills' international ski jumping competition held every New Year. The Olympia Eisstadion regularly hosts international curling and skating competitions but is otherwise open to the public, and other non-ski activities include cross-country touring, tobogganing, sleigh rides and spectator sports such as ice hockey.

With a casino, scores of restaurants, discos and nightclubs with traditional Bavarian or modern music, nightlife is a big part of staying in Garmisch-Partenkirchen. A further endorsement of its charms is that one of its biggest markets is the USA — every winter, hundreds of former servicemen who skied there while in the army return across the Atlantic with their families.

CERVINIA

Cervinia always suffers in comparison with its Swiss neighbour, Zermatt. No, this bustling little town in north-west Italy does not have the quaint old-world charm of Zermatt and, yes, the 'back' of the Matterhorn (Monte Cervino, to the Italians) viewed from this side looks mundane compared with its awesome aspect from the Swiss side. The fact is that it is unfair to compare the two. Each provides a very different ski holiday and Cervinia's plus points are keen prices, an extensive skiing area, excellent restaurants and a carefree attitude to *après-ski*. There is the added bonus of being able to ski on Zermatt's slopes although a separate lift ticket is required. The drawback to skiing in Cervinia is that many of the lifts are in need of modernization (replacement, in some cases) and that queues for early-morning cable-cars are

For all its sprawling mass of hotels, pensioni and apartment buildings, Cervinia is a jolly little town where the fun is non-stop in a convivial atmosphere.

often lengthy, particularly at weekends when hordes of Milanese charge up the valley—it has that in common with Zermatt!

Cervinia was founded in the thirties when Mussolini decided that the Aosta Valley needed another major ski resort and the road which until then had petered out at Val Tournenche, was extended up to the little farming settlement at Breuil. Construction work took the form of throwing buildings together without any discernible pattern with the result that, today, Cervinia is a sprawling mass of hotels, *pensioni* and apartment buildings. So, if you are seeking traditional

alpine charm, forget it. If, on the other hand, you are in search of a ski town where the fun is non-stop, Cervinia is perfect.

The town is set at 2050m (6725ft), which is higher than the top station of many resorts, and there is skiing up to 3480m (11417ft) on the Plateau Rosa which means that despite its south-facing aspect, Cervinia regularly enjoys good snow conditions. There is little to challenge the true expert but, for beginners, intermediates and, especially, families, Cervinia has long and undemanding south-facing slopes including one 22km (14 miles) run all the way down to Val Tournenche.

Most of the skiing is on wide-open snowfields and bowls, centred on Plan Maison, the cable-cars' mid-station at 2565m (8415ft), where there is a little

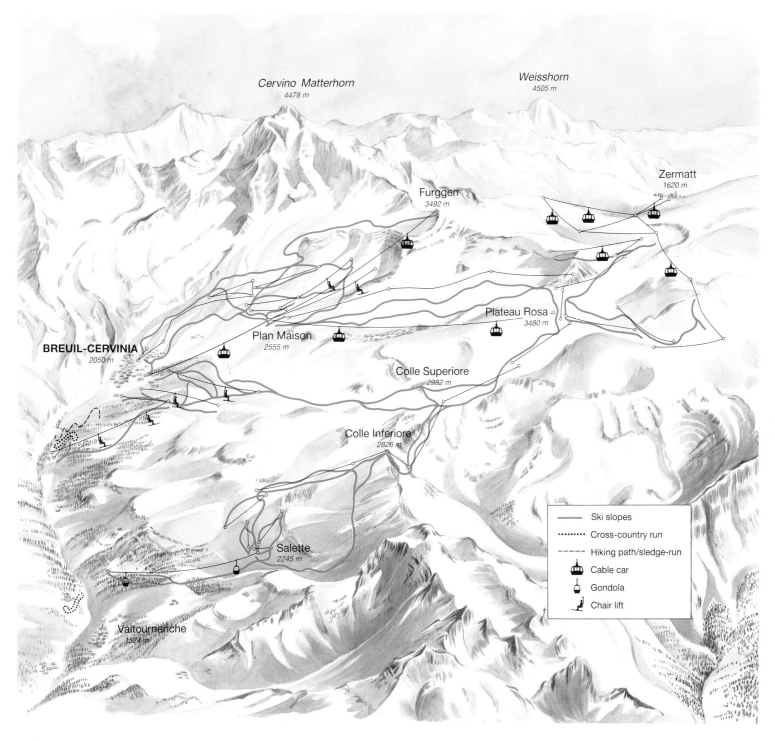

Cervino Matterhorn
4478 m

Weisshorn
4505 m

Furggen
3492 m

Zermatt
1620 m

Plateau Rosa
3480 m

Plan Maison
2555 m

BREUIL-CERVINIA
2050 m

Colle Superiore
2982 m

Colle Inferiore
2826 m

	Ski slopes
····	Cross-country run
----	Hiking path/sledge-run
	Cable car
	Gondola
	Chair lift

Salette
2245 m

Valtournenche
1524 m

snack bar and a hotel, Lo Stambecco, with a dining room open to the public. The skiing in the immediate vicinity is easy on nearly flat slopes, providing the perfect terrain for novices. Below this point there are various descents so that everyone can ski back to town in a gentle cruise or a fast *autostrade* bash.

Above Plan Maison the choice is between a series of three drag-lifts running up to the Theodulpass, a cable-car rising to Furggen (3492m/11457ft) and two more to the Plateau Rosa, all of them on or adjacent to the Swiss border. Of the three, the drag-lifts to Theodulpass afford the easiest return to Cervinia and present the opportunity for playing at being a downhill racer. The little (16-person capacity) cable-car to Furggen has a nasty habit of swaying about alarmingly in high winds and at the top you must walk down hundreds of steps before attacking some demanding skiing with several off-piste variations along the way. The two cable-cars to the Plateau Rosa give the easiest access to Zermatt and an 8km (5 mile) return to Cervinia on the Ventina trail which is the ultimate pleasure for intermediates; an easier route, a traverse, leads less ambitious skiers back to the

runs above Plan Maison. By turning left above the Cime Bianche (2832m/ 9291ft), it is possible to ski all the way to Val Tournenche, a pleasant little village, although an extra lift has been added in recent years to obviate the necessity of making one boring traverse along the way. There is another route (unpisted) to Champolouc. Incidentally, if you are planning to treat yourself to a day in Zermatt, check on likely weather conditions as an overnight stay in Switzerland

can be very expensive. In any case, allow enough time for the return.

There is one other route down from the Plateau Rosa, running directly below the cable-cars. Not many people attempt it as few skiers want to end the day in a wooden box.

Eating on the slopes is a variable experience as some restaurants are over-crowded and others grubby. Fortunately, this is not the case back in town although there are few really grand restaurants

other than in the more luxurious hotels. Instead, good value can be found in the numerous little places where you can replace calories expended during the day's exertions. The centre of town is full of inexpensive eateries, with Copa Pan, Chez Lombard and the Ristorante Lombard among the best. Pasta and pizza dishes are the staple diet in Cervinia, but look out for regional specialities such as *rigatoni* and *polenta* as well as a *fondue valdostana*—much like a fondue any-

where else except that cream and eggs are added. Meals can be washed down with the heady *caffè alla valdostana*, a mixture of grappa, coffee and spices served in a wooden *grolla* friendship bowl.

It is worth taking a five-minute taxi ride to the Cime Bianche. After a hair-raising journey—taxi drivers here are real boy racers—look forward to a wholesome dinner of cold meats followed by a main course of venison, washed down with gallons of wine in a noisy, cheerful atmosphere. A visit to the Cave des Guides, below L'Hostellerie des Guides in the main street, is a treat as it is a museum-like tribute to Cervinia's famed mountain guides and the climbers who set off from the old village of Breuil to attempt the ascent of Monte Cervino and neighbouring peaks. L'Hostellerie des Guides itself also celebrates the art of mountaineering—its tranquil lounge is decorated with pictures of climbing in the Alps and Himalayas—and the Caffe Whymper is another quiet place for a hot chocolate and a pastry. But there is nothing tranquil about most of the bars. Places like The Dragon in the Hotel Pellisier (popular with the British) and La Chimera boom away at full volume until the early hours.

Skiing, eating, drinking and dancing comprise most of Cervinia's attractions but there is an Olympic-specification swimming pool at the Hotel Cristallo, with attendant massage and sauna facilities, and a skating rink behind the ski-school office.

Day excursions to the region's capital, Aosta, can be arranged through the tourist office. On this interesting journey people crane their necks to gaze up at the many castles and tiny chapels perched high above the valley, while in Aosta they can explore remains of the original Roman settlement and some very stylish clothes shops. Day trips for skiing in Courmayeur, which is covered by the same lift pass, are also available. This being said, Cervinia is not well placed for sightseeing, being at the head of a dead-end valley. Instead, its visitors are happy to enjoy the locals' haphazard attitude to skiing and life in general, and to stroll home on a starlit night, pausing to look up at Monte Cervino, its peak picked out by floodlight.

Left: *First-time skiers in Cervinia are able to relax on the easy slopes around Plan Maison while the more accomplished can ride cable-cars to more challenging runs.*

Above: *Skiing isn't the only activity in Cervinia. The bobsleigh run provides thrills for participants and spectators alike while swimming and skating are less frenetic.*

CORTINA D'AMPEZZO

Cortina d'Ampezzo is one of the grand old breed of ski resorts where the Beautiful People gather in their furs and finery each season to admire and be admired by other Beautiful People. Set in a beautiful broad bowl surrounded by the craggy pink Dolomite mountains two-and-a-half hours by road from Venice, it is Italy's most elegant ski resort, rivalling Megeve and Gstaad for its elegance. The atmosphere and style of this sunny town with its designer fashion and jewellery shops is unashamedly Italian with plenty of activities for non-skiers.

The skiing is notable for its great variety and takes place in four different areas, rise to a height of 3243m (10 637ft). It is perfect for all standards with plenty of blue runs and a few steep gulleys for experts. Cortina boasts a total of 52 lifts and 160km (99 miles) of groomed pistes, but the Super Dolomiti Ski Pass gives you access to a total of 450 lifts and over 1600km (990 miles) of well-maintained and marked pistes.

On the mountain there is no compulsion to get involved in the vast Superski Dolomiti complex, but it would be a shame to visit Cortina without trying it on at least one day. Another reason for skiing this area is that one of the best restaurants is at Armentarola which is easily reachable from Falzarego, where the Superski Dolomiti begins 20 minutes by bus from the centre of town.

Locally, there is a choice of four areas, all linked by shuttle bus, the cost of which is included in the lift pass. Most first-time visitors begin on the Faloria (2123m/6963ft), a good place to rediscover your ski legs. Here there are open runs and plenty of restaurants, and a good piste down to the Rio Gere where a cable-car leads up to the Cristallo (3000m/9840ft) which has a good, steep mogul slope back towards the Passo Tre-Crocio. From the San Forca, those who like a challenge can take the gondola to the Forcella Staunies, from where a wonderful run plummets back again to the Rio Gere restaurants.

The major area close to the resort is Tofana (3243m/10 637ft). It is served by numerous lifts and the Freccia nel Cielo (Arrow in the Sky) cable-car, which rises from the centre of Cortina to the Ra Valle. When the snow is scanty elsewhere you will find it up here, and the views from the restaurant at the top are quite stunning, offering a complete circuit of the soaring pink and green Dolomites—a breathtaking panorama in the late afternoon. The runs up here will delight everyone: steep pistes and moguls for experts, a good beginners' piste at Pocol and plenty of everything for those in between.

Away from the slopes Cortina offers curling, skating, sleigh rides, swimming, excursions to Venice, and even steeple-chasing on ice. With 74km (46 miles) of cross-country trails it is a particularly popular resort for devotees of that sport.

Like many Italian centres, Cortina is a hotel resort ... most of the chalets are in private hands and likely to remain so. The great hotel here is the five-star Cristallo, but the smarter set and the older money now assemble at the bar of the Hotel Poste. Other good hotels are the five-star Miramonti, the four-star Ancora and the three-star Olimpia.

There are plenty of first-class restaurants, though meals are more expensive than you might enjoy in other Dolomite resorts. But then, this is Cortina, a place unlike anywhere else. Apart from the bar at the Hotel Poste, the rare birds of the Italian jet set come to roost in the cafés along the Corso Italia, trying not to look too keen to see and be seen. Other night spots include the Valentino Piano Bar, the Ippopotinius and the Orange, to name a few from an extensive choice.

Left: *The glory of the Dolomites ensures that even the most avid skiers stop to gaze at the craggy outcrops all around, their peaks looming at every corner.*

Above: *With 52 lift installations of its own, some dating back to when skiers were less-demanding, Cortina is a part of the 450-lift Super Dolomiti ski system.*

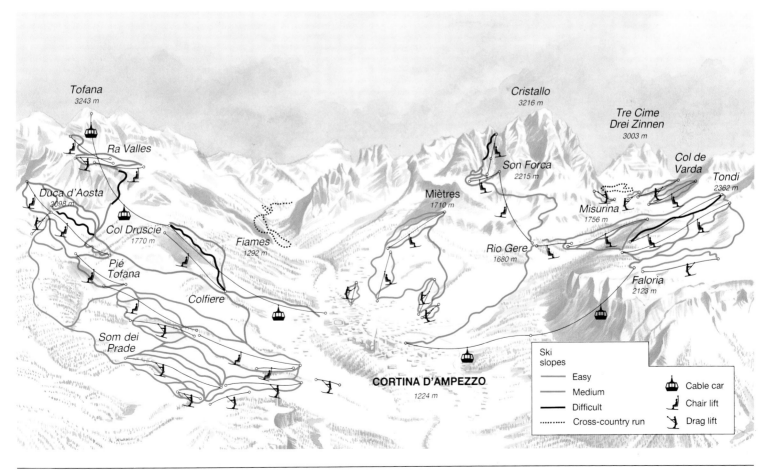

Tofana
3243 m

Cristallo
3216 m

Tre Cime
Drei Zinnen
3003 m

Ra Valles

Son Forca
2215 m

Col de
Varda

Tondi
2362 m

Duca d'Aosta
2098 m

Miètres
1710 m

Misurina
1756 m

Col Druscie
1770 m

Fiames
1292 m

Pié
Tofana

Rio Gere
1680 m

Faloria
2123 m

Colfiere

Som dei
Prade

CORTINA D'AMPEZZO
1224 m

Ski slopes	
Easy	
Medium	Cable car
Difficult	Chair lift
Cross-country run	Drag lift

COURMAYEUR

views are staggering, with Mont Blanc looking down like a giant sentinel.

The bare facts—23 lifts serving some 100km (62 miles) of marked trails—conceal the immense variety of Courmayeur's skiing. By taking a combination of gondolas and cable-cars to Cresta Youla (2624m/8609ft) you have the option of continuing up to Cresta d'Arp for the unpisted run all the way back to

Tucked in beneath Mont Blanc (Monte Bianco) in Italy's Aosta Valley, Courmayeur's outskirts present a bleak first impression. Behind this drab hinterland the village centre is a maze of twisting alleys, each home to dozens of welcoming bars, cafés and restaurants. The combination of cobbled streets and ski boots produces a wonderful clatter in the late afternoon when the whole village fills with the hum of conversation as the day is reviewed to the accompaniment of pastries and cakes, coffee and grappa.

Courmayeur probably ranks at the top of the second division of European resorts in terms of its skiing area, and high in the first division when it comes to atmosphere. Unlike many of its purpose-built counterparts over the French border, Courmayeur has dozens of steamy mountain restaurants doling out huge dollops of delicious pasta and other Italian delights. It is easy to see why the Italians' attitude to skiing is so carefree when luncheon is the main event of the day and dinner is

In Courmayeur a series of lifts rise from Plan Checrouit up to Lago Checrouit and Cresta d'Arp from where Mont Blanc can be seen standing like a giant sentinel across the Val Veny.

the main event of the evening.

The excited chatter of hordes of Milanese on the early-morning cable-car indicates that skiing is meant to be fun. Some go straight to a café on arrival at Plan Checrouit but most want to attack the vast array of runs below the Cresta d'Arp (2755m/9039ft) and above the Val Veny where there are some interesting diversions through the trees. However, apart from one tricky unpisted route to Dolonne, none of the trails leads back to town and so it is necessary to return by the cable-car at the end of the day or to ski to Entreves and catch a bus. The plus points are that the nursery slopes are spread around Plan Checrouit, so that beginners can meet their more accomplished friends for lunch, and that the

Dolonne (check beforehand on snow conditions as it is often closed), or heading for the Val Veny via broad, fast runs on the upper section and lovely tree-lined trails lower down, with scores of off-piste diversions *en route*. The wide bowl beneath Cresta Youla is sheltered although visibility can be a problem as it is above the tree line. The itinerary for the morning can be either a cruising run down to Entreves, which is adjacent to the entrance of the Mont Blanc tunnel, or a fast and bumpy bash to Zerotta where, on sunny days, umbrellas on restaurant ter-

races beckon enticingly. Zerotta is one of the favourite lunchtime destinations for better skiers as the restaurants are less crowded than those around Plan Checrouit. But wherever you choose to eat, prices are affordable, portions huge and service enthusiastic, if occasionally erratic.

One misconception is that the Vallee Blanche, which runs down to Chamonix, over the French border, is strictly for experts. This is one of the great skiing experiences in the Alps, not for its difficulty but for stupendous views and the

constant presence of staggering glacial architecture. The mystique is founded on the length of the run (18km/11 miles) and the fact that it is essential to be accompanied by a guide who will avoid crevasses *en route*. The Vallee Blanche is reached by a three-stage cable-car from the outskirts of Entreves to Punta Helbronner and, although the descent can be negotiated in a couple of hours, most skiers prefer to turn the trip into a day's excusion, pausing for a picnic lunch and to look at and photograph the extraordinary glacial outcrops. The journey back

Mont Blanc
4810 m

Aiguille Noire
3773 m

Chamonix →

Punta Helbronner
3470 m

Val Veny

Courba Dzeleuna
2080 m

Zerotta
1520 m

an Checrouit
1706 m

Pavillon
2130 m

Lassy

Pre de Pascal
1912 m

Tunnel de Mont Blanc

Entreves

Funivie Mont Blanc

Ski slopes
—— Nursery
—— Easy
—— Medium
—— Difficult
Cable car
Gondola
Chair lift
Drag lift

from Chamonix is by bus or taxi.

The top section of the alternative descent from Punta Helbronner down the Toula glacier, on the Italian side, is, however, for experts although the lower reaches, served by the lowest section of the cable-car to Pavillon, are very gentle. The Vallee Blanche run is usually opened in late February.

Lift queues are rare in Courmayeur, other than when waiting for the cable-car (capacity 130) to return home in the afternoon. The two ways to avoid the rush are to ski down to Entreves, and take a five-minute bus ride, or adopt the local practice of sitting in a café until the crowds thin out. The *cognoscenti* hire a locker at Plan Checrouit and leave skis and boots there overnight. Pistes can be very crowded and the Italian method seems to be to take every run as fast, and noisily, as possible regardless of the skier's ability.

Being so close to the Mont Blanc tunnel, Courmayeur is popular with the self-drive market, and there are some interesting day excursions if you have a car. La Thuile is a 20-minute drive away and offers intermediate skiing as well as the chance to ski over the French border to La Rosiere, covered by the same lift pass (which is also usable at Cervinia, incidentally). La Thuile is one of the most tastefully designed purpose-built resorts in the Alps and has a low-key, friendly atmosphere making it popular with families and groups of beginners. Further afield, Champolouc is undiscovered by tour operators making it a perfect place for a day's secluded skiing. Its skiing connects with that of Gressoney-la-Trinite and one of the pleasures is to

cializing in woollen and leather goods. Organized excursions to the region's capital, Aosta, with its fascinating Roman ruins, and to Chamonix, are available through the tourist office.

One of Courmayeur's institutions is the Maison de Filipo at Entreves: gluttons feel that they have reached the Promised

Left: The Vallee Blanche is usually open from mid-February and can be skied by any competent intermediate – it is worth it for the views alone.

Below: Courmayeur ranks high in the first division of European resorts when it comes to atmosphere, food and apres-ski activities.

Land as some 30 courses are provided at dinner, with a huge variety of *antipasti* and pasta dishes, steaks, game (including chamois), fish, cheeses, cakes and fruit, with the meal completed by the passing of the *caffè alla valdostana nella grolla dell' amicizia*, a wooden bowl with spouts for the communal enjoyment of a heady mixture of grappa, coffee and spices. This quite extraordinary establishment continues to defy the appetites of the hungriest of diners. Elsewhere, on a more modest scale, cafés and bars on the via Roma do a roaring trade—quite literally, at times—and the discos and nightclubs are invariably packed with a merry crowd, dancing away as if life depended on it.

pause to gaze at Mont Blanc in the distance to the left, with the Matterhorn looming straight ahead. The local patois here in the Monte Rosa district is based on German while in Courmayeur, once a part of the Duchy of Savoie, it leans towards French.

Courmayeur retains its market-town atmosphere—and the weekly Wednesday market is a treat—so that non-skiers are able to have a thoroughly enjoyable time wandering the streets, stopping for a pastry while contemplating the next purchase in one of the little shops spe-

SESTRIERE AND THE MILKY WAY

There are many circuits in the Alps which seem made to challenge intermediate skiers. Italy has two of these circuits—the Sella Ronda in the Dolomites and the Milky Way in the Western Alps. It is difficult to decide quite where the Milky Way starts: at Sauze d'Oulx perhaps or maybe Sestriere. Wherever it may be, it wanders up lifts and down glades until it finally reaches Montgenevre in France. Passports need to be kept in jacket pockets, for the customs men get quite nasty if the documents cannot be produced on demand. Along the way there are no fewer than 300km (186 miles) of beaten pistes with 100 lifts.

Sestriere has quite a history. It was built by Fiat in the late 1930s on a high and windy col, well above the treeline, as the smart place for the young Turinese to dash up to in their cars at weekends. A big car park in the centre of a bowl, with three main lifts round it gives instant access to three different mountains. And the bowl curves gently at the bottom to bring skiers back with an expert flourish—good ego-building stuff. Gradually

The Milky Way is served by scores of lifts and criss-crosses the French-Italian border taking in Sauze d'Oulx, Sestriere, San Sicario and Montgenevre along the way.

runs and lifts were extended to nearby villages though it was not until after the War that Sauze d'Oulx was built to the north and even longer before it could be reached without a guide, by lift and piste. Sauze became the package holiday haven, buzzing with life, amusement arcades, noisy bars and a great deal of fun. Its slopes are much under-rated. There is a good north-facing scarp with pistes zig-zagging down between the larches.

San Sicario, which links with both Sauze and Sestriere was purpose-built in the seventies. Ultra-modern with a little shuttle to bring apartment dwellers up to the main lifts, it concentrates on rich families who buy upmarket apartments. The children have a safe haven in which to ski and parents can go off on the wide slopes around. The two-storey shop precincts have some of the charm of children's building bricks and it is extremely

convenient with its wide, well-graded road which is skiable when snowcovered.

Claviere and Montgenevre were the two existing frontier towns; in fact, Montgenevre was France's first ski resort and Maurice Chevalier and Mistinguette both visited the old Palace Hotel there. There are still remains of the old ski-jump and though new apartment blocks and facilities have been built, the old village still clusters round the thin-spired church. The main road over the col to Briancon does rather cut the village in two, but it is a pleasant, friendly place with a good English-speaking ski school. There are three nightclubs: Le Boom, Playboy and Ca del Sol. Much the best restaurant is Le Jamy which is owned by the Mayor.

As well as being part of the Milky Way, Montgenevre has linked itself to the ski areas on the French side and it is possible there to buy a Grande Galaxie weekly lift pass which includes a day's skiing each in Grand Serre Chevalier, Puy St Vincent, Les Deux Alpes and Alpe d'Huez—giving a total of 236 lifts and 900km (558 miles) of pistes. Sufficient to satisfy any skier

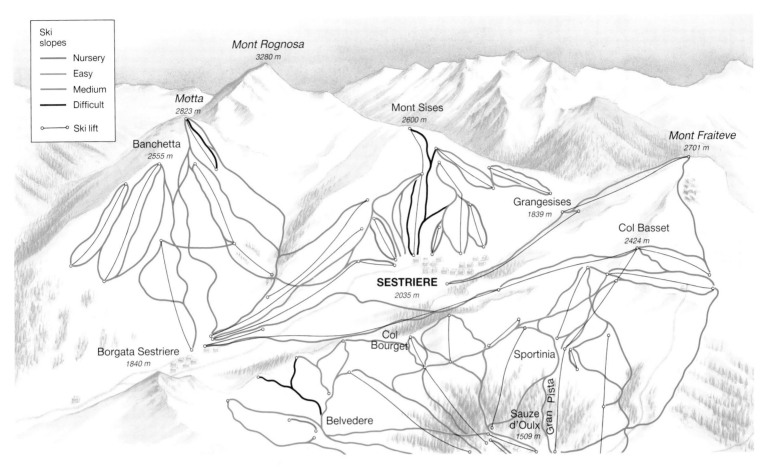

Ski slopes
— Nursery
— Easy
— Medium
— Difficult
∘—∘ Ski lift

Mont Rognosa
3280 m

Motta
2823 m

Mont Sises
2600 m

Mont Fraiteve
2701 m

Banchetta
2555 m

Grangesises
1839 m

Col Basset
2424 m

SESTRIERE
2035 m

Borgata Sestriere
1840 m

Col Bourget

Sportinia

Gran Pista

Belvedere

Sauze d'Oulx
1509 m

with seven-league boots.

Montgenevre also has night skiing, schools that teach mono-ski and ski-surfing, an ice circuit for racing skidoos and a natural ice rink. There is a particularly good off-piste run down to Claviere—though there is no lift back up as yet. A great deal of money has been put into new quad lifts and some moveable snow-cannons.

Sestriere is the queen among all these villages. For a while it lost its connection with Fiat who sold off its two most characteristic hotels—the round towers of the Duchi d'Aosta and the Torre—to Club Mediterranee. Following its usual policy, the Club installed its own staff, ski instructors, food, wine and entertainment, so that its clients were self-sufficient and the rest of Sestriere became rather deserted.

But in the early 1980s Gianni Agnelli of Fiat who had always kept his family chalet in Sestriere (and who also retains an interest in Club Mediterranee) became interested again in the development of Sestriere. One of the village's priceless

assets, the Principi di Piemonte Hotel, which lies to one side in its own forest with its own piste and lift into the main circuit, had begun to look rather run-down. People no longer appreciated that it had been among the first hotels to build an open-air swimming pool, where clients could laze with great mountain peaks all around them—or with snow gently falling onto the warm water. When he took stock of Sestriere the first thing Agnelli decided was that it needed several more hotels and the Principi di Piemonte must be rebuilt. For three years a crane hovered over its roof but finally, in 1987, this great hotel reopened, its rooms prettily decorated, its restaurant and tearoom a delight to eye and palate. Now Ferraris and Range Rovers once more wend their way down its long drive and designer-clad skiers pour out in the morning onto their own lift to set off on the day's itinerary.

Sestriere has also had a long history of racing. It was Italy's base for Arnold Lunn's Arlberg-Kandahar Open Ski Race—joining Murren, St Anton, Garmisch and Chamonix on the race's five-

year cycle of Alpine countries. It has now returned as a World Cup venue, successfully hosting the Super-G, a sort of shortened downhill. Piero Gros, ex-world champion, lives in Sauze d'Oulx and is often to be seen in Sestriere.

To the great benefit of its pampered clientele, Sestriere has always had good machinery on its pistes, ratracs and pistenbullies grooming the slopes night and day. It has also adopted snowmaking, for its altitude at 2000m (6550ft) guarantees sufficiently low temperatures at night, though the bowl traps the Italian sun by day. As many as 600 snow cannons blow out precisely graduated water and compressed air to make sure that the main runs are kept well covered.

Not noted for its shopping (Turin, perhaps, is too near) Sestriere does have other cards up its sleeve. There is tennis, a ski-jump, a cinema, an ice rink and—again in keeping with its motoring links—an ice-driving circuit on which Lancias can be slid, spun and controlled. Lessons are, of course, advisable but it is great fun as well as useful practice for car drivers.

GEILO AND LILLEHAMMER

Four thousand-year-old rock carvings show the ancient heritage of Norwegian skiing, which has a depth of tradition to make the Alps seem like a faddish newcomer. Norway is only now regaining the popularity it held 20 years ago with the British. It has never been nor ever will be a mass-market destination, but with a better exchange rate and the introduction of charter flights it can compete with the Alps for ambience and certainly for snow. While Alpine snow cover in recent seasons has been conspicuous by its absence, Norway's 100 or so ski resorts reported snow business as usual. In the early 1989–90 season the top resort, Geilo, was fully open on a respectable 40–100cm snow cover while in the Alps many resorts were a third to a half open. An ideal combination of snow-making facilities, northern latitude and natural snow gives good skiing well into April and May. In Norway the key to good snow cover is latitude, not altitude.

Sunbathing is a major activity in the long spring daylight. Apart from peak periods pistes are uncrowded. Many come just for the downhill, although Norwegians are as likely to use cross-country skis as downhill skis on the piste.

A scenic three-hour train ride takes skiers from Bergen or Oslo to Geilo which at 800m (2625ft) holds the snow well on ground frozen from November to May. With some 36km (22 miles) of downhill runs, and 29 slopes split between the two main ski areas (Geilohovda and Vestlia), the resort is not large by Alpine standards, but the skiing was varied enough to attract World Cup skiing in 1986 and 1990, with one downhill run of 3km (2 miles) at nearby Sudndalen. There are 150km (93 miles) of cross-country trails in Geilo and 450km (280 miles) in the immediate area; a favourite trip on telemark skis is to take the train to Finse and ski back in a day. Downhill skiing is pleasant but not challenging, the hardest run being more red than black, except a short mogul section of the Vestliaheisen piste when conditions are icy.

A ski taxi service runs between the main ski area and the Vestlia slopes, home of the Trollklubben, a kindergarten where children can be left and entertained for the day by English-speaking nannies. In fact, a friendly family atmosphere prevails in the entire resort. Piste restaurants are functional; many skiers prefer to take a picnic lunch to the slopes.

Geilo's Highland Hotel is a well-appointed and comfortable place to stay with good piste views and conveniently near the lifts. With nine quality hotels, four nightclubs and two discos, there is a fair selection for a week's holiday. Most hotels have a swimming pool and sauna. Particularly enjoyable are the refurbished Dr. Holms Hotel for an *après-ski* drink, and the cosy atmosphere and fine food of the Halling-stuene restaurant.

Lillehammer expects to be the country's premier winter sports centre—for a cost of £25 million it ought to be—by the time it hosts the 1994 Winter Olympic Games. Norway last hosted the Winter Olympics in 1952 at Oslo. The immense task is well under way to provide beds for 40 000 people and direct rail links with Oslo and Gardermoen international airports some 150km (93 miles) and 90 minutes away. Lillehammer has a stable winter climate and a good snow record despite its low altitude. Some 500km (310 miles) of forest and mountain cross-country ski trails will be available at

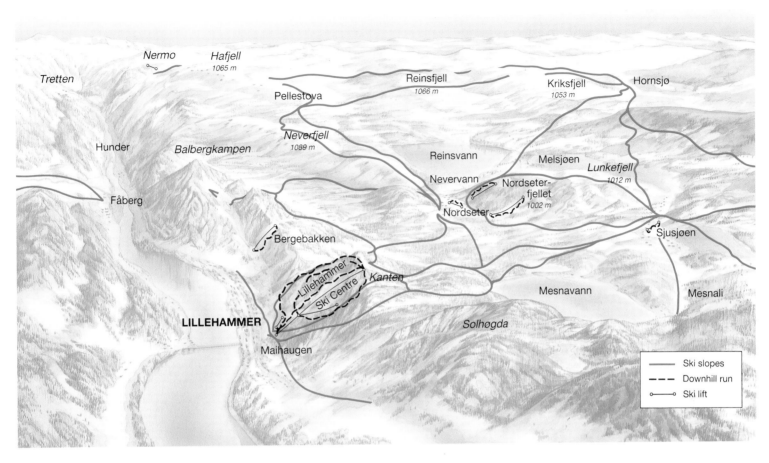

Nermo Hafjell
1065 m

Tretten

Pellestova

Reinsfjell
1066 m

Kriksfjell
1053 m

Hornsjø

Hunder   Balbergkampen

Neverfjell
1089 m

Reinsvann

Melsjøen

Lunkefjell
1012 m

Nevervann   Nordseter-
fjellet
1002 m

Fåberg

Nordseter

Sjusjøen

Bergebakken

Lillehammer
Ski Centre   Kanten

Mesnavann

Mesnali

LILLEHAMMER

Maihaugen

Solhøgda

Ski slopes
- - - Downhill run
o—o Ski lift

Left: *With six floodlit trails near the centre of Lillehammer, the resort is perfect for skiers who can't drag themselves away from the slopes.*

Below: *Lillehammer's attractive resort centre will be the hub of the 1992 Winter Olympics, the first time Norway has been awarded the games since 1952.*

Nordseter and Sjusjøen, reflecting the fact that this long-ski form of the sport is a mass-participation national pastime in Norway. There are six floodlit tracks near the town centre for insomniacs and those for whom there are just not enough hours in the day. About 15km (9 miles) from Lillehammer, Olympic downhill pistes are being developed at Hafjell and Øyer, as yet unknown quantities as ski resorts.

As it is not yet a package holiday destination, even the journey to Norway can be counted as part of the fun. Scheduled or chartered flights from Heathrow, Gatwick, Norwich, Newcastle, Aberdeen and Edinburgh to Oslo or Bergen take about two hours. Onward journeys by train direct to the resorts are reliable and comfortable. A new internal air service from Oslo or Stavanger to Dagali airport will further accelerate transfers. Families of beginner and intermediate skiing standard who do not need the stamina-sapping nightlife of the Alps and prefer relaxing scenic skiing should thrive on the new-look Norwegian experience.

AVIEMORE

Aviemore is situated in the Spey Valley, approximately 80km (50 miles) south of Inverness, and is the focal point of Scotland's largest ski area. Its ski slopes are on Cairngorm, 11km (7 miles) away. Aviemore is both a purpose-built centre and an established highland village. The centre is a collection of hotels, a swimming pool, bars, discos, shops, skating rink, squash courts, dry ski slope and cinema. A fact of life in Scottish skiing is that there always needs to be something to do when not skiing. The weather is its greatest enemy, but when it's good it's excellent. The best time to go is later in the season when the days are longer and the snow cover more reliable.

To reach the skiing there is a regular bus service from Aviemore train station, or you can drive to one of the two car parks at the bottom of the slopes. At weekends and in the high season the Coire Cas car park, servicing the Day Lodge, ticket office, rental shop, restaurant and bar, fills up very quickly, often by breakfast time. And once the lower Coire na Ciste car park fills up, slightly later in the morning, the police normally close the road to all further cars. So for a later start it is easier to take the bus which will drop you right at the Day Lodge. There is also a bus which shuttles between the two car parks.

The ski area is divided into two sectors, Coire Cas, on the 'front' of the mountain, and Coire na Ciste on the left flank. In total there are four chair-lifts and 11 drag-lifts servicing the combined areas. Beginners' slopes are situated at the bottom and, surprisingly, the top. The lower slopes are more restricted, so, weather permitting, the wider, gentle slopes in the Ptarmigan Bowl just below the 1245m (4084ft) Cairngorm summit, are preferable. There is an easy traverse descent from the top down to the Shieling and then down to the Day Lodge car park via the Fiacaill Ridge run. Generally, though, the area is better suited for the intermediate and advanced skiers. Steeper and more challenging runs are on the Coire na Ciste gully and its steep West Wall. The

bumps on the White Lady are deep and sharp enough to tax the most expert skier.

Piste grooming is unpredictable, however, and of disappointingly variable quality. For hill refreshments the choice is fairly limited. The Ptarmigan snack bar at the top might be the highest eating place in Britain, but it is not the best. The Shieling snack bar and picnic room midway down the mountain serves the same fare with no greater success, and so a better bet is to go down to the Day Lodge with bar and restaurant at the car park. A small snack bar at the Coire na Ciste car park caters for those who choose not to go round to the main car park.

At weekends and peak times expect to

wait a minimum of 15 minutes in the queues, though they are extremely well organized. As in the United States there is no queue barging here. The chair-lift company offers tickets to suit all needs and abilities, from one chair-lift run to a full area day pass.

Après-ski at Aviemore is excellent, Scottish hospitality at its best, with a variety of inexpensive restaurants, bars and live entertainment to choose from. Skiing in Scotland should not be compared to that in the Alps but it has a lot to offer. Some may feel more at ease in Scotland than in a resort of foreign-language speakers and strange road-signs. Some may feel the ease of travelling to

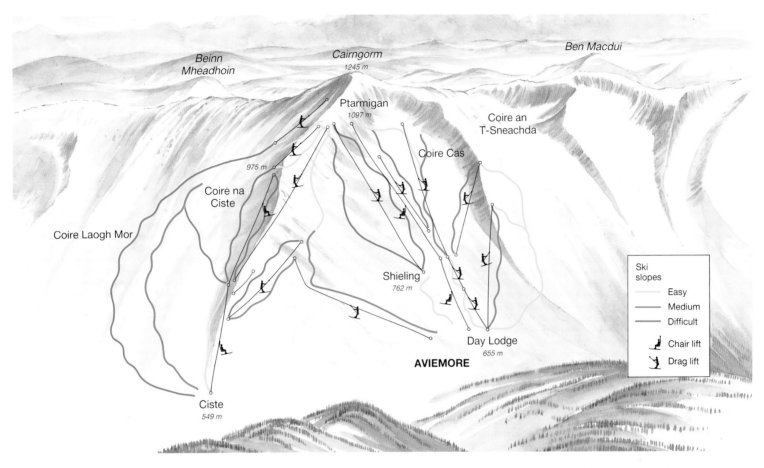

Beinn Mheadhoin

Cairngorm
1245 m

Ben Macdui

Ptarmigan
1097 m

Coire an T-Sneachda

Coire Cas

975 m

Coire na Ciste

Coire Laogh Mor

Shieling
762 m

Ski slopes
Easy
Medium
Difficult
Chair lift
Drag lift

Day Lodge
655 m

AVIEMORE

Ciste
549 m

Left: *Aviemore has several tough descents, notably the Coire na Ciste gully and its West Wall. The bumps on the White Lady are enough to tax the most expert skier.*

Below: *The best time to visit Aviemore is at the end of the season when the weather is better, the days are longer and the snow cover more reliable.*

Aviemore from around Britain a considerable plus, both in transit times and cost.

Accommodation can be found to suit any budget, from caravans and self-catering chalets, to excellent value bed-and-breakfast houses and recently upgraded four-star hotels. Skiers have colonized all the villages of the Spey Valley; Newtonmore, Kingussie and Kincraig are the most southerly group, either on or not far away from the main A9. Likewise, further north Carrbridge, Granton-on-Spey and Boat of Garten have a style all of their own away from the buzz of Aviemore.

Though we have concentrated on Aviemore and Cairngorm there are four other Scottish ski resorts: Glenshee, the Lecht, Glencoe and the brand new Aonach Mor. All offer a variety of skiing. The Lecht is ideal for beginners and families, Glencoe for enthusiasts but with minimum facilities. Glenshee is slightly lower than the others with good skiing for all abilities, and the newest resort at Aonach Mor brings state-of-the-art uplift, wide-open skiing and spectacular views.

CRANS-MONTANA

Crans-Montana is an amalgam of two quite different resorts which joined forces for the soundest of solid Swiss commercial reasons—to make money. In the 19th century, Montana was renowned as a health centre set on a sunny ledge with beautiful views across the Rhone Valley and down to the town of Sierre. It was the sort of place where fashionable doctors from all Europe sent their tuberculosis patients, in the hope that the fresh mountain air at 1500m (4920ft) might effect a cure which medical science could not yet provide.

Only a mile away lay the separate and more upmarket resort of Crans-sur-Sierre which played host not to the invalids or economy-minded family holiday-seekers attracted to Montana, but to the cream of the Swiss trade from Geneva, Basle and Zurich together with a regular handful of well-heeled British golfers. Each resort had its separate market, but neither on its own was big enough. It made sound sense to marry in the cause of Mammon and so the two villages became one, linked by a straggling suburbia to become Switzerland's largest ski resort.

Uninspired architecture and clogging traffic means Crans-Montana has none of the quaint charm of villages like Zermatt,

Villars, Lenzerheide and Arosa. The shops bear smart international designer names like Cartier, Gucci, and Louis Vuitton, but their obtrusive concrete design sets them apart from their namesakes in Rodeo Drive and Bond Street.

Although now united, the two original resorts retain some of their differences and contrasts. While Crans is city chic on snow, Montana has a more parochial air to it with its simple patisseries and fondue restaurants. Crans is stuffed with leather and furs, while in Montana you are more at home in *après-ski* boots and an anorak. Although Crans-Montana has more first-class hotels than any other resort except St Moritz, it has never attracted the international jet-set.

The Grand Hotel Rhodania is considered the best hotel here; the Crans Ambassador has a pool; and the National is a family-run hotel with a good reputation. The hotels range from old to modern, but all are clean, solid and efficient, and the large number of high-rise apartment blocks attracts the more budget-conscious of the Swiss. The small clusters of traditional chalets look sadly anachronistic against the concrete.

Every kind of entertainment is on hand to service the large number of rich cus-

tomers, from a casino and two cinemas to a good variety of restaurants, discos and jazz bars. Top restaurants include Le Chamois d'Or, whose chef works at Maxim's in Paris between seasons, and the Rotisserie de la Reina. More modest meals can be eaten at Le Trappe in the Hotel Cisalpine, and at the Hotel Aida.

The recent ski history of this area starts in 1950 when the first ski championships were held here. And even earlier in 1911 the British founder of modern downhill racing, Sir Arnold Lunn, planned a race from the top of the Plaine Morte glacier down to Montana which developed into the famous Arlberg-Kandahar series.

In more modern times, Crans-Montana hosted the 1985 World Championships, which turned out to be something of a benefit event for the native Swiss racers. Peter Mueller won the men's downhill and Pirmin Zurbriggen both the giant slalom and super giant slalom; Maria Walliser took gold in both the women's downhill and super giant slalom and was followed on to the winner's podium by Vreni Schneider who won the giant slalom and Erica Hess who completed her best season ever by winning the slalom.

Intermediates will rate Crans-Montana one of the greatest places they have ever skied. The variety is quite outstanding. But for beginners opportunities are extremely limited; even the gentler slopes are islands in a red sea of pistes. With the opening of the purpose-built resort of Aminona, the area now boasts a total of 40 interconnected lifts and 150km (93 miles) of prepared pistes.

The ski complex is made up of three main areas: the Cry d'Err/Bella Lui, Violettes/Plaine Morte, and Aminona/Petit Bonvin. The Aminona area is reached by four lifts. From Crans a gondola brings you to Chetzeron at 2100m (6888ft) which was the starting point of the men's super giant slalom. Another gondola goes to Cry d'Err at 2206m (7235ft) which is the heart of the area; this can also be reached by gondola from Montana. The whole area is linked by short free bus rides and fast gondolas,

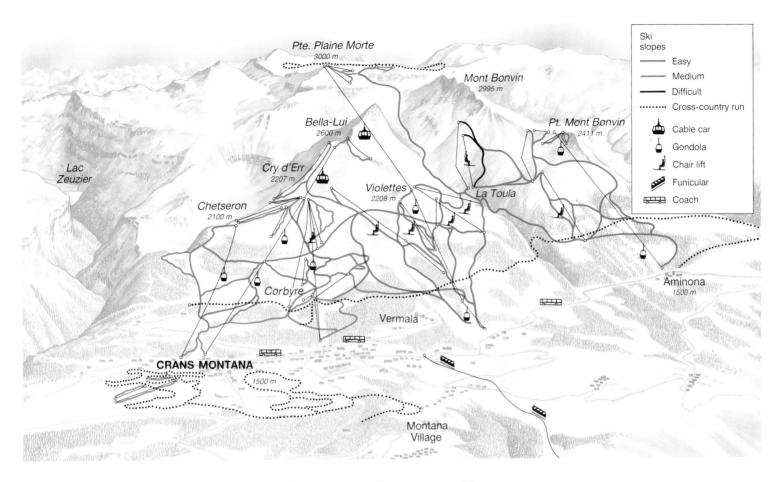

Left: Without the quaint charm of Zermatt, Crans-Montana is perfect for intermediates who will find that it is one of the greatest places they have skied.

Below: Maria Walliser won two gold medals in the 1987 World Championships. Zurbriggen, Mueller Schneider and Hess all added golds to the Swiss tally.

taking skiers all the way up to Petit Bonvin at 2411m (7908ft). Here the ski area is wide open and uncrowded.

Cry d'Err is the most crowded section of the mountain as ten lifts bring skiers to a busy junction. Another bottleneck is near Pas du Loup where four trails come together. From Cry d'Err another route brings you into the intermediate Violettes area, which is separated from the Montana section by a sheer cliff. Across the valley from Violettes is the Aminona area and the La Toula lifts, the former offering wide-open, uncrowded cruising and the latter some testing slopes for the better skier.

Only experts are seriously short of good runs at this resort. There are no steep areas, but there is plenty of off-piste work and skiing through trees. Hot air ballooning ranks high among the off-ski activities. There is also skating, curling and swimming on offer together with tennis and riding. If that is not enough, with 40km (25 miles) of prepared tracks at your disposal you can always take up cross-country skiing.

DAVOS AND KLOSTERS

Davos Dorf, situated in the south-east corner of Switzerland, in the shadow of the Gotschna mountain, started its life as a convalescence centre, but it was also one of the first villages to have been developed as a ski resort. Today it has become a large, international town linked with Davos Platz. All year round it is a conference centre, and in winter it is one of the world's top ski resorts.

Klosters and Davos between them have seven ski areas and a total of 320km (198 miles) of pistes and 55 lifts. The biggest and best-known of the seven areas is also one of the classic ski areas in the Alps, the Parsenn, which has 99 pistes and a huge number of lifts. The wide mountain is topped by the Weissfluhgipfel at 2844m (9328ft), which offers good skiing for both intermediates and experts in search of the off-piste powder. The area is reached from Davos by the Parsennbahn mountain railway which runs every 15 minutes, and from Klosters by the two-stage Gotschnabahn which has now much improved from having been a painfully slow lift with notorious morning queues. The ascent finishes at the Gotschnagrat, where skiers can either traverse to the Parsenn or ski down under the cable-car.

The most testing piste runs here are Kobel and Drostobel off the notorious Gotschnagrat, followed by Meierhofertalli down to Wolfgang (the best mogul field in the area), and Chalbersaas. The notorious Wang run is usually closed due to avalanche danger. Though the majority of pistes are geared towards intermediate skiers, there is also wonderful off-piste skiing to be had all over the mountainside, with opportunities for climbing on skins to reach an interesting mountain hut or even another resort. Experts can find enough varied and challenging skiing for a week, and many return year after year.

Most well known resorts claim to have 'the biggest', 'the longest' or 'the best' run or lift. The Parsenn's fame lies in the length of its main run: 14km (9 miles), which makes it one of the longest in Europe. The skiing meanders through open snowfields and forests, and down to the traditional hamlets of Saas, Sernaus and Kublis. All the villages are connected by the Rhatische Bahn that also serves St Moritz, making it easy to return to Klosters or Davos.

Klosters' second, smaller ski area, Madrisa, is reached by a gondola from Dorf and it has six lifts. It is primarily a beginner's area of sunny south-facing slopes. But it is also the set-off point for ski mountaineering to Austria. A short walk will take you to the starting point for

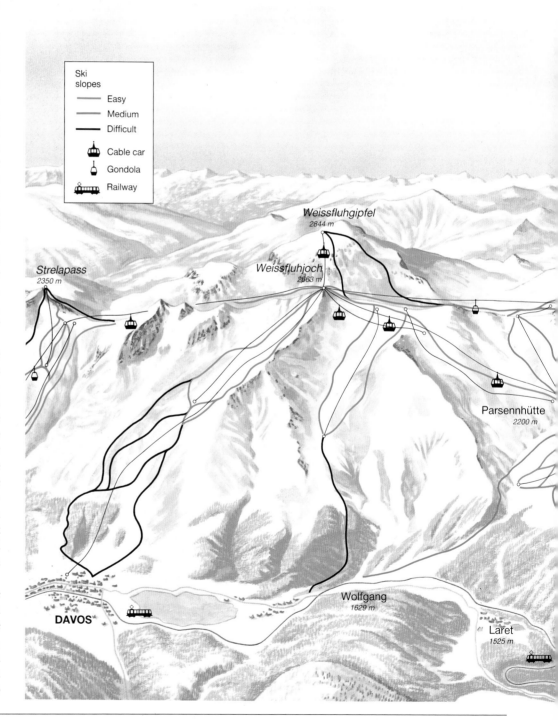

Ski slopes

—— Easy
—— Medium
—— Difficult
🚡 Cable car
🚠 Gondola
🚃 Railway

Weissfluhgipfel 2844 m

Strelapass 2350 m

Weissfluhjoch 2663 m

Parsennhütte 2200 m

Wolfgang 1629 m

DAVOS

Laret 1525 m

The Rinerhorn provides a tranquil change from the buzz of activity around Davos and is reached by the local rail service. Most of the skiing is on wide, open runs with spectacular scenery all around.

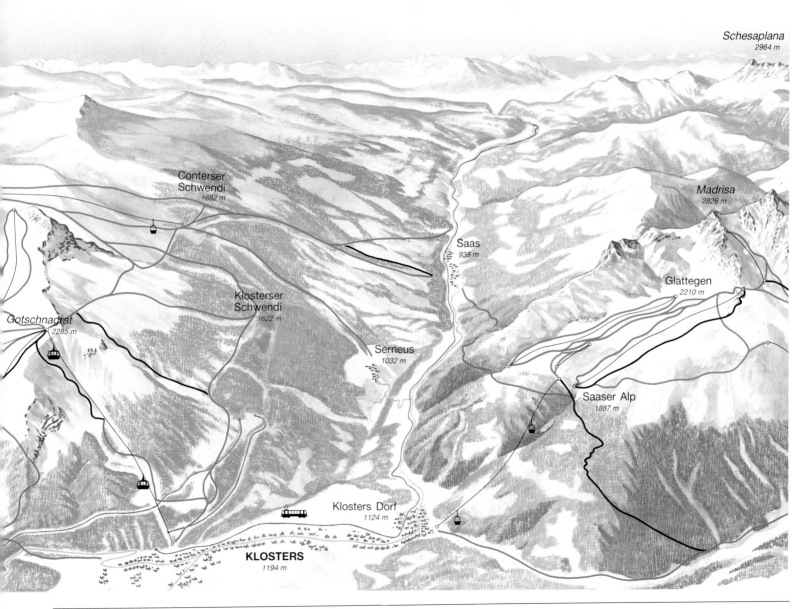

Schesaplana
2964 m

Conterser
Schwendi
1682 m

Madrisa
2826 m

Saas
938 m

Glattegen
2210 m

Klosterser
Schwendi
1622 m

Gotschnagrat
2285 m

Serneus
1032 m

Saaser Alp
1887 m

Klosters Dorf
1124 m

KLOSTERS
1194 m

a fabulous ski down to Gargellen in Austria, returning via St Antonierjoch and St Antonien before taking the bus to Kublis.

Davos has four of its own ski areas apart from the Parsenn. Schatzalp/Strela is on the same side of the valley and joins the Parsenn by cable-car. The other three areas are across the valley, and have the advantage of crowdless skiing even in high season: Pischa is reached by bus from Davos and offers limited runs and some easy off-piste; Jakobshorn is an intermediate area of 14 runs, reachable by cable-car from the town centre; and finally, Rinnerhorn at Glaris, just up the valley from town, is reached by gondola, has 13 runs and some tree skiing ideal for bad weather. All runs end in the valley; those that end further along the valley in Kublis, Saas, Klosters, Wolfgang or Glaris are connected to Davos by free train.

The long sprawling town of Davos is not attractive, but it is lively and offers something for everyone from the 'see and be seen' crowd who pamper themselves in the five-star hotels and spend their time shopping until the *après-ski* hour arrives, to the keen skier who prefers to stay in one of the small hotels or an apartment.

The two luxury hotels are the Fluela in Dorf and the Steigenberger Belvedere in Platz, but other recommended hotels include the Sunstar, the Sporthotel Central, the Derby, the Morosani Park and the Meierhof.

An alternative to the hustle and bustle of a big town is to stay in Davos-Wolfgang or Davos-Laret, which are a hearty walk or a bus ride to the ski area. Staying in Wolfgang is the best way to get away from it all, and it is conveniently positioned between Klosters and Davos. One of Wolfgang's — indeed the whole area's — best restaurants is Jakob's in the Kulm Hotel at the bottom of Meierhofertalli. The restaurant is a firm favourite of Prince Charles, and has good food and atmosphere.

The nightlife in Davos is informal, with a good choice of bars and discos including the Cabanna Club, the Postli Club and the Dischnabar. You can even find tea dancing in the Morosani Posthotel. Apart from skiing, the town has good other facilities, including skating—Davos has a

famous ice hockey team—curling, indoor tennis and squash. It is also a particularly good resort for cross-country skiing with six trails totalling 75km (46 miles).

Klosters is 16km (10 miles) away on a very efficient train service. A small and select group of British families have been coming here since the 1940s, but it was not until Prince Charles's party was caught in that tragic avalanche that Klosters became a houshold name all over the world. It is a straggling village which, like Davos, is divided into Dorf and Platz. Accommodation in Platz is mainly in

Above: *The Parsennbahn rises to 2492m (8176ft). From the top, the choice is between concentrating on the easy terrain in the immediate vicinity or skiing all the way to Klosters via Jakobshorn.*

Opposite: *The Jakobshorn area is immediately above Davos Platz and has fast on-piste runs, mogul fields and plenty of off-piste opportunities.*

private chalets, whereas Dorf has predominately hotels, including the five-star vegetarian Piz Buin and the five-star

Parsenn, plus a number of very attractive medium-priced hotels ranging from the Vereina, the Steinbock and the Alpina, to the Walserhof and the Chesa Grischuna.

Most Klosterites, including Prince Charles, have either stayed in or eaten at the Hotel Wynegg. This quaint and cosy hotel is run on a chalet basis by Ruth Guler, a member of one of Klosters' prominent families and a familiar figure in the resort. Apart from a few good eating places like the Wynegg, Klosters' nightlife is quiet.

JUNGFRAU REGION

If they are not the birthplace of modern alpine skiing then the gentle meadows of the Bernese Oberland are at least its kindergarten. The slopes above the railway village of Lauterbrunnen near Interlaken form one of the great intermediate ski areas of the world.

From their stately positions above, the three sister peaks of the Eiger, Monch and the Jungfrau look down upon a winter playground first discovered by the English before the First World War. Of the three—the Ogre, the Monk and the Maiden—it is the 3972m (13 028ft) peak of the mighty and terrible Eiger which captivates the minds of all who view her. The Eigerwand, the north face of the mountain which towers over the much loved 'British' resort of Wengen, has drawn climbers from all over the world for nearly a century.

In Edwardian times when the funicular mountain railway system—which still today forms the basis of uphill ski transport—was being built, groups of elegantly betweeded gentlemen would gather on the slopes of Kleine Scheidegg to stare up in wonder at the vertical North Wall which rises sheer for over 200 metres (656ft).

Drawn by the danger of this magnificent mountain, dozens of young men have tried to scale it, and died in the attempt. The 'unclimbable' North Face was first conquered in the summer of 1938, but it was not until 1961 that the summit was reached in winter. With them, those early British climbers and hikers brought skiing.

The Jungfraubahn cog railway climbs up through the North Face itself to the 3454m (11 329ft) Jungfraujoch, Europe's highest station. The train winds through a tunnel, stopping at the famous mountain window in the North Face. Many a climber owes his life to the bravery of the Grindelwald guides who have mounted successful rescue operations from here. The trip is not included on the lift pass but should excite even the experienced traveller.

The completion of the Jungfraubahn

meant that British visitors to the area no longer had laboriously to climb on sealskins for many hours for the brief delight of a descent on skis. Instead they could ride the railway up from Wengen to Wengeralp and the Eigergletscher and ski

down. The crazy foreigners who delighted in this formed their own club, the Downhill Only which still flourishes in the resort today.

The train system is a crucial part of the lift network and life in Wengen. Not only

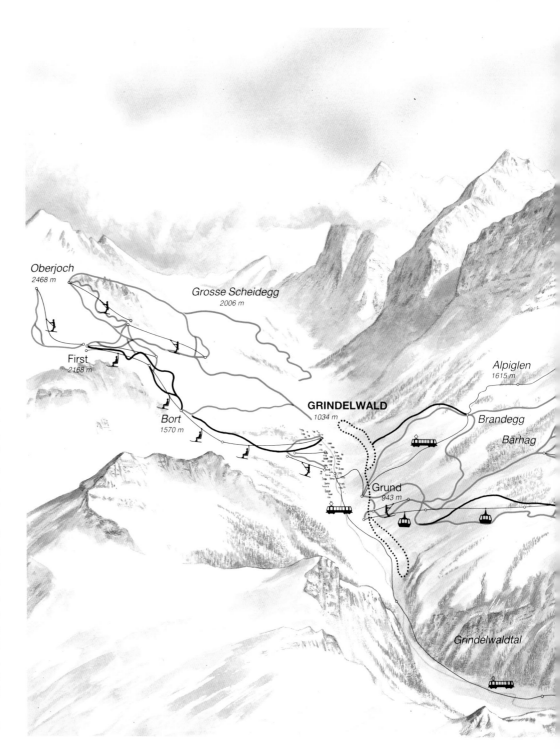

does it bring you to the village, but it also takes you up to different points of the ski area each morning. Commuting up the mountainside to Kleine Scheidegg and the main ski area (a 30-minute ride) feels like

The Jungfrau's quaint railways are supplemented by some excellent, modern lifts which give access to some glorious skiing, high above the valleys.

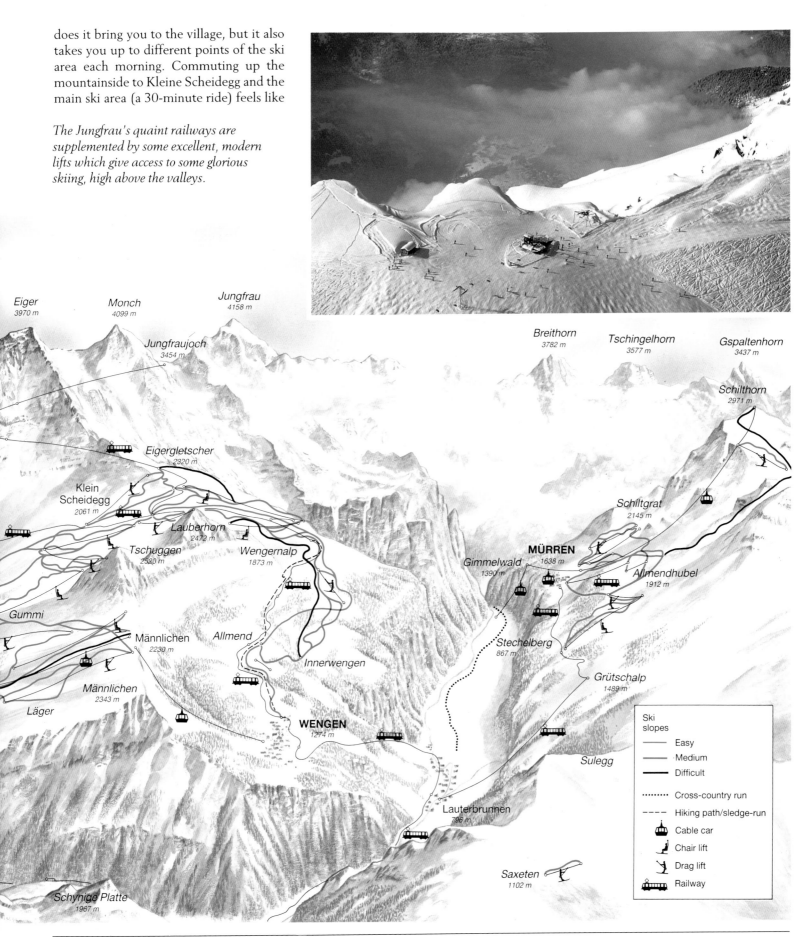

Eiger
3970 m

Monch
4099 m

Jungfrau
4158 m

Jungfraujoch
3454 m

Breithorn
3782 m

Tschingelhorn
3577 m

Gspaltenhorn
3437 m

Schilthorn
2971 m

Eigergletscher
2320 m

Klein
Scheidegg
2061 m

Lauberhorn
2472 m

Schiltgrat
2145 m

Tschuggen
2520 m

Wengernalp
1873 m

MÜRREN
1638 m

Almendhubel
1912 m

Gimmelwald
1390 m

Gummi

Männlichen
2230 m

Allmend

Innerwengen

Stechelberg
867 m

Grütschalp
1489 m

Männlichen
2343 m

WENGEN
1274 m

Läger

Sulegg

Lauterbrunnen
796 m

Saxeten
1102 m

Schynige Platte
1967 m

Ski slopes

— Easy

— Medium

— Difficult

.... Cross-country run

- - - Hiking path/sledge-run

🚠 Cable car

🚡 Chair lift

🎿 Drag lift

🚋 Railway

the ultimate in lazy extravagance. The only disadvantage is that rail travel is much slower than other forms of transport to the slopes which means less hours of skiing per day.

Wengen is one of those resorts still run by real people, not the get-rich-quick merchants of some French, and even some Swiss and Austrian, resorts. In many ways Wengen and the Jungfrau area are caught in a time warp dating back to between the wars. But this gives Wengen its unique flavour—its crumbling Victorian hotels, the railway as its focal point, and a straggling, car-less village.

Like its smart neighbour Grindelwald, Wengen is larger and more cosmopolitan than Murren across the valley. It is also the most central resort of an area which is covered by one convenient lift pass. The main ski area of Kleine Scheidegg/ Mannlichen is shared with Grindelwald. The skiing is aimed at the intermediate, though the centrally placed nursery slopes also make it a good place to learn and it is especially good for children.

Another way on to the slopes is on the long and crowded cable-car from the village centre. From the top of it you can ski all the way to Grund, a suburb of Grindelwald. There are some tree runs to Innerwengen at 1300m (4268ft) as well as more difficult runs next to the Innerwengen and Wixi chair-lifts, and more beside the Bumps drag-lift.

The Eigergletscher station is the start point for some of the most challenging piste skiing in the area together with the best off-piste runs. This is high alpine territory and some slopes are particularly prone to avalanche in certain climatic conditions. Even the experienced foreigner will not know which ones, so a local guide is an important investment for off-piste skiing here.

The best off-piste is to be found on the White Hare, which is approached by climbing on skis from the Eigergletscher towards the site of the base camp of the successful 1969 assault on the Eiger by a team of Japanese climbers. The run down is one of the classic powder runs of the world. It ends with a stomach-wrenching traverse of the roof of one of the railway tunnels and is not for the faint-hearted. Other powder runs to be recommended

are the Wixi and the aptly named Oh God. If your appetite survives this experience, the best lunchtime stop is the popular Jungfrau Hotel at Wengernalp. Try to avoid the crowded self-service restaurants on the Mannlichen.

The village itself is a cluster of slightly faded hotels and smart shops. Recommended hotels include the rebuilt Eiger near the station, the Victoria-Lauberhorn and the Alpenrose. The Hotel Brunner is nearest to the slopes and offers one of the best breakfasts in Switzerland.

Wengen is the home of the annual Lauberhorn World Cup downhill—at around 2min 26sec it is the longest and one of the most difficult on the calendar. The course provides some of the resort's best piste skiing, but only the very brave or stupid will contemplate attempting the 40m (131ft) jump in the middle of the course where racers top 136km/h (85mph). The Lauberhorn ranks second only to Kitzbuhel's Hahnenkamm in the Blue Riband stakes—skiing greats such as Klammer, Schranz, Resch, Weirather and Hoeflehner of Austria, the U.S.A.'s Johnson, Read of Canada, the Swiss stars Mueller and Burgler plus the immortal Jean-Claude Killy of France have all won the Lauberhorn.

Above: *Harti Weirather was one of the Austrians along with Klammer, Resch, Schranz and Hoeflehner who defied the local Swiss challenge to win the Lauberhorn downhill over the years.*

Right: *Olympic Gold Medallist, Bill Johnson of the USA, was a frequent competitor in the Lauberhorn downhill and won this thrilling event in 1984.*

Grindelwald is the biggest of the three resorts and is dominated by large hotels, a big central skating rink and smart shops. It is a sophisticated town with an excellent sports centre and over 50km (31 miles) of cross-country trails. Unlike its two neighbours, Grindelwald does allow cars, which encourages plenty of weekend visitors. As the resort is lower than Wengen and Murren, snow conditions for early or late season skiing are unreliable.

Grindelwald has two separate ski areas: the first is the Mannlichen/Kleine Scheidegg, shared with Wengen, which is reached through a caravan site. The alternative route to Kleine Scheidegg is by train, subject to long queues in peak periods. From Kleine Scheidegg the choices are between skiing back down to Grindelwald on easy runs, skiing the

chair-lifts and drag-lifts on the Mann-lichen side, or skiing down to Wengen via Wixi.

Grindelwald's second area, First, at the other end of the village, rises to Oberjoch at 2468m (8095ft) which is reached by a four-stage chair-lift and is ideal for in-termediates. The runs, including those from the Schilt and Grindel drag-lifts, have numerous routes back to the village. Unfortunately the access point to the area is often closed due to high winds. There are also good off-piste possibilities in the area, with a guide.

Grindelwald is more lively than its two neighbours after dark, with most of the activity centred in the hotels. The most impressive is the Grand Hotel Regina which the ever-strict Swiss Tourist Board accords the full five stars. Others recom-mended include the Belvedere,

Schweizerhof and Spinne. The Bahnhof Hotel is well placed next to the Jungfrau railway. Night spots include the Spider at the Hotel Spinne and the Cava Bar at the Hotel Derby Bahnhof.

On the other side of the valley lies Murren, the third of the Jungfrau resorts. Murren is compact, car-free, quaint, charming and so unspoiled that there are minimal facilities for beginners. The lift system is old-fashioned, the nightlife is nearly non-existent, and the majority of the people who go there like it just the way it is. A large number of those people are British and have been skiing in Murren for generations. They are members of the Kandahar Club, the founding body of alpine ski racing which was established as long ago as 1911 and still plays a part in training young British racers today. Sir Arnold Lunn, an Englishman and the

father of modern skiing, staged the first modern slalom race here in 1922.

Murren is reached by mountain railway from Lauterbrunnen or by cable-car from Stechelberg at the opposite end of the valley. On arrival in the village, everyone is struck by its prettiness — Murren is exactly what the first-time skier imagines a ski resort to look like. It remains remarkably untouched by commercial development, most of the dark wooden chalets are unchanged and new additions blend in without being eyesores. Cars are banned. Almost the only concession to the changing face of a world which now attracts 21 million alpine skiers is a modern sports centre with an indoor football and basketball pitch, squash courts, a swimming pool and gym.

For such a small resort, Murren offers surprisingly good skiing. The most famous

peak is the Schilthorn at 2970m (9742ft) where you will find the famous Piz Gloria revolving restaurant seen more than 20 years ago in the James Bond film *On Her Majesty's Secret Service*. The top section of the run down is difficult, especially the first few turns on moguls which are cut as high as small houses. Many a well-lunched skier has been known to take one look and head straight for the cable-car and a more sedate downward journey. But after the first section the run opens out into the gentler Engetal. Don't be deceived, it is followed by the Kanonenrohr which lives up to its name—a gunbarrel chute between rocks and yawning precipices (fortunately protected by safety nets). The off-piste runs on the Schilthorn are all difficult and can

be dangerous in icy conditions. Never even contemplate them without a guide.

Every January since 1928—with a few exceptions in the 1940s when the participants were otherwise engaged—skiers of varying expertise have thrown themselves from the top of the Schilthorn in what is the biggest, and arguably the longest, downhill race in the world. In one day up to 1450 racers, setting off at intervals, tackle the 14km (8 mile) course which ends in the valley in Lauterbrunnen. The race, known as the Inferno, was invented by Sir Arnold Lunn, and was won that year by his compatriot Harold Mitchell in 1hr 15min. The record today is under 15 minutes, to drop some 2144m (7034ft). Stragglers come panting in having taken more than twice as long.

You don't have to be an expert racer to take part, you just need a crash helmet and a start number. The latter is not so easy to obtain as young bloods from all over the Alps want to enact their World Cup fantasies here. In the week before race day you see them drifting into town like Wild West gunslingers through the glass doors of the railway station opposite the Hotel Eiger. They are easily identifiable by the size of their rucksacks and the five pairs of skis of varying lengths attached somehow to their shoulders.

Although the race is now organized by the Swiss with immaculate precision the Kandahar is still very involved and its younger members usually put in some fast times. The rules have changed very little over the years—you start at the top and

around the Gimmeln and Schiltgrat drag-lifts at the far end of the village, near the base of the cable-car. Here you will find what seem at first to be red runs, but which actually give access to some good black runs like the Kandahar and Black Line. The gentler skiing, in fact the nearest in standard to a beginner area, is in the wooded area above Winteregg, served by chair and drag-lifts, and reached from the village by a train up to Allmend-hubel. The Bob Run back down to the village is not manageable for beginners. All three ski areas meet at a central point, Blumenthal, which is a useful lunchtime rendezvous for friends of different standards. There are a couple of good restaurants to choose from here.

The main hotel is the Residence Sport-hotel Murren, once called the Palace. It was here that Sir Arnold's father, Henry, conceived the idea of contracting rooms for the season to take the first winter package tours. The Murren is the most

expensive hotel, but the old regulars prefer the more intimate atmosphere of the Eiger opposite the railway station, which is renowned for its large Swiss breakfasts. The Bellevue is also known for its good food.

Après-ski life in this tiny village is very limited. The out of season population is less than 500. It has been said that you have to be over 50 to get the best out of Murren by night. A lot of those 50-year-olds' children would not agree, but night-life is very much what you make it. Chalet guests manage to make their own fun at home, while the Eiger and the Jungfrau both have good bars and restaurants. Of the few hotel bars which provide music, the Tachi-Bar in the Eiger is the cosiest. A popular evening activity is to take toboggans up to one of the mountain restaurants, sit down to a fondue with friends, then toboggan home down what seems to be a black run, but is only a blue run in daylight.

Above: *The Piz Gloria revolving restaurant was immortalised in the James Bond film* On Her Majesty's Secret Service.

Right: *The Jungfrau region embodies Swiss chocolate-box charm with tiny alpine restaurants tucked in beneath the folds of the gigantic mountains all round.*

you finish at the bottom. Participants spend a lot of time in the bar arguing about their line and which short cuts they can take. These days a handful of compulsory gates have to be negotiated to prevent serious accidents. Two skiers once tried to ski down the 45 degree tracks of the railway with fatal results.

The main intermediate ski area is

GSTAAD

The internationally famous village of Gstaad is an exclusive cluster of old wooden buildings with some more modern additions, tucked into an attractive valley just two hours from Geneva. Like St Moritz, it is a place where celebrities come to mingle with others equally rich and famous. But, unlike St Moritz, this

Gstaad's chalets are winter home to a glittering array of show business personalities who enjoy the picturesque village for its charm and atmosphere.

discreet little village with only 3000 inhabitants offers a level of privacy much cherished by stars such as Roger Moore,

who actually have a home here.

At a low 1100m (3600ft) Gstaad has a short season — the best time to come here is from mid-January to mid-March. The European jet-set tends to congregate here in January and February, so March can be very quiet. There is no such thing as a cheap hotel in Gstaad. The resort's visi-

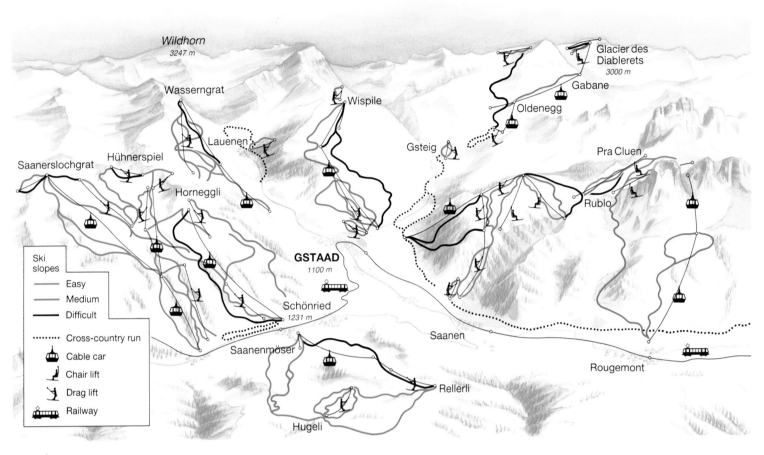

tors come here precisely to avoid such things. The Palace Hotel is synonymous with the resort, but you need to book your room a year in advance. The hotel's grill and *fromagerie* are among the best eating places in town, and its Greengo nightclub is the liveliest and most expensive. Other hotels include the Rossli and the Olden, both with good restaurants.

Because of its rich and famous image, Gstaad is a resort that has never been taken very seriously by real skiers. In fact, for beginners, intermediates, and families who are not on a budget, the gentle pistes may be just what they are looking for. The 250km (155 miles) of pistes is made up of three main areas. Eggli is the largest and connects with the towns of Saanen and Rougemont. The second area, Wasserngrat, is the most challenging of the three and home to the fashionable Eagle Ski Club. The third area, Wispile, is easier and the closest to town.

A total of 11 interlinked villages make up the White Highlands area, all of which are on one lift pass. Gstaad is the most central, with Chateau d'Oex at one end

and St Stephan at the other, but it is the smaller and less expensive villages which attract Swiss weekenders. The skiing everywhere is excellent for beginners, with the best run being the 1253m (4110ft) Skilift Schopfen slope from the gondola station on the Eggli.

If you like the sort of skiing that actually takes you somewhere, rather than up and down the same monotonous runs on one side of a mountain, this place is ideal. The most adventurous skiing is above Eggli at the rocky La Videmanette summit at 2156m (7072ft), from where you can ski through the rocks on black runs down to Rougemont.

The Hornberg has the largest number of interconnected lifts, and is easily reached from Gstaad by bus or train, both of which are included on the lift pass. You can also take the Horneggli lift from Schonried or the gondola from Sannenmoser. There are 14 lifts and the runs are suitable for lower intermediates. Opposite the Hornberg lies the Rellerligrat at 1934m (6343ft), with a good view of Gstaad. But the slopes are south-facing,

starting off icy in the morning and becoming slushy by the afternoon. The restaurant at the top is well worth a visit.

Another good area is from Gandlouenegrat down to Chaltenbrunne, with skiing from expert to intermediate. Be sure to stop for lunch at the Chemi Hutte at Lengebrand above St Stephan. Zweisimmen is another small sector unconnected with any of the others. The gondola from town to the Rinderberg opens up seven runs and five lifts. At the other end of the valley is Chateau d'Oex, also included on the lift pass, but well known in its own right as a centre for finishing schools and hot-air ballooning. Its intermediate ski area has about a dozen runs.

Gstaad and the White Highlands ski area are best enjoyed with a car. Beginners and lower intermediates will benefit from the skiing most of all, but better skiers will also enjoy the variety of terrain to be found here. Just when you think you have seen everything, another tree run or long schüss appears around the next corner.

SAAS FEE

Saas Fee is a chalet-style, car-free village, with only electric taxis and horse-drawn sleighs for transport. For this reason it is frequently compared with neighbouring Zermatt. But here the comparison ends. Zermatt, with its crop of world famous hotels, designer shops and top-class skiing, is ranked among Europe's top five resorts. Saas Fee has a very different image, being a resort for families and intermediates. Where Zermatt can only be reached by train, or car when the roads are completely clear, Saas Fee can

be reached by car. Both resorts lie off the main road between Sierre and Brig *en route* to the Simplon Pass.

Saas Fee is one of the coldest resorts in Europe. With a setting in the centre of an amphitheatre of huge peaks, the village benefits from little sun during the early winter months. The advantage of the altitude and lack of sun — the village is at 1800m (5900ft) and the top skiing at 3500m (11 480ft) — is that this is a safer destination for snow than most.

Saas Fee's most celebrated inhabitant is

Pirmin Zurbriggen, the reigning Olympic Downhill gold medallist, whose home is actually in Saas Almagell a little way down the valley, which has its own tiny ski area. His family owns hotels and other property in Saas Fee itself.

Saas Fee is a sprawl of mainly modern but traditional-style buildings. Further building in the already web-like streets is restricted by avalanche danger. One of Saas Fee's biggest problems throughout the season is lift congestion to the main Felskinn and Mittelallalin ski area. A

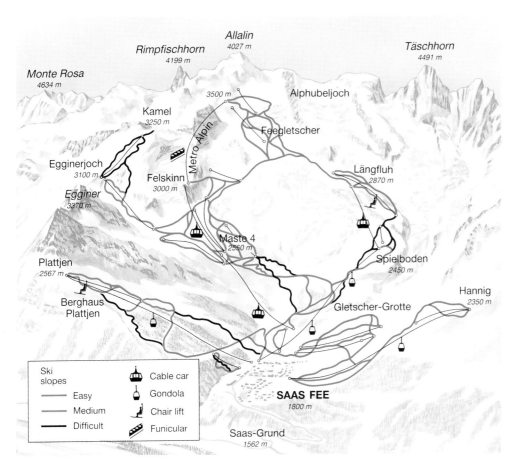

Monte Rosa
4634 m

Rimpfischhorn
4199 m

Allalin
4027 m

Täschhorn
4491 m

3500 m

Alphubeljoch

Kamel
3250 m

Feegletscher

Metro Alpin

Egginerjoch
3100 m

Felskinn
3000 m

Längfluh
2870 m

Egginer
3370 m

Maste 4
2550 m

Spielboden
2450 m

Plattjen
2567 m

Hannig
2350 m

Berghaus
Plattjen

Gletscher-Grotte

Ski slopes		
Easy	Cable car	
Medium	Gondola	
Difficult	Chair lift	
	Funicular	

SAAS FEE
1800 m

Saas-Grund
1562 m

Left: *Car-free Saas Fee boasts several top-class hotels in addition to traditional chalets and apartments; nightlife is livelier than in most Swiss counterparts.*

Below: *Pirmin Zurbriggen is Saas Fee's most famous son having taken gold in the Calgary Olympics and been placed in the top three in dozens of World Cup races.*

crevasses. The seven ski areas make up 80km (49 miles) of piste with mainly red and blue runs and there are good nursery slopes on the outskirts of town, as well as summer skiing on the glacier.

Experts won't find much to amuse them for very long—the best area is around Langfluh at 2870m (9414ft). But there are some excellent opportunities for touring with a guide from the top of Alphubel and Allalin, both of which start with a four-hour climb on skins. The famous Haute Route tour starts from the Britannia Hutte which is reached by a climb from the Plattjen ski area. The tour takes place from mid-April to early June, encorporating Zermatt, Courmayeur and Chamonix.

There are six four-star hotels in town, the best of which include the Ambassador and the Walliserhof. Another well worth considering is the Allalin, with its good restaurant. Other eating places to try are the Fletschhorn, the Hohnegg and the Walliserhof's restaurant. Good mountain restaurants include the Gletscher-Grotte in the woods on the way down from Spielboden.

Compared with many Swiss resorts, Saas Fee has quite a lively nightlife. Night spots to visit include Le Club, the Sans Souci and the Yetti. There is also a modern sports centre.

drag-lift takes you to the start of the Felskinn cable-car, and at the top the Metro Alpin funicular railway runs up inside the mountain to the summit of the ski area. It is able to carry large numbers of people in any weather conditions. It is quick, and it is suitably environment-friendly. It was also the first of its kind and started a trend which was later copied by Val d'Isere, Les Arcs and Les Deux Alpes, among others.

At the breathtaking 3500m summit it is essential to take things very slowly in the thin mountain air. Here, and all around the area, the glacial scenery of blue ice falls is some of the most spectacular in the Alps. It is a very active glacier—the Feegletscher moves at around 30mm, or just over an inch, a year which means the lift pylons have to be regularly moved. Because the glacier is so fast-moving, the off-piste is extremely dangerous due to

ZERMATT

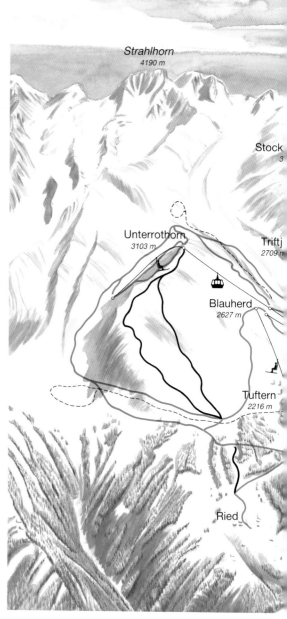

Z ermatt's Tourist Office Director was once quoted as saying, when asked about the resort's publicity activities, that 'with 1.7 million postcards sent from here every year, nearly all of them showing the Matterhorn, who needs publicity?' The Matterhorn is surely the most recognizable and most photographed mountain in the world. Just about every visitor to Zermatt returns home with pockets full of film showing friends skiing (with the Matterhorn in the background), sitting on a restaurant terrace (with the Matterhorn in the background) or strolling through the village centre (with the Matterhorn in the background). Other pictures just show the Matterhorn! Each year, many people die trying to climb this incredible outcrop but most visitors are content to stare at it from across the valley—the mountain absolutely dominates Zermatt

The Matterhorn is Zermatt's ever-present sentinel and the most photographed mountain in the world whose splendour inspires some to climb it.

in a way that no photograph or postcard can portray.

For all Zermatt's natural beauty, its quaint streets and chocolate-box backdrop, it is one of Europe's most demanding skiing areas and attracts keen skiers from around the world. The skiing is on three sections, which are not completely interconnected, and each is reached from a different point in the village. So, if your main priority is convenience, Zermatt is not for you. Horse-drawn sleighs and little electric taxis provide transport between hotels and lifts, although most people quickly become used to a 10-to-15-minute walk at the start of the day. The

fact that the three areas are not connected is not a great problem as each is at least the size of an average resort in its own right.

The Gornergrat—Stockhorn section is the most central and is reached by the old railway; this involves a 40-minute journey to the top although there are a couple of stops *en route*. The section below the Gornergrat (3100m/10 171ft), where there is a hotel, is mostly easy and runs alongside the railway for a while before a decision has to be made as to whether to continue all the way down to Zermatt,

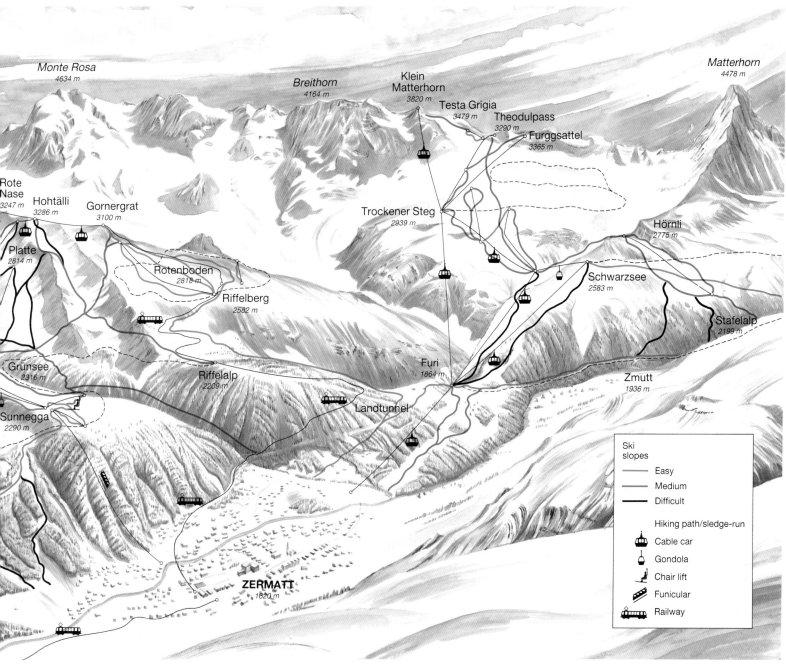

Monte Rosa
4634 m

Breithorn
4164 m

Klein
Matterhorn
3820 m

Testa Grigia
3479 m

Theodulpass
3290 m

Furggsattel
3365 m

Matterhorn
4478 m

Rote
Nase
3247 m

Hohtälli
3286 m

Gornergrat
3100 m

Trockener Steg
2939 m

Hörnli
2775 m

Platte
2814 m

Rotenboden
2818 m

Riffelberg
2582 m

Schwarzsee
2583 m

Stafelalp
2199 m

Grünsee
2316 m

Riffelalp
2209 m

Furi
1864 m

Zmutt
1936 m

Sunnegga
2290 m

Landtunnel

ZERMATT
1620 m

Ski slopes

— Easy
— Medium
— Difficult
∿ Hiking path/sledge-run
🚠 Cable car
🚠 Gondola
🚡 Chair lift
🚞 Funicular
🚃 Railway

jump back on the train at Riffelalp, or veer off to the left for a route through trees to Furi where cable-cars take skiers to the Trockener Steg or Schwarzsee sections—more of which later.

None of this is very appetizing to adventurous skiers, who usually prefer to take the two-stage cable-car from Gornergrat to Stockhorn (3405m/11 171ft), alighting half-way at Hohtalli or continuing all the way. Whatever the choice of destination, the result is the same— hard work all the way down to Triftji or Gant on a variety of relentless, unpisted

and very steep runs which don't usually open until mid-February. There is one relatively easy trail down to Findeln where the reward is a choice of delightful restaurants, notably Enzo's. There are a couple of drag-lifts to enable good skiers to spend all day on the bumps above Triftji, if their knees can stand it, and a gondola runs from Gant to Blauherd (2580m/8465ft).

Blauherd is the mid-point between Sunnegga and Unterrothorn (3103m/ 10 180ft). Sunnegga is reached from town by the ultra-fast Sunnegga Express

which runs through the mountain in just three minutes, rising 700m (2297ft) in the process; compared with riding the rickety train to the Gornergrat, this is like travelling in the next century. Below Sunnegga, there is a short run to Findeln, steep trails through trees back to town or a wide, gentle run to Reid followed by a path down to the outskirts of Zermatt. These last two are end-of-day favourites.

Blauherd is the starting point of a much easier trail to Tuftern, as well as being a staging-post for the journey up to Unter-rothorn from where both medium and difficult trails drop down to Tuftern and others lead back to Blauherd. The views of the Matterhorn from this area are the most striking in the whole region and, in common with everywhere around Zermatt, there are plenty of sunny restaurant terraces from which to enjoy them. Should you visit Zermatt at Christmas, pause at one of the restaurants late in the afternoon on Christmas Eve and listen to the compelling booming of the church bells beckoning parishioners down from the hillsides to worship. The churchyard is bedecked with candles and, if it is snowing, produce a pink, shimmering hue. The bells continue until Mass begins at 11p.m. and are joined during the evening by the tinkling of the little bells of the English church which holds an inter-denominational service on Christmas Eve.

Another fascinating time to visit Zermatt is around 1 August, Swiss National Day. Then the usually reserved Swiss get into the party mood with displays of dancing to the accompaniment of traditional music before a stunning firework display. The walls of the mountains seem to shake and, needless to say, the Matterhorn is illuminated. At this time of year it is still possible to ski all the way down to Trockener Steg from the Klein Matterhorn (3820m/12 533ft) where the glacier provides year-round skiing. Sum-

mer in Zermatt sees the village in another light, quite literally, and rather than the chatter of hordes of skiers, cowbells clunk away in the distance, picnics take place in flower-speckled meadows and walkers roam the hillsides while serious climbers pit their skill, and good fortune, against the mountains. The skiing in summer is as extensive as in some small resorts during the winter and is especially good for first-timers.

The glacial area below the Klein Matterhorn is known as the Plateau Rosa and forms a part of the border between Switzerland and Italy. It is reached from Cervinia on the Italian side and although a separate lift ticket is required for the return journey to Zermatt, many skiers like to zip down to Cervinia for lunch. This is certainly a good idea as Cervinia boasts some excellent restaurants, far cheaper than those in Zermatt, but don't

Right: *A combination of beautiful alpine scenery, several top-rate ski areas, a charming village, restaurants dotting the mountainsides and a very lively apres-ski scene is hard to beat – Zermatt has the lot.*

Below: *Although there are plenty of easy descents, Zermatt is certainly not the best place for beginners as they are simply overwhelmed by the sheer size of the area.*

make the trip if there is the slightest danger of a storm brewing up as Cervinia's upper lifts close when the weather closes in. Many people will testify to the difficulty of finding accommodation when stranded in Cervinia overnight, particularly on high-season weekends when the town is overrun by hundreds of Milanese.

Back on the Swiss side, the skiing on the Plateau Rosa itself holds few terrors, and most routes down to Trockener Steg are easy, but there is some extremely tough work below Schwarzee. This sec-

tion is reached by a network of cable-cars which originate from the outskirts of Zermatt, about 15 minutes' walk from the centre. The first dispersal point is at Furi (1864m/6115ft) from where a 125-person car rises to the Trockener Steg station (from which another continues up to the Klein Matterhorn), a second runs to Furgg (2432m/7979ft) and a third to Schwarzee (2583m/8474ft). The trail map looks like a rather complicated spider's web around here as two more cable-cars complete the network—one connecting Schwarzee and Furgg with the other running between Furgg and Trockener Steg. A highlight of anyone's visit is the final ascent of the lofty Klein Matterhorn, with twisted glacial landscape all around, and views across three countries from the observation platform at the top. A tunnel, leading to the slopes, runs through the Klein Matterhorn and skiers can often be seen leaning against its walls, trying to catch their breath in the thin air.

The start of the run from Furgg down to Furi looks innocuous enough but all too soon it becomes narrow and rock-strewn further down and has frequently forced even the best of skiers to stop to gather their concentration. Moderate intermediate skiers should take the cable-car. There is a similarly deceptive run from Schwarzee to Furi and, as this often resembles a battlefield with fallen skiers trying to reassemble themselves, a sensible option is to take the Weisse Perle route behind Schwarzee to Zmutt and Stafelalp. They provide plenty of challenge but also afford the opportunity to

admire the tranquil valley; make sure that you are travelling fast enough on the last section to avoid having to walk uphill on arrival at Furi.

Like Val d'Isere, Zermatt is a keen skier's resort and while it does not share the French resort's interlinked lift system, nor its connections with a neighbour of the size of Tignes, it remains the perfect alpine resort in most respects. Its disadvantages are that quite a lot of walking is involved, there are frequently long queues for the Furi cable-cars, and the Gornergrat train seems to take a lifetime to get anywhere. Yet these are minor quibbles for most visitors who are enthralled from the moment they gasp in wonder on their first sight of the Matterhorn from the train up from Tasch.

Zermatt is traffic-free other than for electric taxis and horse-drawn sleighs—there is a large car park at Tasch although many visitors prefer to take the train all the way from Geneva, enjoying views

For all its early-morning crowds, Zermatt provides tranquil skiing away from the main areas, with glorious views, and the highest tree-line in Europe, ensuring good visibility if the weather closes in.

across the lake and changing to the branch line at Brig. The stations on this line are like outsize music boxes and the trains are full of locals carrying shopping and avid skiers. The station square buzzes with activity as sleighs and taxis vie for trade from arriving trains and anyone used to French purpose-built resorts, or the condominium complexes of the Rockies, is immediately transfixed by the unspoilt village. Seemingly, every building is complete with intricately carved wooden galleries and even the more modern hotels exude a *fin-de-siècle* opulence.

But, for all its rustic charm, Zermatt is very sophisticated and is certainly not for the impecunious skier. The best hotels such as the Mont Cervin, Monte Rosa,

Alex, Alpenhof, Walliserhof and Schweizerhof are all worth visiting for a drink even if you can't afford to stay in them. The Monte Rosa was Edward Whymper's base when he led the first successful assault of the Matterhorn in 1865 (successful in that Whymper reached the summit, although at the cost of four lives) and a visit to the Whymperstube for a beer is a must. See also the English church, founded by adventuring Britons, which serves as a monument to many who failed to return from their exertions on the surrounding mountains. The Alpine Museum displays enough memorabilia to enthral anyone interested in the history of mountaineering.

The story of Whymper's ascent of the Matterhorn deserves repetition. He had been preparing for the climb from the Italian side when word reached him that another Englishman, the Rev. Charles Hudson, was about to set out from Switzerland. So, Whymper joined him,

along with Lord Francis Douglas and D.R. Haddow, plus two local guides and another, Michel Croz, from Chamonix. They were successful in reaching the summit on 14 July 1865 but disaster struck on the way down when Haddow fell and he, and the three attached to the same rope (Hudson, Douglas and Croz) were left suspended in space until the rope snapped, sending them tumbling to their deaths. A portion of the offending twine can be seen in the Alpine Museum and the written account of Whymper, who watched the entire episode, remains a haunting testament to man's frailty.

For many of the smart people who congregate in Zermatt, shopping is the main *après-ski* activity, with jewellery and fashion at the top of the list. Otherwise, there is skating on an outdoor rink unless the local ice-hockey team has a match.

Although most British tour operators organize a programme of evening entertainments including tobogganing, fondue

Zermatt is expensive but the price is a small consideration for good skiers who trek there pilgrim-like for fast on-piste runs, tortuous mogul fields and, after a heavy snowfall, perfect powder skiing.

suppers and the like, Zermatt's nightlife revolves around cafés, restaurants and nightclubs. Some are desperately expensive but with a little research it is possible to have a good night out without upsetting your bank manager. Elsie's Bar is a Zermatt institution while the general consensus is that Le Mazot continues to be the best medium-priced restaurant. The dining rooms in hotels such as the Mont Cervin are perfect for a romantic, but pricey, dinner with impeccable service. After dinner the main action is to be found in the two discos in the Hotel de la Poste and those in the Pollux and Alex.

Zermatt has the highest tree line in Europe, with foliage up to 2500m (8202ft), not high by Colorado or Utah

standards, but quite luxuriant for the Alps. Every woodland glade seems to conceal a little mountain hut with the proprietors eager to dole out hearty local specialities at lunchtime—lunch is as important as dinner in this region. Some places are spoilt by those ubiquitous poseurs, many of them British, who like to congregate on terraces ostentatiously swallowing bottles of very expensive champagne.

In the main, though, the mountain restaurants are first-class and have an adhesive quality which seems to demand another half-hour spent sipping coffee and *Pflumli* before hitting the slopes for the afternoon's session. There are some 40 restaurants dotted about the mountainsides, probably the largest number in any ski resort in the world.

Zermatt may not be the world's largest ski resort but it remains one of the most atmospheric and beautiful places to ski in the world.

ST MORITZ

Mention St Moritz in Europe or America, and the chances are that most people will have heard of it as the 'top people's resort'. It is without doubt the world's best known ski resort, famous for its luxury hotels, the Cresta Run and as the venue for the Winter Olympics of 1928 and 1948.

It became a winter resort in 1864 when a group of summer holidaymakers from England complained to Engadine businessman Johannes Badrutt about the drizzly British winter ahead of them. When Badrutt offered them hospitality for the winter, he was at the same time planting the roots of St Moritz as a world-famous winter sports centre.

Today Badrutt's descendants run Badrutt's Palace Hotel, a monolith which is also the jewel in the crown of St Moritz's four five-star hotels. Equal in splendour is the Carlton, built for the last Czar at the beginning of this century. The third is the Suvretta House which was built not far out of town. The fourth giant is the Kulm, home to the St Moritz Tobogganing Club since 1884 when the Cresta Run was built. Evening dress is expected in the

The Engadine Marathon is one of the main events on the cross-country skiing calendar. Over 1500 participants set out on the 42km (26 miles) course, much of it across the frozen lake.

major hotels and in the fashionable Chesa Veglia restaurant. It is worth remembering that men must wear suits if they wish to walk through the public areas of the Palace Hotel after 7p.m. Women's dress should be the equivalent.

More than half of the hotels are four- and five-star. Among the best four-stars is the Steffani, which has a good restaurant, dancing and a swimming pool. Cheaper alternatives can be found on the outskirts of town, in St Moritz Bad, and in the outlying hamlets like Celerina, Champfer and Sils Maria, all of which connect with St Moritz Dorf by bus.

St Moritz is actually two villages — Dorf and Bad. Dorf is the smarter of the two,

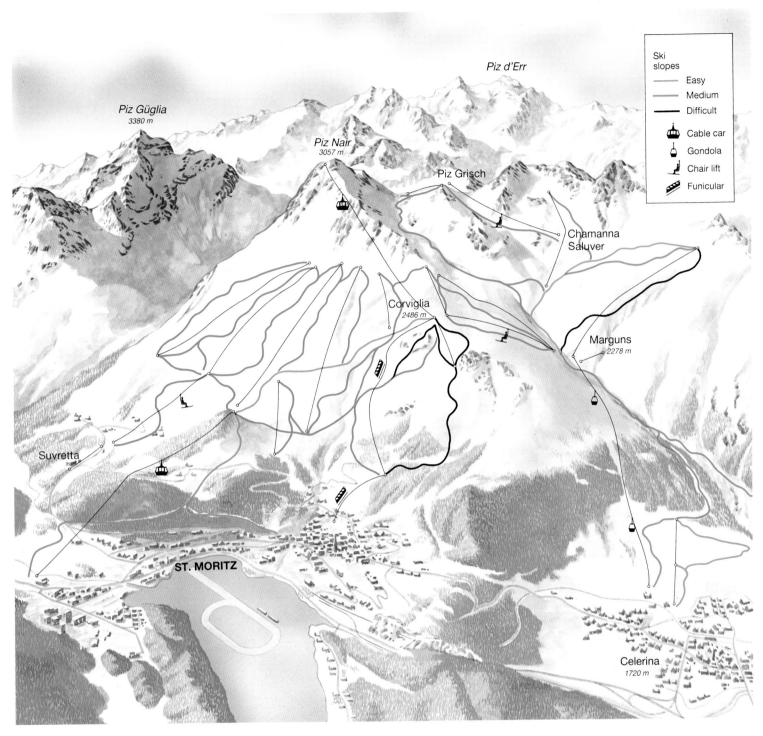

Piz d'Err

Piz Güglia
3380 m

Piz Nair
3057 m

Piz Grisch

Chamanna
Saluver

Corviglia
2486 m

Marguns
2278 m

Suvretta

ST. MORITZ

Celerina
1720 m

Ski slopes
— Easy
— Medium
— Difficult
🚡 Cable car
🚠 Gondola
🚡 Chair lift
🚞 Funicular

with the best hotels and shops, and *the* place for seeing and being seen. Bad, which straggles on to the end of Dorf, is the centre of cross-country skiing. Social events in both Dorf and Bad are numerous, including golf and polo on the frozen lake and Skijoring races with horses pulling skiers across the ice, and the Engadine Ski Marathon (cross-country) every second Sunday of March.

One of the top sports of St Moritz is to drink a Bullshot (consommé with vodka) in the warm safety of the Cresta Club while watching your friends go down the 1212m (3975ft) ice canal at speeds of up to 140km/h (87mph). Apart from the Cresta bobsled, there is also a four-man Bobbahn which takes two passengers.

Lunch is taken either at the Corviglia Club, which is the Suvretta Hotel's

mountain restaurant, or at La Marmite at the top of Corviglia. If you are skiing — and many St Moritzites do not — make sure you stop for a hot drink and *Apfel Strudel* at Hahnensee at the bottom of the long run down from Corvatsch. Another compulsory stop is at Café Hanselmann, in town, one of the best known *après-ski* places in the Alps. A visit to the King's Club in the Palace Hotel is essential, and

Gunther Sachs' Dracula Club is also popular. Other nightclubs include the Disco Spotlight and the Vivai. For a quieter evening, the Hotel Steffani's Cresta Bar and the Kulm's Sunny Bar are popular.

Glittering resorts with luxury facilities tend to attract a rich and famous clientele. They fly into St Moritz in their private jets and stay in their own or their friends' chalets. One of the most romantic ways to arrive is by the famous Glacier Express from Zermatt, a 240km (150 mile) crossing which takes just under eight hours.

Bad is an ancient spa town where visitors can stay in apartments and generally cheaper hotels, as well as benefit from the less crowded connections into the St Moritz lift system. This is also where some of Switzerland's best cross-country skiing takes place, up and down the hills around the lake. Pontresina, along the valley floor, also has good cross-country skiing, plus some of the most difficult alpine skiing in the area. Unlike St Moritz, which has a mixture of architectural styles, Pontresina still has many old Engadine-style buildings.

Above: It is estimated that only 40 per cent of winter visitors to St Moritz ski which means that there is a tranquil atmosphere in the mountains, especially away from the main skiing areas.

Right: St Moritz and its neighbour, Pontresina, provide plenty of opportunities for derring-do skiing. An excellent record of sunny days and pristine snow assures keen skiers of a great time.

St Moritz's skiing is often placed second after the social life. In fact it often has the best snow in Switzerland. St Moritz's ski area has varied runs on 350km (217 miles) of piste, serviced by 56 ski lifts, with plenty of steep off-piste around the Piz Nair which can be really challenging after a new snowfall. Extra-warm clothing including hats, neck gaiters and sometimes even face masks are vital here as conditions can be very unpleasant at the top. The best time to ski is first thing in the morning when the slopes are almost empty—life in St Moritz starts late and finishes late. However, by mid-morning some of the skiing areas do be-

come crowded, especially on a sunny day.

The resort is at a high 1856m (6088ft) with the highest ski runs starting at 3304m (10 837ft). The ski area is divided between four main mountains; Corviglia, Corvatsch, Diavolezza and Lagalb, and there is also some skiing at Zuoz and Muottas Muragl. Day trips to Livigno in Italy are easy. The most popular of these is Corviglia, with its two access points—

one a train right in the centre of town, and the other a cable-car from Bad. Beginners are taught on the gentle pistes at the top of the railway.

The other areas need to be reached by bus. The biggest, Corvatsch, is a 15-minute bus ride from St Moritz, and like Piz Nair it is often very cold. The skiing here is more varied than Corviglia's, with good off-piste skiing and a long black run down open slopes and through the trees. Lagalb and Diavolezza, a 45-minute bus journey from St Moritz Dorf and 15 minutes from Pontresina, face each other across the valley. These are the two smaller, but more challenging, areas. Lagalb has some of the best mogul skiing in the area, and Diavolezza is surrounded by stunning glaciers including the Morteratsch glacier which can be skied down by adventurous intermediates and experts. Over the back of Diavolezza is a very demanding off-piste run.

Apart from polo and racing on the lake, cross-country and downhill skiing, and the Cresta Run, other activities include para-gliding, sleigh trips to the Roseg and Fex valleys, skating and curling. Summer skiing takes place at Corvatsch and at Diavolezza.

VERBIER

Skiing at Verbier has developed into a cult activity among well-to-do young Britons over the last few years. Many spend a two-week vacation there every winter and visit for another three or four weekends during the season; others visit once and vow that they will never return, having been appalled by the attitude of their rowdier compatriots whose only winter sports achievement is making a noise. Either way, it cannot be denied that Verbier has some brilliant skiing and the fact that it connects with Haute Nendaz, Super Nendaz and Thyon 2000 makes it one of the largest interconnected ski areas in the Alps. This resort in the Swiss Valais should be high on the shopping list of any keen skier.

Do not expect a Swiss idyll of chocolate-box chalets complete with balconies inhabited by locals whose life style has remained unchanged for centuries. This is, instead, a modern, but not unattractive sprawl ranged around a plateau above Le Chable, 128km (80 miles) from Geneva. It is far better to regard the village of Verbier merely as the base for some spectacular skiing. If you are happy to be in the company of the finest flowers of British youth who congregate here all winter long, fair enough — otherwise, keep your own counsel or travel with a group of friends.

The four valleys which make up the skiing area of Verbier and its neighbours are full of challenge, and a few surprises, for experts and intermediates. Beginners would be best advised to go elsewhere as although there are some nursery slopes just outside the village, there is little chance of novices progressing to the very demanding terrain above. There are several sectors with easy skiing but there are few comfortable runs all the way back to the base of the lifts.

The village is set at 1500m (4921ft) and the Mont Fort top station is at a heady 3300m (10 827ft), meaning that the vertical drop is about 1800m (5900ft); given the right conditions, it is occasionally possible to ski all the way down to Le Chable which is set at 821m

(2694ft), giving a drop of almost 2500m. There are 320km (200 miles) of marked trails served by 86 lifts. The statistics indicate the sheer size of the area. What they do not reveal is the exciting quality of the skiing at Verbier.

Anyone who wants good ski credibility heads straight for Mont Fort to attack Tortin. Too many find that it is they who are being attacked by a relentless, seemingly never-ending slope which has reduced more than its fair share of timid

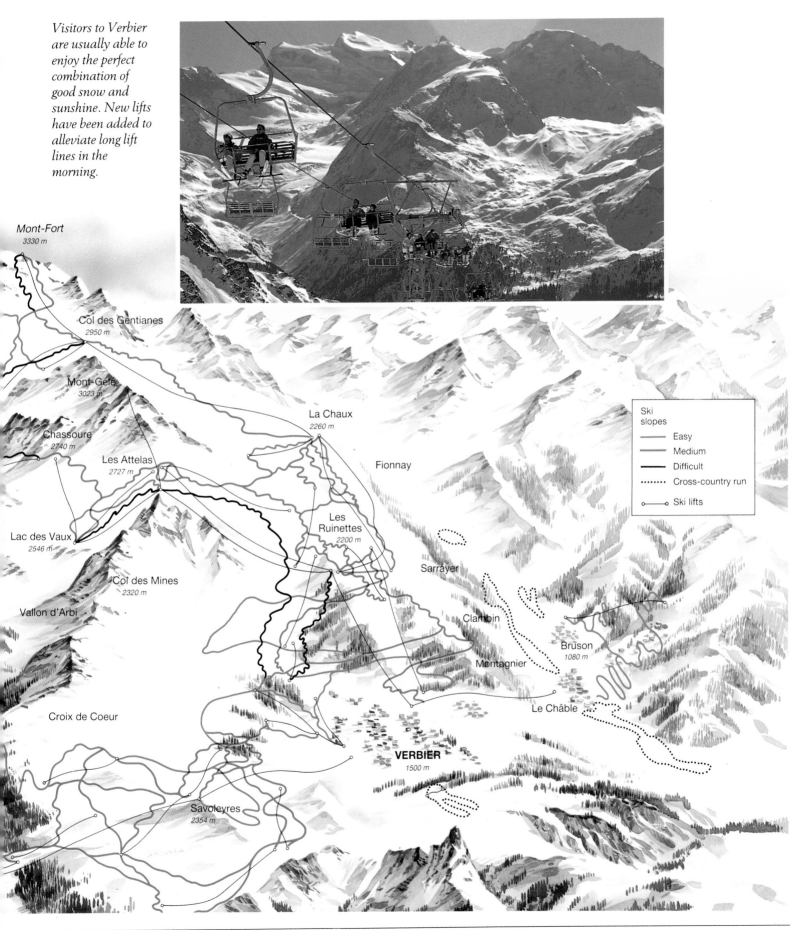

Visitors to Verbier are usually able to enjoy the perfect combination of good snow and sunshine. New lifts have been added to alleviate long lift lines in the morning.

Mont-Fort
3330 m

Col des Gentianes
2950 m

Mont-Gelé
3023 m

La Chaux
2260 m

Chassoure
2740 m

Les Attelas
2727 m

Fionnay

Lac des Vaux
2546 m

Les Ruinettes
2200 m

Col des Mines
2320 m

Sarrayer

Vallon d'Arbi

Clambin

Bruson
1080 m

Montagnier

Croix de Coeur

Le Châble

VERBIER
1500 m

Savoleyres
2354 m

Ski slopes

Easy

Medium

Difficult

Cross-country run

Ski lifts

skiers to jelly over the years. If you fall, you fall a long way – 400m (1312ft) to be precise – although Tortin is frequently speckled with huge moguls to slow you down.

Moderate intermediates are better advised to head for Savoleyres during their first couple of days in Verbier as this section, which is not linked with the rest of the pistes, is less intimidating and provides less congested skiing and shorter lift queues. The tree-lined run down to La Tsoumaz is delightful and there are plenty of restaurants at the bottom, many with terraces for a languid lunch on a sunny day.

Most of the skiing is reached from the opposite end of Verbier and most of that is reached by a gondola-lift which occasionally has appalling queues in the morning, especially during high season and at weekends. Les Attelas is the main dispersal point and gives access to the area above Lac des Vaux, where there are plenty of alternatives for intermediates, and down to Les Ruinettes, where the skiing is more difficult. There are, fortunately, a couple of easy routes from Les Ruinettes back to town. A small cable-car rises from Les Attelas to Mont Gele from where some of the best off-piste skiing in Switzerland is to be found. Tortin is accessible from this point.

The base of Tortin is also the connecting point for skiing on to Super Nendaz, even less atmospheric than Verbier and certainly less lively although there are a few good mountain restaurants in this part of the Four Valleys network. There are two options here: take the Plan-de-Fou cable-car to ski above Haute Nendaz or take the easy off-piste run to Priaron and down to the valley where a bus can be caught back to La Tsoumaz and thence to Verbier via Savoleyres on skis. Otherwise, a network of lifts gives access to Thyon 2000, a modern resort from where it is possible to ski down to Les Collons, Mayens-de-l'Ours and Veysonnaz. Thyon 2000 has some very good skiing for modest intermediates, and is one of the better places in the region for first-timers. It is a good alternative to Verbier for skiers who want extensive terrain without the hassles of Verbier's lengthy lift queues and high prices. The better skiing is,

however, closer to Verbier.

There are so many variations when skiing Verbier's vast array of challenges that several circuits of the system are recommended for varying grades of skier. An intermediate's itinerary could be as follows: take the gondola to Les Attelas for the run to Tortin, then go by cable-car to Col des Gentianes for the long and undulating trail down to La Chaux before choosing between skiing back to Verbier via Les Ruinettes or taking the route through Lac des Vaux to La Tsoumaz. Experts have endless possibilities but one of the best itineraries for a half-day's skiing is to get to the top of the Mont Gele cable-car before the crowds assemble and ski down part of the Tortin descent, stopping at the next cable-car to rise to Col des Gentianes and then up to Mont Fort. Then it's all the way down to Tortin—and good luck! After this, everything will seem easy and the rest of the morning can be spent amusing yourself by taking an off-piste run back to Verbier from above Lac des Vaux.

Verbier is one of the premier resorts for visitors who want staffed chalets although

Above: *Most of Verbier's skiing is above the tree line, affording spectacular views across the valley – many visitors pause to look at the views as an excuse to recover from the tough skiing all around.*

Right: *The Mont Fort cable-car gives access to some of Verbier's most exhilarating and demanding skiing.*

there is plenty of self-catering accommodation in apartments as well as some good hotels, of which the Vanessa, Les Chamois, La Poste and the Rosalp are among the best. The Restaurant Pierroz in the Rosalp is one of the better places to eat and Verbier as a whole is blessed with dozens of excellent restaurants and loads of little pizzerias and cafés for an informal snack. The sports centre has an indoor swimming pool, Jacuzzi, solarium, squash courts and a skating rink and the cinema occasionally shows English or American films. At night, Verbier really does swing: the famous (or infamous!) Farm Club, La Luge, the Nelson, the Tara and Au Fer à Cheval are among the more popular watering holes.

VILLARS

Villars was one of those resorts, along with Klosters, Murren and Arosa, where generations of British families learned the joy of skiing; typically, there were the older, well-heeled visitors in their luxurious private chalets and smart hotels, and teenagers from the local finishing schools. But in the mid-seventies the ski market changed: the new conception of what a holiday should cost and how many hundreds of kilometres of piste people should get for their money led to a decline in Switzerland's popularity, and particularly so in smaller resorts such as Villars.

More recently Villars has seen a sudden recovery in its fortunes. The tour operators have returned, along with British families and Club Med members. One of the main attractions is the short hour-long drive from Geneva, making it—along with France's La Clusaz—one of the most accessible resorts for traveller's outside the continent. The magnet which has newly attracted the tour operator is the flattering, sunny mountainside which suits beginners to intermediates and provides ideal skiing for family groups. On the slopes you cannot get lost as everthing centres around Bretaye. The green route from here to the village makes a wonderful last run of the day. The pistes in the immediate vicinity of Villars are gentle enough for beginners to learn on and for intermediates to perfect their technique, but they also offer some interesting challenges to experts after a good snowfall.

Villars and Les Diablerets share 120km (74 miles) of piste and 48 lifts. The most popular way up the mountain in the morning is on the crowded cog railway to Bretaye, but the gondola to Roc d'Orsay at 2000m (6560ft) is an alternative and much faster ascent. Roc d'Orsay down to Bretaye is a gentle blue run. The Grand Chamossaire and the Petit Chamossaire are good intermediate areas with a variety of red, blue and one black run back to Bretaye. Petit Chamossaire is the more challenging of the two. The opposite side of Bretaye, around Chaux de Conches and Chaux Ronde, has some excellent off-piste skiing, including some good tree skiing for bad weather days, though beginners are also catered for.

In recent years Villars' ski area has joined up with Les Diablerets, adding a black run and a glacier with a top height of 2970m (9742ft) which is useful for the poor snow years and summer skiing. The link is not an easy one, however, and a supplementary lift pass is needed. Apart from the glacier skiing, the two ski areas at Les Diablerets are easy, extensive and crowdless. The Isenau area, which rises to 2120m (6954ft), is mainly for beginners to intermediates, though the skiing under the Pierres Pointes gondola between the glacier and Isenau is some of the most challenging around. Villars also links up with Barboleusaz, which has uncrowded skiing for all standards including experts who can ski off-piste under the Gryon gondola. There are seven mountain restaurants in the area.

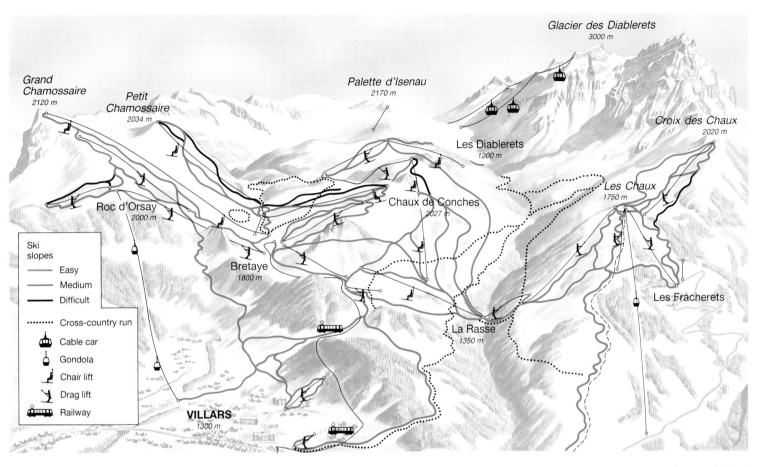

Left: *The skiing around Bretaye is mostly easy and it is possible to ski all the way back to Villars from this point. There are several restaurants in the area.*

Below: *The cog-railway to Bretaye is the most popular way up from Villars in the morning. The gondola to Roc d'Orsay provides an alternative if it is too crowded.*

Villars itself is a large but subdued resort, lying at a relatively low 1300m (4264 ft). It has somehow managed to keep its alpine, though rather eclectic, style over the years, keeping the architectural monstrosities to a minimum. Hotels include the luxurious Grand Hotel du Parc, the Panoramic, Le Popular Renardiere and the attractive Alpe Fleurie. There are all the usual village shops, restaurants and bars. The other activities on offer to the holidaymaker include an excellent sports centre with indoor tennis and squash, as well as an indoor swimming pool, a bowling alley and a skating rink.

Les Diablerets is a chalet-style village with some newer buildings constructed in an alpine look to blend in with the original ones. Accommodation is mainly in chalets and apartments and there is little nightlife. *Après-ski* both here and at Villars is quiet, more suited to families than singles or couples. In Villars the best discos are the New Sam and the El Gringo, while the Bridge Pub is a lively nightspot too.

THE AMERICAS

Any skier visiting the United States or Canada for the first time is inevitably struck by the two factors which make the North American continent an extra-special experience: a big country with stunning scenery and genuinely friendly people who really do want you to have a nice day. Visitors really are treated as honoured guests – a situation far-removed from the monosyllabic grunts which greet skiers in certain French resorts.

The resorts in the eastern states of the USA exude a 'chipper' atmosphere, in keeping with the demeanour of the citizens of Boston and New York who use them as winter playgrounds; those on the California-Nevada border are far more laid-back (except at night when the clinking of gambling chips makes for a heady atmosphere of anticipation and, often, disappointment); the ski towns of Colorado, New Mexico, Utah and Wyoming reflect their history of mining for gold and silver, and skiers are thrilled by the prospect of skiing the famous 'Champagne' powder and invariably enthralled by the grandeur of the Rockies.

Grandeur is almost an understatement when describing the resorts in Alberta and British Columbia. Most resorts in the Canadian Rockies are set in National Parks, where elk and long-horned sheep roam free, and the vast pine forests provide the perfect backdrop for either heli-skiing, cruising perfectly manicured slopes or attacking steep and deep powder bowls.

LAS LENAS

At the height of the European summer, the reverse seasons of the Southern Hemisphere bring winter to the Andean snowfields in a ski season lasting from June to October. Las Leñas, Argentina's premier ski resort, has high season in July and August. European tourists are an increasingly common sight in the capital Buenos Aires and on the Las Leñas slopes. In South America tourism is the pursuit only of the very rich; more widespread development is hampered by the absence of a tourism infrastructure.

The resort's claimed annual snowfall of 635cm (250in) is perhaps optimistic — the Chilean Andes have had better snow in recent seasons. But the snow at Las Leñas is reliable enough for many national teams to train there in our summer months. It is the first South American resort to gain World Cup accreditation and is now the opening venue of the World Cup season.

The purpose-built resort was created in 1983, and has the look one would expect from imported Franco-Swiss technology, with an exclusive and trendy upmarket feel and prices to match its blue-chip

Purpose-built Las Lenas has borrowed French and Swiss technology to produce a trendy, exclusive and up-market ski station.

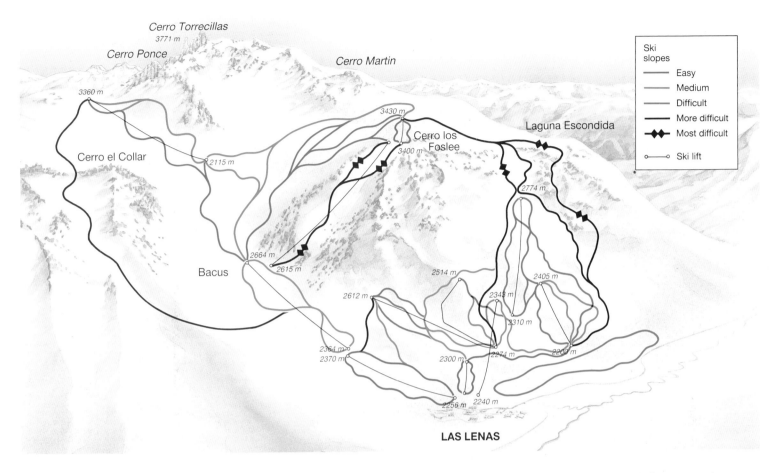

Cerro Torrecillas
3771 m

Cerro Ponce

Cerro Martin

3360 m

Cerro el Collar

2115 m

3430 m

Cerro los Foslee

3400 m

Laguna Escondida

2774 m

2664 m

2615 m

Bacus

2514 m

2405 m

2612 m

2348 m

2310 m

2364 m

2274 m

2200 m

2370 m

2300 m

2256 m

2240 m

LAS LENAS

Ski slopes
— Easy
— Medium
— Difficult
— More difficult
♦♦ Most difficult
∘—∘ Ski lift

Mendoza sponsors. It lies in red rock Dolomitic scenery above the natural tree-line and above San Rafael in the appropriately named Valle Hermoso (beautiful valley), 250km (155 miles) and three hours' drive south of Mendoza. Pistes go from 2250m (7382ft) up to 3400m (11 155ft) — highly respectable by alpine standards but only of middling altitude here in the Andes, the second highest mountain range in the world. The resort can sleep 3000 visitors and claims to be able to shift 9000 skiers per hour through its lift systems. Despite this, at peak season it can be uncomfortably busy.

Four first-class hotels, 305 self-catering apartments and convention-style facilities all open directly on to the pistes. The new Piscis hotel has luxury accommodation for 200 with a European-style casino and indoor-outdoor pool. A shopping arcade, restaurants, bars and a disco are conveniently placed for *après-ski*. Slightly cheaper accommodation is available in the Hotel La Huenca at Los Molles, a bus ride from the resort.

Modest by alpine standards, Las Leñas has a ski area of 39 square km (15 square miles). Eleven lifts serve 39 downhill runs (totalling 64km/40 miles) providing 1200m (3937ft) of vertical descent and a longest continuous run of 8km (5 miles). There are 16km (10 miles) of cross-country tracks as well as guided off-piste skiing, some of which is extreme. The main disadvantage of such a spectacular mountain range are frequent strong winds which tends to close the higher lifts and turns the otherwise champagne powder to crust. Moguls, gullies and motorway reds are rare, but there are some black runs worthy of the name — particularly the 40 degree Marte which often carries deep, light, flattering powder. Names of other runs are suitably galactic for a resort of such purpose-built lunar appearance: Venus, Neptuno, Vulcano, Minerva, Apolo, to name but a few. Three new chair-lifts are being built for 1991.

Ski hire equipment is excellent — modern and new. The ski school is also good, with English being widely spoken (Spanish is the official language). Most credit cards are taken, and as elsewhere in South America, dollars are the most useful foreign currency, whether they be notes or traveller's cheques.

Access is by plane to Buenos Aires plus a 90-minute internal flight to Malargue airport, followed by a 70km (43 mile) bus transfer to the resort. The extravagance of skiing at very high prices can be mitigated by extending the holiday and taking in some of the excellent side trips such as the Iguaçú Falls, whale watching on the Valdez peninsula (September) or riding on the gaucho *estancias* (ranches on the pampas).

There are some other points to note before venturing to ski in Argentina. Health standards and drinking water are generally good in the main Argentine tourist centres but take your own water supply before travelling if a journey off the beaten track is intended. The Argentine currency is the Austral and in recent years has often been devalued. In economic crises, which are frequent, credit cards can be suspended, so take enough cash. The internal telephone system is erratic but international calls and telex are more reliable.

BANFF

In common with most resorts in Canada, skiers are treated as friends, not a visiting nuisance, at Sunshine Village, a 20-minute ride from the centre of Banff via the free bus service. Every morning, a group of ski hosts and hostesses congregates at the foot of the lift system. The group, known as 'Twinkies', comprises unpaid volunteers who, in exchange for a free lift pass, act as on-piste guides for the day. Anyone can choose to join them for a day's fast cruising around the mountainsides or a gentle potter about in the glades below the mid-station. The Twinkies are, in the main, residents of Calgary who find the draw of the Banff National Park irresistible and their delight is to show visitors around the hills and to enjoy good company on chair-lifts and at the luncheon table. This system works particularly well for couples of differing abilities and aspirations as each can ski with a like-minded group for the day.

Sunshine Village is the larger of Banff's two ski areas, and the more varied. It has been developed over the years so that there is plenty of accommodation in the immediate vicinity, mostly in the village complex, close to the top station of the gondola. Various packages are available that include accommodation, unlimited use of the lift system, 90 minutes of tuition every day, day-care facilities for small children, a ski tour with a Twinkie, entertainment every night and a last-night party. These deals certainly appeal to people who want the convenience of doorstep skiing plus a ready-made *bonhomie* but the majority of visitors prefer to stay in Banff itself where there is more variety in the choice of restaurants and nightclubs.

Sunshine Village's lift system rises from the valley (505m/1658ft) to a top station on Lookout Mountain at 2730m (8954ft) and the final section, the Great Divide chair-lift, follows the line of the Continental Divide and criss-crosses the border between Alberta and British Columbia with stunning views of the Canadian Rockies all around. Most of the skiing above the Sunshine Village mid-

station (2160m/7082ft) is also above the tree line and every lift affords a choice of descents. There are several options at the top of the Great Divide double chair: the South Divide and Red 90 trails are both for intermediates but the near-vertical

Bye Bye Bowl is, as its name suggests, a heart-stopping feature. Similarly, the Standish double chair gives access to the gently-rolling Creek Run, intermediate trails such as Big Bunkers and tortuous descents like Headwall, Larynx and Stan-

Colorado and Utah don't have a monopoly on good powder. The Canadian Rockies regularly have big dumps of snow which assure powder hounds of a great day.

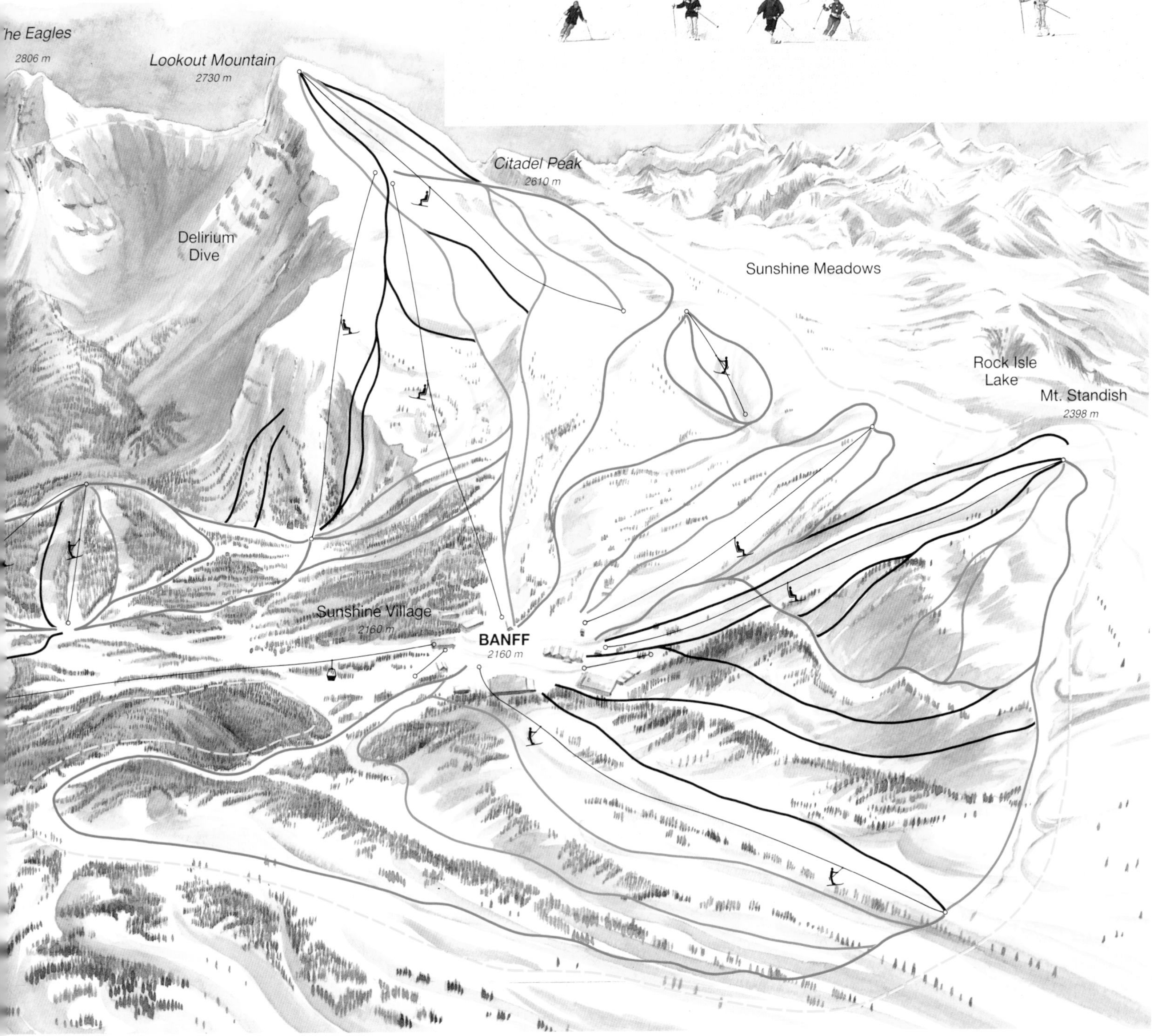

The Eagles
2806 m

Lookout Mountain
2730 m

Citadel Peak
2610 m

Delirium Dive

Sunshine Meadows

Rock Isle Lake

Mt. Standish
2398 m

Sunshine Village
2160 m

BANFF
2160 m

dish face, the lower section of which snakes down narrow routes through trees back to the Sunshine Inn where bathers in the huge hot tub watch skiers make their descents.

The longest run is from the top of Lookout Mountain all the way back to the valley, some 8km (5 miles) in length and incorporating a vertical drop of 1070m (3514ft). This is a lovely run at the end of the day and provides several interesting diversions through the trees.

In addition to good skiing for all adult skiers, Sunshine Village provides excellent facilities for children through the Kids Kampus Daycare Centre (19 months–six years) and the Wee Angels (three–five-year-olds) and Young Angels (six–12-year-olds) skiing programmes. Adult beginners can take advantage of a package that includes equipment rentals, lift ticket and tuition. At the other end of the scale, Sunshine Village regularly hosts top-quality amateur and regional professional races.

Mount Norquay, Banff's second skiing

area, is a very different proposition. The installation of two new four-seater chair-lifts and an extra 28 hectares (70 acres) of skiable terrain has added the missing middle-ability ground to what was previously either extremely difficult or beginners-only territory. Being just 6km (4 miles) from the centre of Banff, a 10-minute journey by bus, it remains a perfect place for beginners while experts delight in achieving mind-boggling daily 'verticals': 27 runs from top to bottom adding up to a total descent of 10.5km (35 000ft), qualifying skiers for membership of Club 35000 and a gold pin if they manage it in a day. Over half of Mont Norquay's skiing is designated as of 'black diamond' difficulty and 35 per cent is covered by artificial snow-making equipment. There are licensed lodges at the base and top of the lifts, babysitting is available for children over two years and, in addition to equipment hire, ski clothing can be rented.

With a top station at 2133m (6998ft), Mount Norquay is by no means the

Above: *Banff is a friendly little town with plenty of hotels, bars and restaurants, set in the Banff National Park with two good ski areas in the immediate vicinity.*

Right: *Tomba the 'Bomba' took gold twice in the 1988 Calgary Olympics for Italy, in the slalom and giant slalom events, capping a successful season in World Cup races.*

highest resort in North America and it is far from being the largest, but its reputation for providing some of the most challenging skiing on the continent is justified. The steep trails from the top of the Norquay chair-lift — North American, Bowl and Lone Pine — all sound innocuous enough but should only be attempted by thoroughly competent and confident skiers. The lift ticket includes floodlit skiing until 9p.m. three nights a week and the resort provides a variety of programmes including children's and adults' learn-to-ski sessions, recreational racing, Telemark skiing and snowboarding. There is a season-long racing pro-

gramme including many all-comers' events. Both Sunshine Village and Mount Norquay have their own lift passes and there is one also covering Lake Louise.

One of the big features of Canadian skiing, heliskiing, is also available from Banff. This entails an early-morning departure and a two-hour coach journey through Kootenay National Park to Panorama Resort in British Columbia before flying into the Purcell Mountains. Groups are organized according to ability and instruction in powder technique and snow craft is provided.

Banff offers a good range of accommodation, from the sumptuous Banff Springs Hotel to the well appointed but more-affordable Banff Park Lodge and Charlton's Cedar Court, as well as plenty of little places offering room only. There are some 70 cafés and restaurants in town—quite extraordinary for somewhere with a population of just 6500—and options include French, Italian, Greek, Mexican and Japanese cuisine as well as a variety of standard ribs and burger joints. The Silver City is a popular disco while the Rose and Crown is a self-styled 'English Pub', complete with dartboard. Other non-ski activities include tours of Banff National Park, sleigh rides, hiking, ice climbing, snowmobiling, dog sledding, skating, curling, ice fishing, racketball and squash. Shopping is a rewarding pastime with a fine selection of locally made and imported jewellery, Canadian jade, Cowichan fashions and Indian artefacts.

Although Banff and its neighbours comprise Alberta's main skiing area, the Calgary Winter Olympics of 1988 took place at Mount Nakiska, about 30 minutes' drive from the centre of Calgary. It was there that the Italians celebrated in rumbustious fashion when Alberto Tomba took gold in the slalom and giant slalom, and Swiss cowbells echoed around the valley in recognition of Pirmin Zurbriggen's victory in the men's downhill and Vreni Schneider's two wins, in slalom and giant slalom. In all, the Swiss won nine medals in Alpine events and were followed by the Austrians with six. Local passion was fuelled by Karen Percy's two bronze medals for third place in both the downhill and super giant slalom.

LAKE LOUISE

Following the sun around all day is an easy prospect at Lake Louise where four ski sections face in different directions. Named after Queen Victoria's daughter, Princess Louise, this little resort doesn't look much on first impression: just a collection of gently rolling tree-lined runs leading back down to the Whiskyjack Lodge resort complex. What is not immediately apparent is that there is a lot more on offer than the Whitehorn section (top station 2672m/8765ft) immediately to the fore. The Top of the World high-speed quad chair-lift and the Summit Platter Poma both serve the Back Bowls and are the immediate targets of avid powder hounds; the Ptarmigan section has wide open skiing on its upper reaches, with a full range of marked trail below, while the Larch area provides some long, fast trails as well as the delightful winter wonderland of the Marmot trail with its easy skiing on gentle terrain, snaking its way through forests.

Set in Banff National Park, 40 minutes from the town of Banff, Lake Louise has another big advantage over rivals in that it is set in some of the most remarkable scenery on the continent. The view across the Bow Valley, with a quartet of four sturdy mountains (Temple, Fairview, Beehive and White) arrayed sentinel-like above the lake, and with the intricate Chateau Lake Louise peeping out from the conifers, is enough to make even the keenest of skiers stop in his stride to gaze at the majestic landscape. Kicking Horse Pass, which leads from Alberta to British Columbia, is in the distance to the right.

This is the view portrayed on a Canadian $20 bill and continues to catch the breath of the most hardened visitor. This grandeur gives way to a stark landscape in the Back Bowls where the deep powder snow lies throughout a season which generally lasts from mid-November until the end of May. The Ptarmigan and Larch sections are different again, very pretty and well sheltered from the elements.

Lake Louise is a user-friendly resort in that other than on the Back Bowls, every lift has at least one easy route down from

Left: *The grandeur of the Canadian Rockies is the perfect backdrop for off-piste skiing. Being set in a National Park, there are no boundaries and skiers are free to roam at will.*

Below: *The base lodge houses a self-service cafeteria and a (slightly) more formal restaurant to fuel hungry skiers. The lifts rise from a few yards away and the nursery slopes are alongside.*

the top. A couple of skiers of different abilities, for example, can ride the Eagle chair-lift, which connects the Whitehorn and Ptarmigan sections, and then choose between the Pika run which meanders in a traverse through trees across the hillside and then down to the valley, or the thigh-burning descent of either the Ptarmigan, Raven or Exhibition mogul fields. The Temple Lodge is conveniently situ-

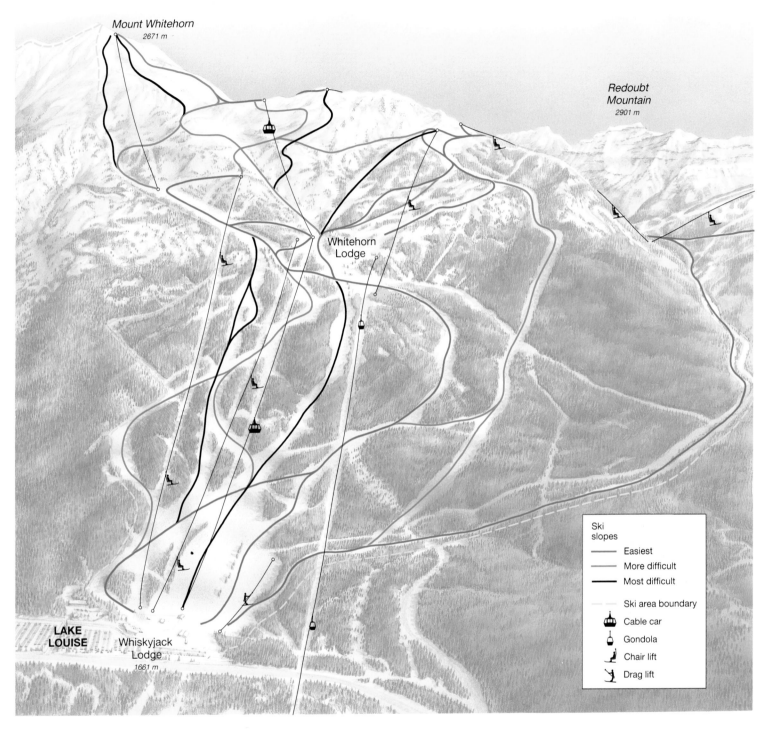

Mount Whitehorn
2671 m

Redoubt
Mountain
2901 m

Whitehorn
Lodge

LAKE
LOUISE

Whiskyjack
Lodge
1661 m

Ski
slopes

Easiest

More difficult

Most difficult

Ski area boundary

Cable car

Gondola

Chair lift

Drag lift

ated as a rendezvous point for a mug of hot chocolate or a hearty lunch. Similarly, the Whitehorn section provides plenty of choice: the high-speed Olympic chair deposits skiers at 2301m (7550ft) from where experts can test their ability down the World Cup men's or ladies' downhill courses while their less accomplished, or less ambitious friends can cruise down the lovely Wiwaxy run which is another of

Lake Louise's long, gently rolling tree-lined trails.

In addition to its excellent and extensive on-piste skiing—49 marked runs served by 14 lifts plus some 182 hectares (450 acres) of unmarked terrain on the Back Bowls—Lake Louise offers a great variety of cross-country skiing with trails graded according to difficulty. Also to be found are heliskiing in the Purcell Moun-

tains, top-quality nursery and day-care facilities plus the Friends of Louise, volunteer ski guides who show visitors around the mountains.

In addition to the Chateau Lake Louise, glimpsed in that view across the Bow Valley, there are another half-dozen hotels and lodges in the immediate vicinity although most visitors to the area stay in Banff where there is more nightlife.

WHISTLER

Whistler gets its name from British Columbia's whistling marmots. This is two resorts in one—Whistler Mountain and Blackcomb are two separate skiing areas whose lifts originate just yards from each other at a plaza on the outskirts of the smart, modern village.

Myrtle Philip was the first settler, opening the Rainbow Lodge in 1914, recognizing that the gold prospectors travelling on the Pemberton Trail from Howe Sound to the interior of British Columbia needed a place to stay and this custom was quickly augmented by fishermen who enjoyed their sport on Alta Lake. They travelled from Vancouver to Squamish by steamer and thence by rail. It was not until 1965, when Whistler's first ski-lifts opened, that road access was completed, the result of Canada's Olympic Committee bidding for the winter games.

Today, Whistler and Blackcomb operate as two separately owned lift companies but, thankfully, they provide a

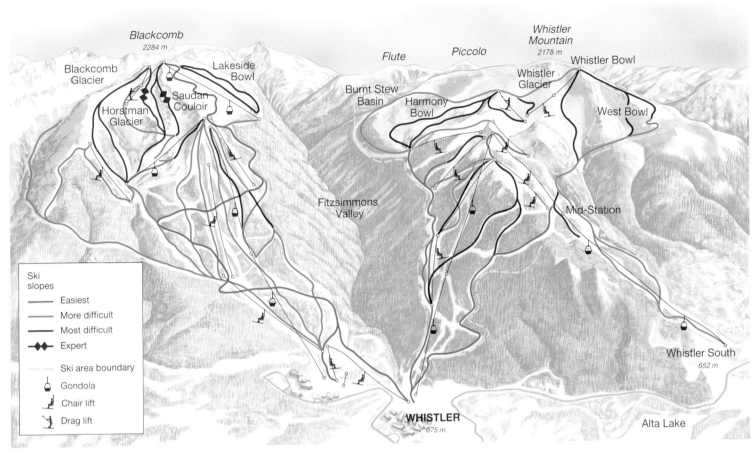

Ski slopes

— Easiest
— More difficult
— Most difficult
◆◆ Expert

- - - Ski area boundary
🚡 Gondola
🪑 Chair lift
⛷ Drag lift

Top left: *Whistler and Blackcomb have some justification in giving names such as 'Seventh Heaven' to parts of the skiing area as, after a heavy snowfall, that is how skiers feel.*

Bottom left: *Whistler's own Rob Boyd won the World Cup downhill on his home mountain in 1989 to the delight of the whole of Canada.*

joint lift pass to facilitate the exploration of both areas, although you can purchase day tickets (and half-day tickets) for each if you want to confine your activities to one or the other.

The village is an attractive ramble of mostly three-storey buildings with nearly all accommodation in luxury hotels which boast vast (by European standards) bedroom suites and efficient yet relaxed service. Shopping for high-quality clothes and souvenirs in the form of vivid T-shirts is one of the major *après-ski* activities although eating in any one of a score of restaurants and cafés is nearly as popular a diversion.

There are plenty of oriental specialities to be found, notably at Sushi Village and Teppan Village, as the Japanese constitute one of Whistler's biggest markets. Vancouver is served by direct flights from Tokyo and the transfer time from the airport is just two hours. If sushi isn't to your taste there are plenty of other places doling out huge portions of Mexican food, burgers and giant sandwiches.

On the mountains, Blackcomb and Whistler are similar in scope although experts tend to favour the former for its 'double diamond' (most difficult) trails below Horstman Hut (2284m/7494ft). This section is styled as Seventh Heaven and its runs, like those around Xhiggy's Meadow, are above the tree line and are the big attraction for off-piste *aficionados* after one of the frequent heavy snowfalls. Otherwise, apart from a few off-piste diversions, most runs on both Blackcomb and Whistler are tree-lined and one of the pleasures is to explore the woodlands, taking the paths which criss-cross the areas between trails and branching off into uncharted territory.

The two ski schools operate separately but, in the interests of harmony and attracting groups of mixed ability, they run a Ski Esprit scheme which, as well as providing tuition, puts the emphasis on exploring the mountains in the company of skiers of similar ability. This arrangement is perfect for couples, one of whom wants to hit steep and deep powder bowls all day while the other is content to meander about through the trees.

Since its humble beginnings, Whistler and its friendly rival, Blackcomb, have developed into one of Canada's most sophisticated skiing areas. Popular with well-to-do Vancouver residents, many of whom have weekend lodges, Whistler Village boasts one of Canada's best racers as its own—the great downhiller, Rob Boyd, lives here and it was with great pride that he won the 1989 World Cup race on his home mountain. Whistler holds a World Cup downhill every two years and is also the home of the double Olympic medallist, Nancy Greene, who is frequently to be seen skiing with guests staying at the Nancy Greene Lodge.

THE ASPENS

Aspen, the 'crystal city of the Rockies' is the most famous ski resort in North America. Even without the skiing, to visit this old silver-mining town nestling in the Elk Mountains in Pitkin County's White River National Forest is an experience that exudes an evocative cocktail of class, cash, glitter, gaucheness, brash showmanship and raunchiness almost unique in the U.S.A. This is doubtless one of the reasons why so many of its visitors rarely actually ski. They come to see and, even more important, to be seen. The place is a real honeypot for celebrities.

It is a very different place today compared with the one encountered by miners who trekked across the harsh Independence Pass from Leadville on their Scandinavian-style snow-shoes in the early 1870s, to suffer at the hands of the Ute

Aspen's gold rush day are over but its smart winter clientele enjoys the old Western ambience and architecture which is sympathetic with the town's history.

Indians and severe weather. But when the Ute Chief Duray made peace, the miners persevered and discovered one of the world's richest silver veins in the narrow, glacial valley. By 1879 most of the Utes had been banished to reservations.

Aspen — originally Ute City — complete with banks, schools, a hospital, an opera house, six newspapers, ten churches and a flourishing red-light district, started taking shape. At its peak, the town was served by two railroads, the Denver and Rio Grande and the Colorado Midland, and a 3.2km (2 mile) horsedrawn streetcar system. It was at this time Jerome Wheeler built the Opera House and the

Hotel Jerome. The silver mining boom collapsed in the 1890s, however, when gold became the principal medium of monetary exchange. More than three-quarters of the silver mines were forced to close. By the 1930s the population had shrunk from 12 000 to 400.

The Second World War led directly to Aspen's prominence as a ski resort. A Swiss avalanche expert, Andre Roche had already carried out a survey for a group of investors headed by Ted Ryan and Billy Fiske, a bobsled racer, who wanted to turn the town into a ski resort. (Tragically Fiske was to be killed in the Battle of Britain.) Roche formed the Roaring Fork Winter Sports Club and the first ski trail on Aspen Mountain was named after him. Early skiers were carried by horse-drawn sleigh to the top of Richmond Hill for one exhilarating run through Little Annie

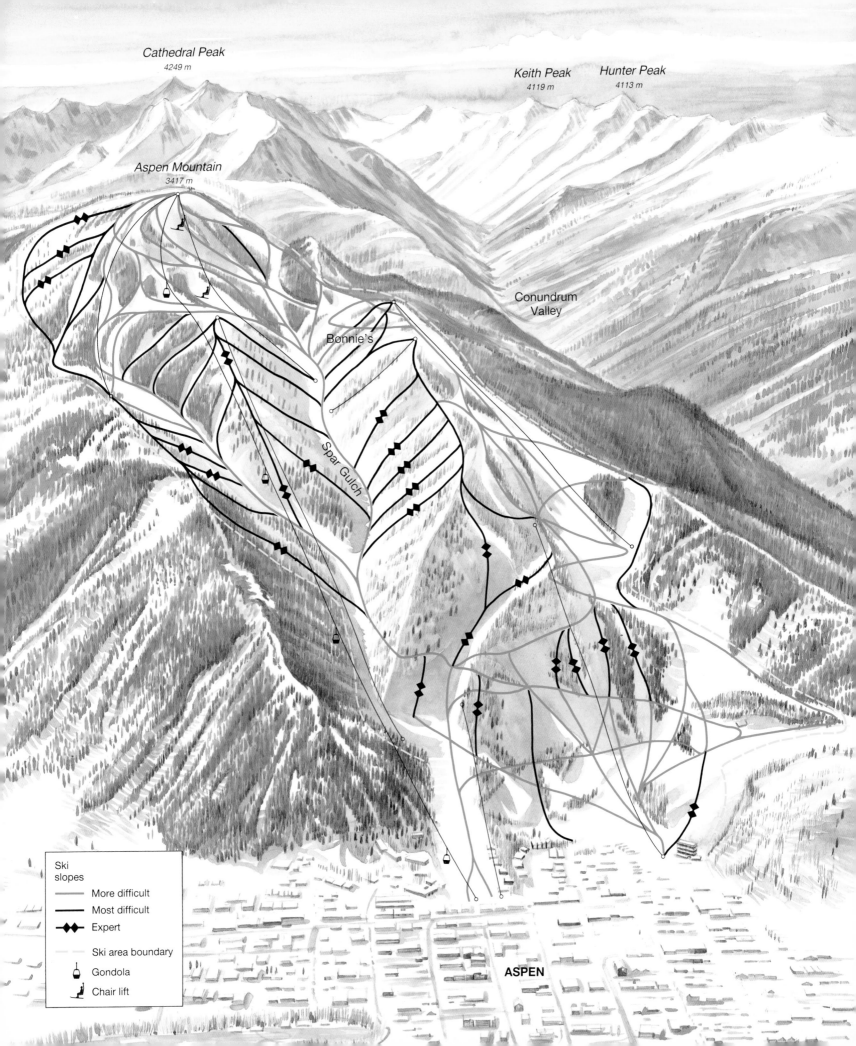

Cathedral Peak
4249 m

Keith Peak
4119 m

Hunter Peak
4113 m

Aspen Mountain
3417 m

Conundrum
Valley

Bonnie's

Spar Gulch

Ski
slopes

More difficult

Most difficult

◆◆ Expert

Ski area boundary

Gondola

Chair lift

ASPEN

Basin. Although the National slalom races were held there in 1941 the infrastructure was still pretty basic.

When America entered the war, the 10th Mountain Division troops, based 51km (32 miles) away at Camp Hale on Tennessee Pass, trained at Aspen and in the Vail Valley. Many of the soldiers discovered an affinity with the mountains and with skiing. One of them, Friedl Pfeifer, once a ski instructor in Hannes Schneider's celebrated ski school in St Anton, went into partnership with a Chicago industrialist, Walter Paepcke, and by 1947 the resort's first real ski-lifts were in operation. In 1950, America's first World Alpine Championships were held there and for the first time European racers competed in the Rockies.

There are actually four ski resorts within a 19km (12mile) radius in Roaring Fork Valley: the original, Aspen itself, based around Aspen Mountain (often known as Ajax); Aspen Highlands, little known to many visitors, 3.2km (2 miles) away; the bland area of Buttermilk, the easiest skiing area of them all, a further mile down the road; and Snowmass, 19km (12 miles) from Aspen which used to live in that resort's shadow but now caters for more skiers than the other three put together. All are linked by a shuttle bus service.

Altogether the resorts offer more than 260 trails and 1497 hectares (3700 acres) of skiable terrain served by more than 40 lifts. Although Aspen no longer entertains the largest number of skiers in the valley, it provides almost all the mystique. Unlike the cult skiing area of Alta, Utah, which has been almost eclipsed by its audacious young neighbour Snowbird, Aspen is still a huge crowd-puller.

You can avoid the long transfer from Denver by flying straight in to Aspen airport, which is almost on the ski slopes. With Snowmass, Aspen has more than 100 restaurants serving the entire spectrum of world cuisine, plus 200 shops, and 30 art galleries dotted around its cobbled alleyways. With all-winter-round fairy lights sparkling on street corners in trees and in shop windows, and the muffled clip-clop of horses drawing sleighs, there is a permanent atmosphere of Christmas.

One of Aspen's most famous watering holes, Little Nells, a quaint, high quality glorified 'greasy-spoon' shack at the very foot of Ajax, has been pulled down to make way for a huge new hotel of the same name (both mountain and hotel are named after local silver mines). The joy of the old establishment was its folksy breakfasts and its wonderfully funky atmosphere when skiers gathered on the sundeck at the end of the day, screwed up their eyes in the fierce sunshine of late afternoon, rolled up their sleeves and downed beers to the sound of heavy metal rock music reverberating round the mountain. A far cry from the *lederhosen* and Tyrolean evenings of the Alps. Some say the new establishment will be just as good in time, but for many people Little Nells, and Aspen, will never be the same.

Until recently, Aspen has both enjoyed and suffered the reputation of being too tough for beginners. It is still claimed there is no beginners' skiing. But this is not strictly true. The problem really was that there was no easy way *down* the mountain for beginners. Thus they risked being skittled by macho skiers hurtling home like guided missiles down runs such as Copper Bowl. But since the prestigious Silver Queen Gondola was built, timid skiers can now take the 13-minute ride up to Sundeck (3360m/11 200ft), ski around on some of the reasonably flat terrain at the top of the mountain, and then descend again by gondola. At least they can have a taste of the skiing on this legendary mountain. Nevertheless, beginners would undoubtedly feel less daunted and make more progress at Snowmass or Buttermilk. The lift pass, with minor adjust-

ments, is virtually interchangeable.

Now for some of this resort's skiing statistics. Aspen has a vertical drop of 980m (3267ft). The longest run is 4800m (3 miles) from One and Two Leaf right down to Little Nell, via North Star and Gentleman's Ridge. Although the average snowfall is some 762cm (300 inches), there is snowmaking provision on one-third of the terrain (85 hectares/210 acres). There are 75 trails covering 247 hectares (625 acres).

Aspen Mountain is long and narrow. They say that from the town you can only see the base of the iceberg. Its principal features are two north-south ridges—Gentleman's and Ruthie's—plus Bell, a 'mountain within a mountain'. Most of the trails in the 'more difficult' category feed from the summit and off Ruthie's Ridge. The 'double-black diamond' runs (blacker-than-black, steep and often tree-lined mogul runs) peel off from the edges of the ski area so that you are unlikely to stray on to one by mistake. There are five steep and tough examples in a row known

as The Dumps running parallel off the International Trail close to Ruthie's on the western edge: Bear Paw, Zaugg Dump, Perry's Prowl, Last Dollar and Short Snort. They were originally created by miners pushing slag and rubble down the mountain from the mine workings.

Across on the eastern boundary, three excellent tough double-diamonds—Walsh's, Hyrup's and Kristi—have recently been reclaimed from beyond the ski boundary and opened to the public. Both the back and face of Bell Mountain are for advanced skiers, but its tree-lined slopes are very useful during periods of flat light or snowstorms. There is access to Copper Bowl which, with Ruthie's, provides some of Aspen's fastest and most exhilarating skiing.

Aspen also features some excellent back-country skiing by snowcat, a sort of poor man's heliskiing because in a slow-moving snowcat you cover less ground than you would using a helicopter. On this excellent day trip you can explore the backwoods and powder snowfields to the

south-east of Aspen. There are 567 hectares (1400 acres) of glades and bowls to ski, with runs such as Gold Mine, Ptarmigan and Little Annie's, even one called Watch Out For The Road!

Aspen figures strongly in competitive skiing. It held the World Championships in 1950 and first featured on the World Cup scene in the 1967/68 season when the Austrians, Nenning and Messner, took the first two places in the downhill ahead of Jean-Claude Killy, while America's own Billy Kidd won the slalom. Nancy Greene, Canada's star of the 1968 Grenoble Winter Olympics, took the women's giant slalom. Ruthie's Ridge, the downhill course, is one of the fastest on the international circuit and is now a regular scene of World Cup races.

Aspen Highlands is the odd one out of the four resorts because it is privately owned and not part of the Aspen Skiing Company. And proud of it. Here, they like to point out, 'lift lines are as rare as designer furs' (although furs are now frowned on even in Aspen). But although

the Highlands is something of a maverick resort, you can buy a four-mountain pass which enables you to ski all four resorts. Because the skiing goes as high as 3597m (11 800ft), the vertical drop of 1158m (3800ft) is higher than Aspen Mountain's—in fact the highest in Colorado. And while trendy skiers pack Aspen Mountain's slopes, less fashionable Aspen Highlands often revels in relatively uncluttered trails.

It has just about everything: wonderful roller-coaster runs like Golden Horn and Thunderbowl can be almost deserted at times, leaving you to gasp with an exhilaratingly heady sense of freedom. There is plenty for the discerning expert, with plunging trails like Moment of Truth, Lower Stein and The Wall. Keen bump skiers will enjoy Scarlett's, and chute skiers will find the Steeplechase runs at Castle Creek really challenging.

If it is bowl skiing you seek, Olympic Bowl is excellent, with Pyramid Peak and Maroon Bells providing a spectacular backdrop. Half-Inch Chair is a good

beginner area, and Red Onion and Exhibition are superb greens. The Highlands has similar run-length and snowfall figures to Aspen's, but there are more lifts—11 serving the 55 trails on 223 hectares (552 acres); the lifts close at 4p.m.—half an hour later than Aspen's. Snowmaking is restricted to 16 hectares (40 acres) at the bottom.

Buttermilk—named after the refreshing drink enjoyed by loggers in times gone by—almost speaks for itself. For those who want to enjoy the sights and sounds of Aspen without tackling the tough trails of Ajax, this is where to learn. And if you happen to be 70 or more, you can ski here for nothing. For all its easy skiing, Buttermilk is far from dull. In fact admirers stress that it has a lot of excellent and picturesque skiing for everyone, and attracts significantly good powder. But Buttermilk closes at the beginning of April, a couple of weeks before Aspen and Snowmass.

The easiest trails account for more than one-third of the area, but a quarter of the

terrain is described as difficult. The skiing goes up to almost 3000m (9843ft) and there is a vertical drop of more than 600m (2000ft). There are 45 trails spread out across its 166 hectares (410 acres) of ski terrain which are served by six double chairs.

Buttermilk divides into three regions: Main Buttermilk, Tiehack and West Buttermilk. Tiehack has most of the difficult terrain, with black trails like Javelin, Sterner, the long, forested Timber Doodle Glade (a tree-skier's delight, especially in powder) and Tiehack Parkway, perhaps the most picturesque trail on the mountain. The other two areas have ample delightful skiing for beginners. Main Buttermilk has such green trails as Homestead Road, No Problem and Oregon, all guaranteed to build up a beginner's confidence. Ridge Trail starts out green but turns blue, to suit skiers as they build up a little courage. More difficult trails include Bear's, with smooth banked terrain, Jacob's Ladder and Friedl's. There is a sign by the ramp at Lift 2 which says:

Right: *Aspen has some vivid trail names. Big Burn, The Edge and Steeplechase are intriguing for their names alone while good skiers can enjoy the views from the top of The Wall.*

Left: *The Rockies are gorgeous after a snowfall with avid skiers desperate for their uphill journey to finish so that they can get at pristine powder in the trees.*

'The Wall of Death: The World's Shortest Black Run!' (It's three moguls long!) There are even special adventure runs in the forest like Black Hole specially for children, with child-sized trail signs. West Buttermilk is even easier. You can't find many easier or more scenic runs than Larkspur, Red's Rover, which follows a delightful little gulch, Tom's Thumb, and Westward Ho.

With its vertical drop of 1102m (3615ft), Snowmass spreads along the front of Baldy Mountain in four self-contained areas: Big Burn, High Alpine, Elk Camp and Sam's Knob, which has its own subsection, Campsite. Snowmass was built in 1967 with the aid of a computer which calculated the density of skiers in this vast skiing area: 5 experts, 10 intermediates or 15 beginners, per acre.

Known traditionally as a predominantly intermediate area, more difficult skiing has gradually been opened up, giving the resort a stronger profile. Its overall skiing terrain is huge: more than 800 hectares (2000 acres) — more than the other three

put together — served by 16 lifts. Its most famous run is still Big Burn, a wonderful multi-run romp dotted with trees spread far enough apart not to be a serious problem for cautious skiers but a bonus for faster-moving powder freaks. Served by Sheer Bliss Lift 9 and the Big Burn Superchair, it extends for more than 6km (4 miles) right down to Sam's Knob Lift 3 or Elk Camp and Alpine Springs. From here you can hike to the experts-only area at The Cirque around 20 minutes away. One of the most popular routes is the Headwall, with several steep, treeless runs to choose from.

Big Burn is so wide and so long that almost any skier could make something of it, especially inexperienced intermediates who really want to get their teeth into a good long run without killing themselves. This is really several runs in one: Whispering Jesse, Wineskin, Dallas Freeway, Mick's Gulley and, lower down, Powder Horn, a continuation of Sneakey's which follows the western edge of Big Burn and commands some superb

mountain views. The Burn got its name from one of Colorado's famous grudge-fires in which the Ute Indians are said to have set fire to the forest to discourage settlers. Today the wide open spaces they created in the trees encourage skiers.

The High Alpine area is almost entirely difficult-to-expert skiing. However Green Cabin, a long, sweeping descent from top to bottom with some superb scenery is fairly mild for a blue.

By far the toughest skiing is the Hanging Valley Glades and Wall, both double-black diamond areas opened up only in recent years. They gave Snowmass a much-needed tough ski area to complete its portfolio of skiing. The opening up of Hanging Valley, once the secret playground of the ski patrol, provided something meaty for experts.

The Hanging Valley Glades are entered from a gate off a black run called The Edge. The Wall requires a 20-minute uphill walk from High Alpine Lift 12, but the view from the top is outstanding. So is the skiing. AMF (it could mean Adios My Friend, but no one seems certain) is a dramatic gully that is not on the trail map; next to it is Goudy's which is even more radical, and Possible is another double-black which perhaps should be renamed Possible? — Discuss. Its precipitous upper chute gradually widens out but remains steep. You will be relieved to find yourself at the top of Naked Lady Lift 15 where the skiing becomes much more probable than possible.

The Elk Camp area lies below Hanging Valley; its runs are all blue, so one can relax and enjoy the scenery. The view from the top is one of the finest in the Rockies. On the opposite boundary, the Sam's Knob trails include quite a few good steep cruising black runs, such as Campground and Powderhorn.

The annual snowfall in Snowmass is 762cm (300in), and there's snowmaking on 22 hectares (55 acres) where the skiing is at its busiest. Nine per cent of the area is designated for beginners, while some 40 per cent is described as most difficult or for experts. Thanks to Hanging Valley, there can be no one who can now dismiss Snowmass as merely one huge intermediate playground. Hanging Valley is for serious skiers.

ALTA AND SNOWBIRD

Alta, known as the Cadillac or Grande Dame of Utah skiing, is the oldest of the resorts in the Salt Lake City area. You could be forgiven for assuming that the main attraction in Little Cottonwood Canyon, where the Mormon pioneers quarried granite for their temple, was the bright, breezy and slightly brash resort of its next-door neighbour, Snowbird. Indeed, you could spend your entire holiday in Snowbird without noticing sleepy Alta's existence. Alta may look a little like a ghost ski town, but things are not quite what they seem. As the *cognoscenti* will tell you, lurking in the mountainside are some of the finest ungroomed trails in the Rockies.

It has not always been so peaceful. Like Aspen, Park City, Breckenridge and Telluride, Alta is an old mining town. Barroom brawls and even shoot-outs around Grizzly Gulch were common. It had one of the highest murder rates in the country, with over 100 shootings in the Bucket of Blood saloon alone. Sometimes miners

Utah's 'Champagne Powder' is light and feathery so that even the most timid off-piste skier is flattered. True powder hounds head straight for the steeps and deeps.

wearing snowshoe skis used to slide down the mountain from the workings, and at weekends people from Salt Lake used to hike up and do the same. Huge snowfalls would frequently disrupt mining activities. Around 75 miners were killed in snowslides between 1872 and 1911. Fire destroyed the town in 1878 but it rose again only to be engulfed on one catastrophic day in the 1920s when most of the buildings were swept away by a 'snowquake'—a huge avalanche which came hurtling down. It seemed even then that the mining days were numbered.

In January 1938 the first transport system for skiers rather than miners was opened at Collins Gulch, albeit a converted mine tram. With Sun Valley, Idaho, and Stowe, Vermont, Alta had become one of America's first ski resorts.

Snowbird, by contrast, was built as recently as 1971 by Dick Bass, a Texan oil-millionaire and phenomenal climber who scaled the highest peaks in every continent.

The architecture of the resorts is totally different. Alta has a handful of traditional lodges with such evocative names as Goldminer's Daughter and Rustler Lodge, and just two condominiums: Hellgate and Powder Ridge. Snowbird's purpose-built lodges—The Inn, The Iron Blosam, Cliff Lodge and The Lodge—give the resort an almost French feel. But the skiing is similar. Both resorts have superb chute skiing on steep, untracked routes through the trees or down the side of the open bowls. Snowbird has Peruvian Gulch and Gad Valley which can be reached by taking an eight-minute ride on one of the fastest trams (cable-cars) in America to Hidden Peak (3353m/11 000ft). Alta's chutes are even more plentiful.

On paper, Alta has a modest vertical drop of only 615m (2050ft) and only three rope tows and eight double chairs, whereas Snowbird's vertical drop is 944m (3100ft) from a height of 3353m (11 000ft), but it only has seven double chairs and its famous 125-passenger tram. This gives you no real idea of the treasures, both easily accessible and hidden, to be plundered in its 688 hectares (1700 acres) of skiing. Alta has Baldy Chutes, the runs off High Rustler, and a whole clutch of chutes you can pick off one by one from Spiny Ridge on the back side of Point Supreme. Sidewinder and So Long are also excellent. West Rustler to the left of the main ski area and Wildcat on the right provide one huge, steep gulley-shaped valley with such delights (or terrors) as Wildcat Face, Supreme Challenge and Stone Crusher, plus endless challenging variants through the trees. These are very ably served by the Wildcat, Collins and Germania lifts.

The Cecret/Greeley area, accessed by the Sugarloaf lift, offers the Greeley Bowls, a couple of excellent black runs (Amen and Extrovert) and Glory Hole

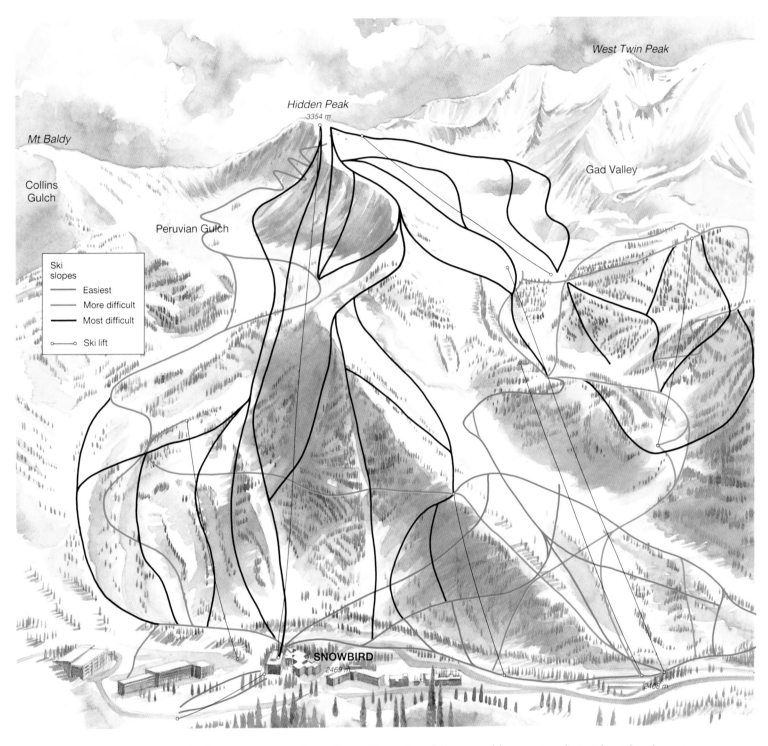

West Twin Peak

Hidden Peak
3354 m

Mt Baldy

Collins
Gulch

Gad Valley

Peruvian Gulch

Ski
slopes

Easiest

More difficult

Most difficult

Ski lift

SNOWBIRD
2469 m

2408 m

where one chilling variant—which starts steep and gets steeper—is aptly named Angina Chute. To reach some of Alta's best skiing, you must take your skis off and hike up. For example, Yellow Trail and East Greeley are reached after a five-minute walk from Germania. You must also walk to get to Gunsight and Eddie's High Nowhere. Don't bother to look for them on the lift map. They are

not there. You will need to follow an old hand who knows where he is going and what he is doing.

When Alta is swamped with snow in one of its celebrated storms the resort's tranquil atmosphere can be shattered by a barrage of hand-grenades and cannons setting off a dozen controlled avalanches. Helicopters whirr this way and that as if in a war zone. They take these things

seriously in Alta. They have to.

Most of Snowbird's 850 hectares (2100 acres) of skiing flanks Hidden Peak. The long, sweeping Chip's Run is the easiest way down with a looping variant called Chip's Bypass. Chip's is a good idea when there is a blizzard blowing at the top. Otherwise select from a clutch of blacks: Primrose Path, Cirque Traverse leading into Peruvian Cirque and the two Regulator alternatives Johnson and Traverse.

Snowbird's toughest runs are coloured yellow on the trail map. Silver Fox, Great Scott and Upper Cirque are superb, steep and exciting ungroomed descents which come hurtling down from Hidden Peak, with another formidable group below Peruvian Cirque. Hold on to your hat if you take on runs like Dalton's Draw, Upper Mach Snell (a good place to find secret areas of unskied powder), Wilbere Bowl and Chute, Barry Barry Steep and Gad Chutes. Two of Snowbird's most exciting powder areas are not even on the map: Baldy Face is right on the boundary with Alta, and Thunder Bowl is on the opposite boundary close to White Pine Valley.

To reach the Peruvian area from Gad Valley, ski to the central area of the Mid-Gad Restaurant and then take Big Emma to Bass Highway. The reverse journey is accomplished by taking Rothman Way, a blue trail. Below the chutes, where the terrain levels out in the mouth of Gad Valley, the main beginner area is dominated by Big Emma, perhaps the widest, biggest and most spectacular trail for novices in the Rockies.

Alta and Snowbird both open around Thanksgiving in mid-November. Alta normally closes in April, but Snowbird stays open for May and even into June. Half of Snowbird's skiing is advanced, with 30 per cent suitable for intermediates and a fifth for beginners. Alta has 25 per cent beginner slopes, 40 per cent for intermediates and 35 per cent for advanced skiers. In spite of its reputation as a Shangri-La for experts, Alta has some good areas for novices, especially around the Albion, Sunnyside and Cecret lifts with trails such as Patsey Marley, Crooked Mile and Sunnyside linking up with Sweet'n Easy and Rabbit in the Alpenglow area.

Another great contrast between the two resorts is the cost of a lift pass. For a major resort Alta's is extraordinarily low, in a country where passes are much pricier than in Europe. Snowbird's passes are more the American norm, although you can buy a reduced rate lift pass at Snowbird if you don't use the tram.

Below: *That Rocky Mountain High is instantly achieved on-piste after a snowfall when the pistes are groomed to flatter and the snow glistens seductively.*

Right: *Avalanche control has reached state-of-the-art status in both Alta and Snowbird. Safety precautions on- and off-piste are rigorous in resorts in the USA.*

SUMMIT COUNTY

Colorado's triumvirate of Keystone, Copper Mountain and Breckenridge are Summit County's major resorts. The Ski the Summit lift pass includes all three along with North Peak, which connects with Keystone and Arapahoe Basin, 15 minutes away by the free shuttle bus. Without the international cachet of Aspen and Vail, the Summit County resorts provide affordable skiing, an energetic nightlife and a friendliness which invariably surprises European skiers. Visitors from Europe are astonished when, on their first visit to the Rockies, they are treated as honoured guests and not as an unwelcome intrusion. Pushing in lift lines is virtually unknown, and the lift attendants offer a cheery exhortation to have a good day.

All three of the major centres are within 128km (80 miles) of Denver's Stapleton International Airport, with most of the journey on the I–70 freeway, and each is within 20 minutes of the others on the highly efficient free shuttle bus service. Breckenridge is the oldest, and most atmospheric. An old silver-mining town, its main street is wide enough to turn a covered wagon and the 'gingerbread' architecture of the old buildings has been painstakingly restored while recent construction work has been

Breckenridge is the most atmospheric of the Summit County resorts and has some of the toughest skiing – trail names such as Mustang and Spitfire speak for themselves.

cleverly designed to blend with the original. Western saloons and modern hotels sit happily together, Mexican taverns and hamburger joints nestle alongside and the relaxed attitude of the locals is proof that tourism is regarded very highly. Shopping for western clothing and Indian artefacts is particularly rewarding.

Breckenridge's skiing is on three mountains which connect with each other and provide some extremely tough work as well as lovely long trails for timid intermediates and beginners. Another aspect of skiing in the United States which entertains European visitors is the vivid naming of the runs (or 'trails', in America). Black trails are marked with a diamond—two diamonds mean that you should stay away unless you are a true expert—but names such as Mach 1, Psychopath, Tiger, Mustang and Spitfire need no markers as they speak for themselves. Similarly, you can be sure of an easy run down Freeway, Homestead and Flapjack, while Four O'Clock leads all the way back to town at the end of the day and is within the scope of everyone.

Peak 8
3722 m

North Bowl

Back Bowls

Horseshoe
Bowl

Peak 9
3493 m

Contest
Bowl

North
Face

Bergenhof

Beaver Run

BRECKENRIDGE

The town is at 2927m (9603ft) and Peak 8 rises to a heady 3723m (12 213ft) from where the easy routes are via Ptarmigan and Pika and thence Northstar and Claimjumper to the Bergenhof restaurant complex. Alternatively, turn left at the top of the T-bar for Contest Bowl and Horseshoe Bowl, each of them steep and deep and the only sections of Breckenridge's skiing above the tree line. Both Peak 9 and Peak 10 have plenty of unchallenging descents but the North Face of Peak 9 is a relentless web of experts' trails with ominous names like Quandary, Too Much and Amen.

All-comers' races are held every day and there are self-operated, electronically-timed slalom courses on Peaks 8 and 9, while the 45km (28 miles) of cross-country trails in the vicinity provide a tranquil antidote to the non-stop activity on the peaks.

Copper Mountain was opened in 1972 and is able to boast a top station (3767m/ 12 360ft) higher than that of its neighbour. As well as providing downhill skiing similar in scope to that of Breckenridge, it is one of Colorado's major centres for snowboarding (surf skiing) with a big programme of tuition and racing.

Orientation is easy as all of the tough skiing is to the east and the easy stuff to the west below Union Peak, with intermediate trails comprising the middle ground. Again, trail names are self-explanatory with Easy Feelin', Fair Way and Woodwinds being restful runs while there is no respite on Widowmaker, Formidable and Sawtooth. Pooh Corner is the nursery area for children. Without the old western ambience of Breckenridge, Copper Mountain is a favourite among families and has made heavy investments in new lift systems.

Keystone has the lowest base elevation of the three—a mere 2834m (9300ft)—but neighbouring Arapahoe Basin, which is hard by the Continental Divide, rises to 3795m (12 450ft). The beauty of staying in Keystone is that there are three separate skiing experiences available during the day with a fourth, floodlit skiing, at

Right: *Copper Mountain is a favourite among families with its nursery area, Pooh Corner, designed for little ones, and orientation of the upper slopes is easy.*

Below: *Most of the tougher runs are on Copper Mountain itself while novices are advised to confine themselves to Union Peak where there are no terrors.*

night. Arapahoe Basin ('A Basin', in local parlance) provides excellent powder skiing on the East Wall, the opportunity to leap from the Cornice on to the West Wall and tortuous trails through trees on The Alleys. North Peak's skiing almost entirely consists of thigh-thumping mogul fields, while Keystone's own skiing is tree-lined and, generally, on well-pisted rolling runs, Go Devil and Last Hoot being the notable exceptions. The novelty is being able to ski until 10p.m. with 13 slopes (81 hectares/200 acres) being illuminated by 300 high-pressure sodium lights for the entire season of mid-

November to early April. The Skyway gondola cars are heated, the top-station restaurant serves fondue suppers and late risers can buy a lift ticket valid from midday and allowing 10 hours' skiing. Despite its altitude, all of Keystone's 202 hectares (500 acres) are covered by artificial snowmaking equipment.

Keystone's accommodation is set around a lake which in winter months becomes North America's largest natural skating rink, and consists of self-catering apartments, sumptuous condominiums and hotels. Skiers used to minuscule apartments in France are amazed at the size of American condos. Dining in the hotels can be a rather formal affair but there are plenty of modest places for a beer, burger or pizza.

Arapahoe Basin is no more than a ski station, with no accommodation, and really comes into its own late in the season, which has occasionally lasted until early July. Pop music blares a booming welcome across the mountains and hungry skiers flock to the mid-station restaurant for huge helpings of ribs and salads, many finding themselves ensconced several hours later.

A trip over the Continental Divide to Loveland Basin is an interesting day's excursion. Take a taxi to the Divide and follow tracks meandering through woodlands until the road reappears. Then hitch-hike the last couple of miles—hitch-hiking is a quite acceptable method of transport in these parts. Loveland Basin is not covered by the Ski the Summit lift ticket but is worth a visit for the journey alone. It is popular with day skiers from Denver as it is close to the freeway and provides easy skiing on Bennett's Bowl and Sunburst Bowl, and bump runs designed to give your knees a severe testing down Tiger's Tail and Zoom.

HEAVENLY VALLEY

With up to 1270cm (500in) of snow falling each winter, Heavenly Valley hardly needs any more, yet the resort boasts the largest artificial snowmaking system in the world.

The name of this resort is not a complete exaggeration. It is extraordinarily beautiful, and the skiing is undeniably excellent. Add this to one of America's largest ski areas and a lot of wonderfully sunny Californian weather and you have a location that no one would be ashamed to call heavenly — except that there is something far more earthly lurking on the other side of the mountain: Nevada, with its vast gambling centres, casino hotels and legalized brothels. By road, the Nevada border is only minutes away. Cannon International Airport at Reno is an 88km (55 mile) journey, while the local airport at South Lake Tahoe connects with San Francisco, San Jose and Los Angeles.

What makes Heavenly so stunning is Lake Tahoe. A minor ink blot on the map, it is breathtaking when you see the real thing. As the Gunbarrel chair-lift takes you higher and higher, the enormity and grandeur of the 38km (24 mile) stretch of cobalt blue water increasingly dominates the landscape until it fills more than half of your field of vision. At the top of the Sky lift, the scenery becomes even more magnificent.

As you make for the Nevada side of Monument Peak, Lake Tahoe is spread below you. In dramatic contrast, the arid, almost sinister Nevada desert is 1524m (5000ft) below you on your right. You have to stop to take it all in. Taking a camera is a mixed blessing, for you are forever stopping to gawp and snap. Best to leave it in your hotel if you want an uninterrupted day's skiing.

Once you have forced your eyes away from the lake, you will notice that much of the skiing terrain is dotted with charming stunted fir trees. They are conveniently distributed to enable skiers to glide round them with plenty of space in between. These are rare Western White-Barked Pines which only grow above a certain altitude. In winter, like frozen gnomes, they freeze into surreal shapes. Heavenly's extensive tree skiing is one reason for its claim to be America's largest ski area. But in the absence of good snow, the tree areas can be fairly unskiable, thus removing large sections of ski terrain.

With or without its tree skiing, however, there is no doubt that Heavenly is one of America's biggest and best resorts. Its publicity material is highlighted by superlatives: the highest, at 3079m (10 100ft), the largest vertical drop, at 1097m (3600ft), the longest run, of 8.8km (5.5 miles). Although these all refer to Heavenly's premier status in the Tahoe region, which has some 18 ski resorts scattered round its shores, Heavenly now also claims the world's largest snowmaking system, with 59km (37 miles) of piping. The skiing is served by 24 lifts, including a 50-seat tram. And one must not forget Heavenly's 'superstar nightlife'.

In many ways the two sides of the mountain are similar. On the Nevada side, from the recently installed Comet detachable quad lift, two new runs, Aries and '49er provide an extra mile of skiing. Aries links with Orion's run, and '49er provides improved access from Nevada back to California. Thanks to new facilities on Ellie's, Liz's and Lower Waterfall, there is now snowmaking from top to bottom on the Californian side.

From the Californian base the gateway

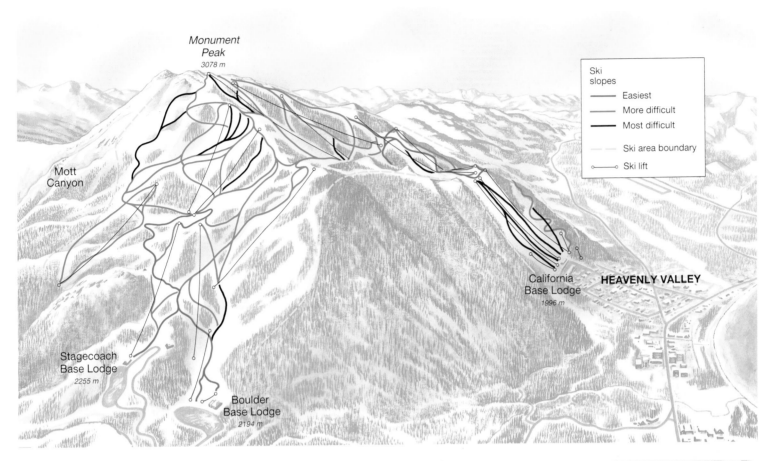

Set above the South Shore of Lake Tahoe, Heavenly Valley has 24 lifts giving access to some fabulous skiing on the California-Nevada border amidst nine peaks.

to the skiing is either the tram or the Gunbarrel and West Bowl lifts. Next take Waterfall which will give you access to the Sky Chair, which takes you to the top of the mountain. You can take the Skyline Trail to the Nevada side of the mountain where a cat's cradle of plunging blue runs dominates the skiing. Dipper Knob brings you hurtling down to Big Dipper Bowl and from here you can choose from Big Dipper, Orion, Crossover, Comet and Olympic Downhill. If you fancy your chances in Mott Canyon (designated for 'super experts'), Milky Way Bowl is your route. The only really easy skiing—thoughtfully displayed on the lift map with a broken green line to signify the easiest way down—is Way Home and Edgewood. In fact, half of the area is intermediate skiing, with the rest equally divided between novice and expert.

To return to the California side, take either Comet or Dipper, which link with Von Schmidt Trail or California Trail. Much of the California side's black terrain (East and West Bowls, and Gunbarrel) is near the bottom. Apart from Ellie's, Waterfall and part of Betty's, the high runs—such as Canyon, Liz's, the upper section of Betty's and Ridge Run—are blue. Most of the green trails, like Mag-

gie's, Swing Trail and Mombo are in mid-mountain.

Heavenly's season starts at Thanksgiving and usually continues until late April or early May. The average snowfall is between 762cm and 1270cm (300–500in). And there is one final heavenly touch—'Heavenly Hostesses' can be provided to show you round the mountain.

JACKSON HOLE

Jackson Hole is a resort like no other, a massively challenging mountain near a small Wyoming town with the authentic flavour of the Wild West. Rendezvous Mountain, a part of the spectacular Teton range, has the only vertical drop in excess of 1200m (4000ft) in the United States, but its magnificence lies at least as much in the variety of its terrain as in its height. The runs are spread across a mountainside 4km (2.5 miles) wide, providing a mixture of open bowls, glades, skiable trees and chutes, especially steep, narrow, difficult chutes with immense allure for

America's bands of radical skiers in search of 'air', which can be roughly translated as large rocks to jump off. 'If there is a better ski mountain in the United States, I have not seen it,' says Jean-Claude Killy. Most visitors would agree with him, adding that Jackson is also a lot of fun.

The first sight of the majestic Teton range, rising dramatically out of the wide flat plain, comes as the aeroplane dips into the snowfields of the Snake River valley to land at Jackson Hole airport. The valley itself is the 'hole'; Davey Jackson was a tough early 19th-century trapper

Teton Village is 19km (12 miles) from Jackson Hole and many prefer to stay here for immediate access – others prefer the Wild West atmosphere of Jackson.

who gave it his name. The airport is served by direct connections from Salt Lake City, Denver and Chicago. In the 1980s, the terminal was a simple wooden structure but the concept of Jackson Hole as 'America's world class resort' is catching on fast at home and abroad, and a sleek modern building has been unveiled for the new decade.

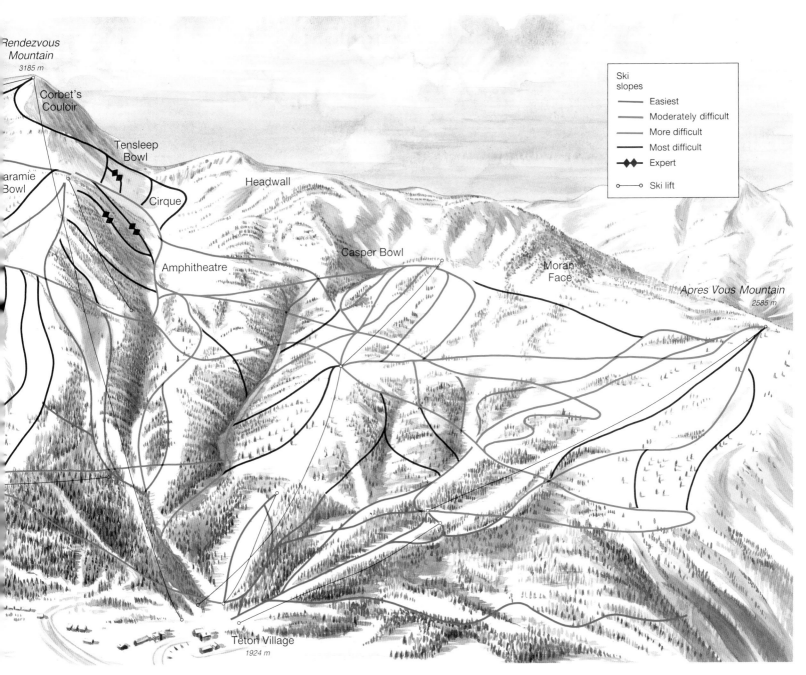

Rendezvous
Mountain
3185 m

Corbet's
Couloir

Tensleep
Bowl

Laramie
Bowl

Cirque

Headwall

Amphitheatre

Casper Bowl

Moran
Face

Apres Vous Mountain
2585 m

Teton Village
1924 m

Ski
slopes

——— Easiest
——— Moderately difficult
——— More difficult
——— Most difficult
◆◆ Expert
o—o Ski lift

The town of Jackson, a popular sum-mer destination for visitors to neighbour-ing Yellowstone National Park, lies 16km (10 miles) to the south down a road that passes the National Elk Refuge, a huge compound that provides winter quarters for thousands of moose (elk). That's a lot of discarded antlers as can be seen in Jackson's Town Square: its main features are the intricately constructed elk horn arches at the corners of the central area and the boardwalks that run along the sides of the square.

Teton Village, the base camp for the

Jackson Hole ski area, lies 19km (12 miles) further along the valley at the bottom of Rendezvous Mountain. The resort is the brainchild and the creation of Paul McCollister, a Californian who first came hunting elk hereabouts in 1942. Having learned to ski in the 1950s, he sold his family advertising business to move out here permanently in 1957. Jackson Hole opened for business in 1965 and built up an immediate reputation as a tough, gutsy place catering for intrepid expert skiers. Before long, the Jackson Hole Barnstorming Pioneers created

myths out of their derring-do. One of them was Barry Corbet who gave his name to the resort's most famous leap. The degree of difficulty of Corbet's Couloir varies greatly according to how much snow there is in it and although he was, in fact, the first to ski it after climbing up Rendezvous on skins, it was ski patrolman Lonnie Ball, a legend in his own lifetime, who first launched himself into the fearsome void.

Nowadays visitors queue up anxiously to peer over the edge of the cornice into the rock-sided gully below. Most amateurs decide to wait for a more propitious day but the professionals leap joyfully downwards, straining to make the first crucial left hand turn that will prevent an ignominious slide to the bottom of the slope. Next to Corbet's Couloir is S & S, the initials of the first two men to go over a rock face of such height and menace that it is unimaginable that it should be skiable. But it is: in Jackson Hole, air is for flying through.

The resort had one of America's first aerial trams (cable-cars), now something of a museum piece but still running to the top of Rendezvous Mountain. As it only takes 60 people, and at a rather leisurely pace, the high-season queues are long but it does give the most immediate access to these and other corridors, among them the Expert Chutes near Tower Three and the Alta Chutes below Cheyenne Bowl. An added bonus for aspiring powder hounds are the Hobacks, a wide expanse of steep, tree-studded snowfields, within bounds but ungroomed, which give almost limitless scope for practice.

As the intermediates who make up the majority of skiers were rightly terrified of these hazards, it wasn't long before McCollister discovered that he had overstressed the ferocity of his mountain. To tone down its image, he developed the gentler adjacent slopes of Casper Bowl and Apres Vous for intermediates and beginners. Moose are a familiar sight on the beautifully prepared and extremely benign nursery slopes at the bottom of Apres Vous but be warned that it is extremely dangerous to come between a cow and her calf.

The whole 1012 hectare (2500 acre) ski area is integrated and served by five double chairs, one triple and a poma as well as the aerial tram. McCollister has plans to supplement the system with a high-speed quad and a poma, arrangements that will relieve pressure on the tram by making it possible to ski Rendezvous from top to bottom without using it. Today McCollister can boast without fear of contradiction that Jackson Hole has more intermediate terrain than ninetenths of America's ski resorts while still providing the ultimate challenge for the radical minority.

The Jackson Hole Ski School is run by

Pepi Stiegler, an Austrian Olympic Silver Medallist in 1964. Besides supervising the 'ski off' which decides which class everyone will be in, he skis a couple of runs each afternoon with anyone who cares to meet him at the top of the Casper chair at 1p.m., giving advice as he goes. Classes are small, a maximum of eight but more often five or six, but the standard of the instructors is fairly uneven and Europeans will be surprised by the lack of consistency in the teaching of the American Training Technique. Highly recommended is the daily three-hour session which concentrates on skiing the powder whenever and wherever possible. More extreme powder experiences are provided by the heliskiing trips on offer.

Although the hourly shuttle bus service between Jackson and Teton runs from 7a.m. until midnight, all visitors are faced with the dilemma of whether to stay in town where the nightlife is extremely lively or in the much quieter Teton Village with its ski in, ski out facilities.

Jackson's smartest hotel is the Wort. Its Silver Dollar Bar, named for the 2032 coins embedded in its long counter, is a hot night spot featuring live music of variable quality. There are also a number of motels, several of them members of the

Above: The opening of more lifts over the years has meant that Jackson Hole has become manageable for families – off-piste freaks still head for the steeps and deeps.

Right: The Grand Tetons loom above Jackson Hole and provide what the Americans describe as 'radical' skiing. There are plenty of wide open trails.

Best Western group, which provide high levels of creature comfort and service but without much atmosphere or taste. The most expensive food in Jackson is served at the pretentious White Buffalo Club, the best at the Blue Lion next door. Its menu includes seafood and elk Wellington as well as the inevitable steak. When in the mood for high quality red meat, book into the Steak Pub; the smart choice is the table in front of the open fire. The pick of a large number of low cost fast food diners is The Bunnery.

In Teton Village, the grandest establishment is the Alpenhof, one minute's walk from the lifts and meticulously modelled on a fairly upmarket Austrian hotel. The food is of a sophistication that is fairly rare in these parts and the breakfast, in particular, is excellent. Dietrichh's Bar on the first floor makes a

welcoming lunch or *après-ski* stop: there is a roaring log fire and corn chips and salsa are provided free as accompaniment to happy hour drinks. The rather larger Inn at Jackson Hole, a three-minute walk to the lift, is also recommended. The Crystal Springs Inn and the Sojourner are more downmarket alternatives.

Life in Teton Village revolves around the Mangy Moose, a complex selling everything from local artefacts to giant pitchers of beer and lethal cocktails. It is by far the most popular meeting place once the lifts close and the large high-ceilinged restaurant, with its cheap and cheerful decor and its huge platters of nourishing all-American food, ensures that the jollity continues at maximum velocity until about 10p.m. After that Teton Village is abed; it really is a ski addict's town.

The Spring Creek Ranch, a complex of condominiums, inn rooms and conference facilities perched on a hill between Jackson and the village has the most impressive views of the Teton Range. Nearer to Teton Village is the Racquet Club Resort, both a conference centre and a private athletic club offering tennis, basketball and volleyball plus a full range of fitness facilities. Those who prefer self-catering

will find a wide choice of lodgings in the Teton Village condominiums, of which all run their own complimentary shuttle bus services to the lifts.

Teton Village has an encouragingly flat cross-country circuit laid out on the valley floor beside the river and both Spring Creek Ranch and the Racquet Club Resort have their own nordic touring centres. There are also two further downhill options. Snow King, the town hill overlooking Jackson itself, is much favoured by the locals. Known as a training ground for American racers, it celebrated its 50th anniversary in 1989. Its steep, north-facing slopes are floodlit for night skiing from Wednesday to Saturday but the cold can be intense.

More interesting is Grand Targhee which lays claim to deeper powder than at Jackson Hole, amounting to a massive total of 1270cm (500in) a year. It lies on the other side of the Teton range and can be reached, after a loop through Idaho, in two hours by car or bus. No one would go to Grand Targhee for the architecture

Below: *Teton Village is at the base of Jackson Hole's lift system, immediately below Rendezvous Mountain from where there is a 1219m (4000ft) vertical drop.*

Above: *As well as giving access to some of the best skiing in the Rockies, Teton Village is home to the Mangy Moose complex with restaurants, bars and shops.*

which has been accurately described as 'neo summer camp' nor for the groomed runs which are limited and intermediate. However, powder hounds should take advantage of the excellent service offered by the Grand Targhee Peaked Express, a 12-passenger open snowcat that takes skiers to the virgin slopes.

Non-skiers are particularly well served in the area. Jackson has surprisingly good

shops, among them a Ralph Lauren establishment on the corner of Town Square that sells seconds direct from the factory at extremely competitive prices. High quality local leatherware is widely available: if you've ever wanted a pair of elkskin cowboy boots, this is the place to buy them. Mind you, it might be tactless to wear them when you go to the National Elk Refuge. As keepers have been providing the herds with winter fodder since it was established in 1912, generations of animals have become accustomed both to gathering close to the source of supply and to the horse-drawn sleighs that bring

visitors right into their midst (45-minute trips departing every 20 minutes, daily except Christmas, 10a.m. to 4p.m.). Another must is a dog sled tour: 12 Alaskan huskies driven by a fur-clad musher pull up to 10 people silently over the snow at 32km/h (20mph). Buffalo skins are provided for much needed warmth.

No one can expect to be alone in Yellowstone National Park during the summer months but the coming of winter allows for much more exclusive visits to such celebrated attractions as Old Faithful. It was the discovery of this fountain of

boiling water and steam jetting 39m (130ft) into the air that inspired President Grant to create the world's first national park in 1870. The geyser is only the most spectacular of many thermal activities including hot springs and mud pots; only the smell is against them. Yellowstone, lying just an hour's bus ride from Jackson, also plays host to many species of wildlife, among them bison, deer, and moose, and 250 kinds of birds. The environmentally conscious can tour the park on cross-country skis; others will enjoy speeding through it at up to 96km/h (60mph) on a snowmobile.

KILLINGTON

Killington never suffers from lack of snow. The lifts open in October even if no snow has fallen, and do not close until June. If enough flakes do not float out of the sky, they are pumped out of snow cannons which work reliably in the low temperatures of Vermont. Then the trails are groomed with great tillers until the only bumps are those left on purpose for mogul-lovers.

With millions of people living in the cities of the eastern states, and longing to get out into the fresh air and exercise of the mountains, Killington realized that it must give them the sure snow and entertaining instruction. As well as preparing its slopes well, it has one of the best ski schools in the world for teaching beginners. They take the fear out of skiing by preparing classes with videos, transporting beginners by shuttle to the slope (no

struggling up slippery paths carrying skis) and then instructing them in tiny classes. Killington's Accelerated Learning Method guarantees beginners that they will be able to ski down from the top of the mountain after only three days' instruction. Children as young as three can start at the school, and have a lot of fun at their own village centre and on the fenced-off practice slope.

Many long green trails wind down the six peaks which are networked with lifts. The signposting is excellent, with pictograms set like inn-signs so that bears, suns or rams' heads show the way. And where the trails divide there are signs pointing to the easiest way down.

But Killington is not just for beginners. The mountains rise from 286m to 1292m (938–4238ft) and nearly a third of the 112km (70 miles) of trails is challenging

to experts who enjoy steep chutes and testing moguls. Outer Limits on Bear Mountain is renowned for the size of its moguls (traditionally described as the size of Volkswagens). There are no red runs in the United States (they call them blue) but the intermediate skiing carries skiers down through glades networking the interlinked peaks. And the school, too, has 'learning stations' tucked among the trees where good skiers can learn to get better in small classes, right up to racing standard. Four entry point lifts along the access road help to keep the queues short.

Vermont is a beautiful state with old wood-fronted inns and high-spired churches in pretty clapboard villages. Killington has built a village of condominiums and the Snowshed Lodge at the bottom of its slopes but many visitors prefer to live in the surrounding country-

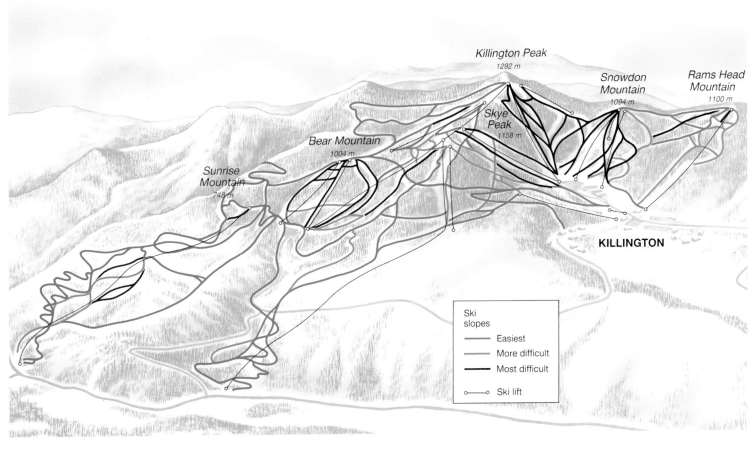

Killington Peak
1292 m

Snowdon
Mountain
1094 m

Rams Head
Mountain
1100 m

Skye
Peak
1158 m

Bear Mountain
1004 m

Sunrise
Mountain
748 m

KILLINGTON

Ski slopes	
——	Easiest
——	More difficult
——	Most difficult
o——o	Ski lift

Left: *Killington has the longest gondola (5.6km/3.5 miles) in the USA and the ski school ensures that beginners can ski from the top after three days.*

Below: *Vermont's natural beauty continues to be the State's main asset in attracting visitors and skiing through the trees is one of Killington's joys.*

side. In the area there is swimming, skating, tennis and dozens of restaurants with no fewer than eight health clubs. There is live music in the many discos.

Killington has the longest gondola (5.6km/3.5 miles) in the United States and this sort of protection is a comfort in the bitter cold. Open chairs can be bleak but everything is done to speed them up so the skier gets back quickly on to his skis. And there are lodges and warming huts on the mountain for the coldest days.

Killington is easily reached by air to Rutland just 32km (20 miles) away, and flights come in from New York, Newark, Philadelphia and Boston. There is a frequent bus service (the Vermont Transit) from New York and Boston. The resort has long been used by business people as a place for a quick weekend's tune-up after a working week in New York. With its reliable snow and challenging skiing it is worth considering for much longer. A week or a fortnight might even give time to ski all its 107 trails, and some hours in its concentrated ski school will transform an indifferent skier into a good one.

LAKE PLACID

Some resorts bid in vain, time after time, to hold the Winter Olympics just once. Lake Placid has hosted the games twice—in 1932 and 1980. Lake Placid's Whiteface Mountain is New York State's favourite winter playground, providing a lot more than skiing down championship courses. You can take the opportunity to ride the Olympic bobsleigh run (with a professional driver and brake man, you will be pleased to hear!) and to enjoy tobogganing, cross-country skiing, dog sled tours of the surrounding countryside and spectator sports such as freestyle skiing and ice hockey matches. Despite all this, Lake Placid's claim to be 'Winter Sports Capital of the World' is a bit of an exaggeration. Still, a full programme of activities for both adults and children make it a good base for a winter holiday, particularly for families.

With a vertical drop of 978m (3216ft), the greatest in the eastern states,

The Adirondacks form the backdrop to New York State's favourite winter playground. There is skiing for all grades plus a host of non-ski activities in and around Lake Placid.

Whiteface has eight lifts serving 37 trails of various descriptions and, thanks to artificial snow-making equipment covering nearly all the skiable area, is able virtually to guarantee skiing throughout the winter. There are runs for experts and intermediates running from top to bottom and most visitors want to emulate the 1980 Olympic champions, Austrians Leonard Stock and Anne-Marie Moser-Proll, on the men's and women's downhill courses although it is all too easy to lose concentration as the views of the Adirondacks are compelling. Paron's Run is one of the best intermediate trails, leading from the summit to connect with Excelsior and then all the way down to the valley—a run of nearly 5km (3 miles).

Parkway and Thruway, both steep at the top and gentler lower down, are favourites among strong intermediates. Mountain Run and Wilderness provide the best bumps runs while three lifts serve the lower sections of the mountain and thence some nursery slopes.

Parents can deposit their children at the spacious and well-equipped nursery where day-long care, plus lunch, is provided. Alternatively, the little ones can be enrolled in full-day and half-day Play & Ski programmes for three- to six-year-olds. Again, lunch can be provided and skiing takes place on the Bunny Hutch 'snow playground'. A separate Junior Development programme, for 7- to 12-year-olds, is intended to provide top-quality coaching and exploration of the mountain in an atmosphere designed to make skiing enjoyable.

Lake Placid is a quaint little town ranged around the shores of Mirror Lake,

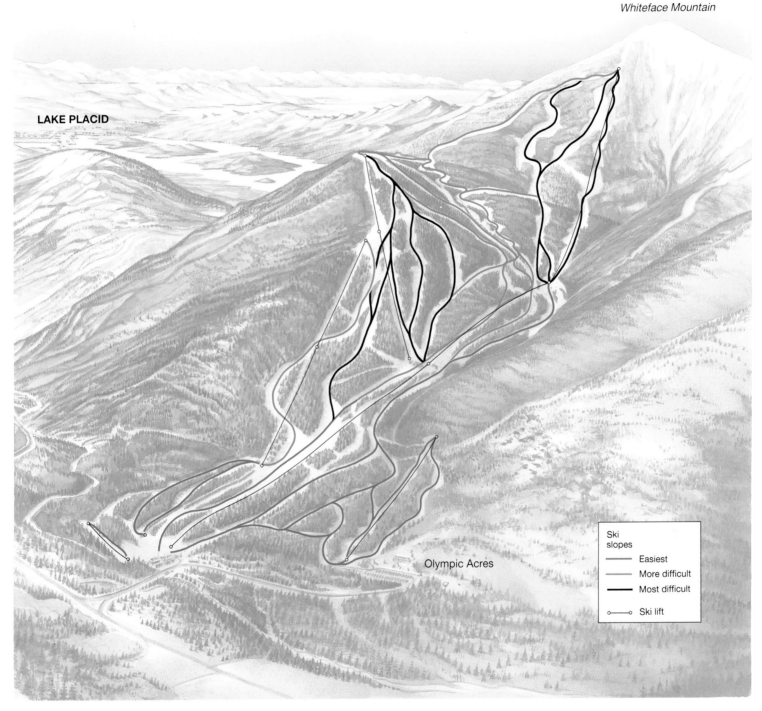

Whiteface Mountain

LAKE PLACID

Olympic Acres

Ski
slopes

—— Easiest

—— More difficult

—— Most difficult

∘—∘ Ski lift

which becomes a giant skating rink during the winter as well as being the scene of dog sled rides and tobogganing. The atmosphere during the evening is relaxed, informal and centred on congenial bars and nightclubs, and there are three cinemas plus dozens of restaurants—typical American ribs and burger joints happily nestle alongside French *haute cuisine* establishments. To counter the effects of

high living, there are several health clubs with indoor pools, saunas and Jacuzzis.

During the day, there are plenty of alternatives to skiing on Whiteface Mountain. Mount Van Hoevenberg's Olympic cross-country trails, 10 minutes' drive from the centre of Lake Placid, provide 53km (33 miles) of marked trails for novice, intermediate and expert skiers. These are complemented by countless

unmarked routes through the Adirondack back-country. The Olympic complex is the centre for riding down the luge and bobsleigh courses—the latter is described as being the 'Champagne of Thrills' in the local publicity literature. Well, the truth is that it is certainly a thrill to hurtle to such terrifying speeds, but most participants need a tot of something stronger than champagne at the finish!

PARK CITY AND DEER VALLEY

Colorado does not have a monopoly in American skiing. Utah is its biggest rival. And Salt Lake City is its skiing capital. This bizarre but beautiful city with its Mormon Temple and Tabernacle is surrounded by mountains, salt flats and the vast greeny-grey, almost lifeless salt lake that from the air looks like a Venusian landscape. It is also ringed by excellent ski resorts, none of them more than an hour away by road, and all glorying in what they insist is the 'greatest snow on earth'. And masses of it—as much as 1400cm (550in) a year.

The snow is often dumped indiscriminately in different canyons so that one resort might be swamped while its neighbour fails to receive a single flake. So the ideal way of finding the best snow each day is to base yourself in Salt Lake and tune in to the snow reports on the radio. Having selected your resort, just head down Interstate 80 (known locally as 'Winterstate 80').

Five of the resorts—Park City, Snowbird, Brighton, Solitude and Alta—can be skied in a one-day back-country tour called the Interconnect, the only real outing in America to compare with touring in Europe. Other resorts include Park City's neighbours Deer Valley and Park West, and the little known but excellent resort of Snowbasin.

Salt Lake City is America's choice for the 1998 Winter Olympics. The international airport is served by 13 airlines and has more than 500 daily arrivals and departures. Although Park City—Utah's largest ski area, 43km (27 miles) east of Salt Lake—is a newish ski resort, there's a strong whiff of the industrial revolution hanging over it. Indeed, the main street, one of the few areas that has survived from the old mining days, looks so authentic that it takes little imagination to picture yourself walking through the time barrier straight into a bar-room brawl.

Park City is the home of the US Ski Team and promises 'brave and bustling' skiing on its 85 trails, half of which are for intermediates and one-third for experts.

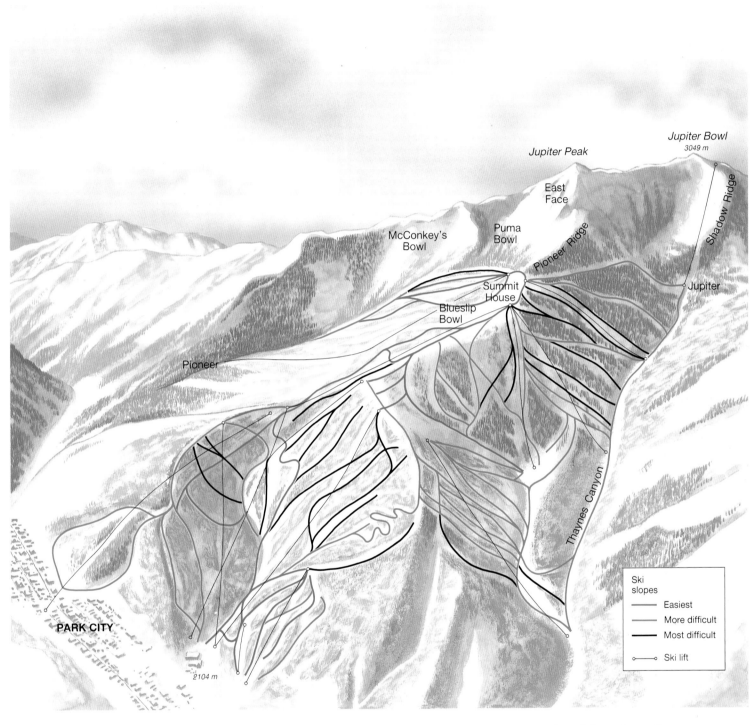

Jupiter Bowl
3049 m

Jupiter Peak

East
Face

McConkey's
Bowl

Puma
Bowl

Shadow Ridge

Pioneer Ridge

Jupiter

Summit
House

Blueslip
Bowl

Pioneer

Thaynes Canyon

PARK CITY

2104 m

Ski
slopes

———— Easiest
———— More difficult
———— Most difficult
○——○ Ski lift

In its day, Park City had the largest silver-mining camp in the whole country, a settlement described as 'a wonderful mixture of precariously perched homes, false-fronted shops, smoky saloons, theatres, churches, a red-light district and a Chinatown'. More than 60 of the original buildings are still there in some shape or form. The rest of the constructions are clever and tasteful replicas. The

overall effect is uncanny. Altogether there are 21 bars and clubs and 45 restaurants. In the old mining days there was a challenge that no one could visit every bar in Main Street and arrive at the other end still standing. History suggests that not a single person ever succeeded.

Park City ski area in the heart of the Wasatch mountains started out in 1963 under the name Treasure Mountains. (It

recently celebrated its silver anniversary with a 25-bomb salute!) Much of its 890 hectares (2200 acres) of skiing is on land riddled with almost 1600km (1000 miles) of tunnels from the old silver mines. In the early days skiers were taken on a bizarre journey into the depths of the mountain on a miners' train and then lifted 540m (1800ft) vertically on a unique mine hoist elevator to the site of the

present Thaynes chair-lift. Even today you find yourself skiing past abandoned mine workings. And many of the trail names are linked with the mining days.

Park City's skiing is brave and bustling, as you would expect in a resort chosen by the U.S.A. national ski team as its home since 1973. There are 89 trails, almost half of which are for intermediates and over one-third for experts. There are two new quad lifts, Prospector Express (high speed) and Cresent, and thanks to a million-dollar programme in 1988, there is now snowmaking on 142 hectares (350 acres) of the resort.

The resort is particularly strong on bowl skiing, with some 263 hectares (650 acres). There are some exhilarating runs, such as Six Bells, Portuguese Gap, Silver Cliff, Indicator, O.M. Zone and the West Face. Jupiter Bowl is named after Jupiter Peak where in Park City's industrial days millions of dollars' worth of silver ore was eventually removed.

Other fine bowls include Scott's. Blue-

slip and, after a longish hike, Puma, and McConkey's. Other good runs for advanced skiers include The Hoist, Silver Skis, The Shaft, Thaynes, Double Jack, Ford Country, Glory Hole and Silver King. Beginners and less-experienced intermediates have an entire area to themselves served by the First Time and Three Kings chairs. By riding the gondola they can also ski Claimjumper to the Prospector lifts. And, since 1967, there is skiing seven nights a week on Payday, claimed to be the longest lighted run in the Rockies.

Between them the adjacent resorts of Park City, Deer Valley and Park West have more than 175 runs and over 1600 hectares (4000 acres) of skiable terrain. Natural snowfall averages 889cm (350in). Although lift passes vary in price in each resort, you can purchase an interchangeable book of vouchers which can be exchanged for each area's tickets.

Deer Valley, opened in 1981, is a prettier, more alpine-looking resort with a lot more greenery than Park City. It is one

Above: *In addition to the bowls for powder freaks, Park City has plenty of manicured, tree-lined trails for the less-ambitious skier, many of them named after the mines.*

Right: *Disused silver mines dot the landscape and remain a testament to Park City's mining days – there are more than 1000 miles of tunnels beneath the slopes.*

of the more luxurious and elegant of America's ski areas. Not surprisingly, its lift pass is one of the most expensive. The trails are groomed to perfection, which is one reason why it is a favourite haunt of skiers 'of a certain age' who like being pampered and, what is more, can afford to pay to be. This well-heeled clientele also enjoys some of the best cuisine at any altitude anywhere in the United States.

Two mountains dominate Deer Valley—Bald Mountain (2820m/9252ft) and Bald Eagle Mountain (2520m/8268ft). The easiest runs, such as Success, Rosebud and Wide West, are at the bottom of

Bald Eagle, although this mountain has two black runs: Lucky Bill, and the long and exhilarating Know You Don't. Bald Mountain's skiing is mainly more difficult, with the chance of good powder and glade skiing in Mayflower and Perseverance Bowls. Narrow Gauge and Morning Star are both testing and exciting runs off the bowl areas. A third mountain, Flagstaff, is open for snowcat skiing.

Deer Valley has a 660m (2165ft) vertical drop and 45 trails, in a good variety of degrees of difficulty. The longest run is 2.3km (1.4 miles). Seven triple chair-lifts and one double serve the skiing areas, and snowmaking facilities have recently been improved.

The skiing at Park West, which opened in 1968, is not in the same price range as Deer Valley's, but it is no less good for

that. Almost half the 344 hectare (850 acre) area is designated 'advanced'. There are 50 trails and an abundance of off-piste skiing, challenging bowls, powder chutes and mogul runs. Some of the names say it all: Massacre and Geronimo Ridge are two examples. Altogether seven chair-lifts serve 50 runs spread over four mountains, with a drop of 660m (2200ft). The longest run is 4km (2½ miles).

SQUAW VALLEY

Walt Disney was in charge of the special effects when the 1960 Winter Olympics opened at Squaw Valley—and when you see the resort's six mighty peaks jostling shoulder to shoulder it is tempting to speculate as to whether he might have built them as well. They look too good to be real, perhaps a polystyrene backdrop for the extraordinary spectacle which accompanied the opening ceremony: thousands of pigeons, fireworks and balloons going off in all directions while 1285 instruments and 2645 voices united in harmony, in a suitably Disneyesque exercise in understatement.

But the mountains are real enough, as you quickly find out when you slither down KT-22 (2499m/8200ft) on your backside. This is superb, dramatic and challenging ski country. KT-22, arguably the most difficult of the peaks, is so named because the wife of the original owner was forced to execute 22 kick-turns to make her descent. The other mountains are Red Dog, Squaw Peak, Emigrant, Broken Arrow and Granite Chief, the highest at 2758m (9050 ft).

There is a huge area of skiing—3359 hectares (8300 acres) altogether. The concept is mainly open-bowl skiing, chutes and gulleys rather than marked trails. And, unusually, the main beginner's area, served by East Broadway, Belmont, Links and Bailey's Beach lifts, is perched way up on Emigrant Peak at High Camp so that novices can have the exhilaration of skiing high up in the most spectacular part of the mountain—with views of the High Sierras and beautiful Lake Tahoe—rather than languishing right at the foot of the slopes as they do in so many resorts. And the Homerun slope from Times Square Rock has recently been widened to 15m (50ft) for a good, long section to ensure a gentle ride down for beginners who don't want to come down in the gondola.

The resort's toughest skiing (almost a third of the terrain) is spread across Red Dog, KT-22, the upper reaches of Squaw Peak and Granite Chief. Most of the intermediate terrain, which represents 45 per cent of the skiing, is on the lower sections of Squaw Peak, Broken Arrow and on Emigrant. In the unlikely event of your requiring further challenges, it is possible to make the testing descent into the excellent neighbouring resort of Alpine Meadows, providing you notify the ski patrol first. There is also night skiing three times a week off the Searchlight and Exhibition lifts.

The skiing in general in Squaw is fairly uncompromising and, apart from the High Camp area, not for the faint-hearted. But if you enjoy a challenge, superb scenery and Californian sunshine, it is an excellent ski area, probably the best in California. It opened in 1949 with the world's first double chair-lift and two rope tows, and now has a total of 32 lifts,

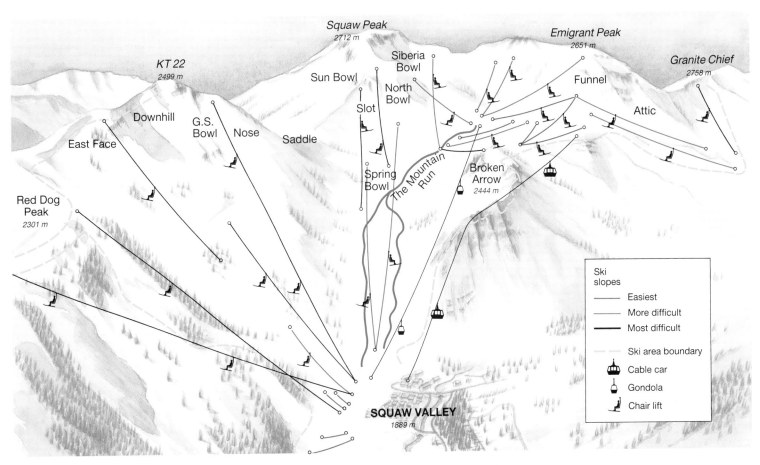

- Squaw Peak 2712 m
- Emigrant Peak 2651 m
- Granite Chief 2758 m
- KT 22 2499 m
- Siberia Bowl
- Sun Bowl
- Downhill
- North Bowl
- Funnel
- G.S. Bowl
- Nose
- East Face
- Saddle
- Slot
- Attic
- Red Dog Peak 2301 m
- Spring Bowl
- The Mountain Run
- Broken Arrow 2444 m
- SQUAW VALLEY 1889 m

Ski slopes

⎯⎯	Easiest
⎯⎯	More difficult
⎯⎯	Most difficult
– – –	Ski area boundary
🚡	Cable car
🚠	Gondola
🎿	Chair lift

Left: *The few beginners' slopes are on Emigrant Peak so that first-timers have the exhilarating pleasure of skiing at altitude with spectacular views of the High Sierras.*

Below: *Squaw Valley's skiing is not, in the main, for the faint-hearted and is for good skiers who enjoy a challenge, superb scenery and Californian sunshine.*

more than any other resort in the U.S.A. They include a 150-passenger tram. The lift network shifts almost 50 000 skiers an hour, meaning few lift-queues. The resort also has 27 snowcats, which, it claims, means 'au revoir killer moguls and Sierra cement (Californian snow at its worst)!' Rocks that begin to show through the melting snow at the end of the season are painted red and flattened later.

Squaw is a 45-minute drive on Interstate 80 from Reno, Nevada. It has an average snowfall of 1143cm (450in), and normally opens between mid-November and the end of May. The vertical drop is 869m (2850ft) and the longest run 4.8km (3 miles).

As for evening entertainment, Lake Tahoe and Tahoe City are close by, but the real nightlife is across the other side of the lake in Nevada at Stateline, a scaled-down Las Vegas with a huge gambling area. This can be reached by road—a 56km (35 mile) journey that takes you past the startlingly beautiful Emerald Bay area—or take a trip across the lake on the *Tahoe Queen* paddle steamer 'ski shuttle'.

TAOS

Taos is an enigmatic, beautiful, exotic, heady, mystical and compulsive cocktail. It is almost as though a little Swiss mountain village has been picked up in a whirlwind and transported to a high and remote part of New Mexico. Even the names of some of the hotels and apartments are in keeping with such an illusion: the Kandahar, Edelweiss and St Bernard, for example. The food is a somewhat exotic mix of American, European and Mexican. All this is hardly surprising since Taos Ski Valley was the brainchild of Ernie Blake, a German-born Swiss, who built it in 1955.

Taos is an extraordinary place. The scenery is spectacular, the sky the same deep shade of blue as seen at high altitude from Concorde, the sun sweltering and the air as fresh as the day it was made. D.H. Lawrence, who made his home on a nearby ranch in the mid-1920s, described the town thus: 'It was beauty, beauty absolute at any hour of the day, whether the perfect clarity of morning, or the mountains beyond the simmering desert

at noon, or the purple lumping of northern mounds under a red sun at night.'

It seems bizarre that a ski resort should exist here in such an arid, desert-dominated state, let alone tower above the desert sagebrush and terracotta buildings at such a height—2806m (9207ft). Once you have travelled there you will surely feel a very strong magnetic attraction to return.

The skiing is almost universally tough. At its best it is utterly spectacular—on the outer limits of what is manageable by a good recreational skier. Tucked away in the remote Sangre de Cristo mountains, Taos is not the easiest ski resort to get to. But for those who relish challenges the skiing, especially off the Ridge, make every hour and every mile of travel worthwhile.

Taos towers above the surrounding desert landscape, an incongruous outcrop of snow-clad peaks amidst the trees. Half of the runs are for experts and the rest for beginners and intermediates.

Much is made of Al's Run, named after Blake's friend Dr. Al Rosen, a ski instructor who used to ski with an oxygen tank strapped on his back after a heart attack. This is a very long and punishing mogul field right under the two main lifts up the

Ski slopes

━━━ Easiest

━━━ More difficult

━━━ Most difficult

◆━◆ Expert

○━○ Ski lift

mountain from the village. It is the first run you see when you arrive in the car park and it looks so disconcertingly steep that Blake erected a sign reassuring alarmed arrivals: 'Don't panic. From this point you can see only one thirtieth of Taos Ski Valley!' Mind you, there would be no guarantee that if they could see the other twenty-nine thirtieths, they would feel inspired with any great feeling of confidence. There is even a story about a truck-load of Texans who drove through the night to get here only to turn tail when they saw the skiing terrain. But it would be wrong to suggest that there is no skiing for beginners here, only that the expert trails are so dominant that you tend not to notice anything else.

Much of the best skiing at Taos is down fierce but exhilarating mogul chutes, often through the trees. From the ski patrol headquarters at the top of Lifts 2 and 6 you have a breathtaking choice. While beginners and unambitious intermediates can enjoy Bambi and Honeysuckle, serious skiers tense themselves for a whole series of gruelling descents. As they move down Bambi, the big challenges line up on the right: Walkyries Chute, Sir Arnold Lunn (one of Taos's

Kachina Peak
3804 m

TAOS

most difficult trails, dedicated to the British alpine skiing pioneer) and Lorelei, with its Werner Chute variant.

Lower down the mountain off Whitefeather and Porcupine, you will find more of the same: Rhoda's (named after Blake's wife); Inferno; a superb and little-used steep expert run through the trees called Jean's Glade, named after the ski school's technical director Jean Mayer, a former French junior champion who runs the St Bernard Hotel (his brother Dadou, who was also in the French junior team, runs the Edelweiss); and of course the run where we came in — Al's.

Across on the far edge of the ski area, reached by Kachina Lift, black runs like

High Noon, Lower Rubezahl and El Funko offer a similarly stiff challenge. Again, novices are not left out; they can survey some of the more startling skiing from the safety of Honeysuckle and Totemoff (named after Blake's long-time Indian friend and associate Pete Totemoff). And brave intermediates can take a brief leap into Streetcar, a less severe black that links two greens: Winkelried (the lower version) and Rubezahl, not to be confused with Lower Rubezahl which is for experts only.

Another little nest of greens includes Trip, Japanese Flag and the upper Winkelried run. Intermediates skiing on this part of the mountain will enjoy Hunziker

Bowl, Shalako, Baby Bear, Patton, Lone Star and Upper Totemoff.

It is hard to believe that there are only seven chair-lifts in such an exceptional ski resort, plus a couple of tows. But Taos has an impressive 72 trails, about half of which are expert runs. The other half are divided equally between beginners and intermediates.

I have saved the best until last. Hold on to your hat, and your skis. You'll have to if you want to experience the ultimate in Taos. A stiff walk up to Highline Ridge and West Basin Ridge brings you to a skiing Nirvana. Cutting a direct fall line through the trees are a dozen or so sublime descents that chute skiers will

Left: *Taos Ski Village is modern, with some 1000 beds although many skiers prefer to stay in the old adobe town of Taos, just under 20 miles (32km) away.*

Right: *Al's Run is named after Al Rosen, the instructor who skied with an oxygen tank after suffering a heart attack. It is a punishing mogul field leading back to the village.*

remember for the rest of their lives. Ernie Blake, who was involved in Allied Intelligence and helped to interrogate Goering and Speer, named some of these runs after the generals and officials involved in the unsuccessful attempt to assassinate Hitler in July 1944. Stauffenberg, Fabian and Oster all fan out from the High Traverse. If you turn right at the top of the Ridge, there are three exciting runs through the trees: St Bernard, Thunderbird and Hondo. In strong sunshine and deep powder, these descents are unforgettable. Because it takes quite an effort to reach them, these runs are pristine.

If you are fortunate, you might find Kachina Peak open, at the far end of Highline Ridge. This 3744m (12 481ft) mountain has no uphill transport except for skiers' legs. From time to time there have been suggestions that a lift might be built in order to give the resort an official vertical drop of 900m (3000 ft) — an increase of 120m. Blake always resisted this idea, saying: 'Americans are too lazy. The hike is good for them.' This has pleased die-hard skiers who don't want their special mountain turned into an instant mogul field.

There are only about 1000 beds in Taos Ski Village, and many skiers stay just under 32km (20 miles) away in the old adobe town of Taos (the name is based on the Tiwa phrase meaning 'place of the red willows'). There is a *pueblo* of 1500 Indians on the outskirts of Taos, which is 2327km (147 miles) from Albuquerque and one of America's more remote ski areas. The average annual snowfall is 820cm (323in).

Early in 1989, the late Ernie Blake's ashes were scattered on Al's and Snakedance by two Corsair fighter-bombers from the local Air Guard at Albuquerque. It confirmed what we all knew — Taos will always belong to Ernie.

VAIL AND BEAVER CREEK

For thousands of Europeans a visit to Vail, high in the Rocky Mountains, is their introduction to American skiing. It would be hard to find a better one. Sometimes criticized unjustly for its ersatz Austrian chalet architecture, the village has a pleasantly familiar European feel to it. But there the similarity ends. From the old village popcorn stand to the ritualistic 'have a nice day, now' which assaults you at every turn, this is America.

What is the largest ski resort in Colorado, and one of the most extensive on U.S. side of the Atlantic, is reached in less than two hours, depending on your income, by express bus or stretched limo from Denver's Stapleton airport. The stretched limo, complete with video, cocktail bar, pile carpet and a liveried chauffeur somewhere up front is clearly the more sensible option. It is certainly less fraught than a Geneva transfer coach and it is less expensive than it looks.

Vail lies in the Gore Creek Valley, named after Lord Gore, an eccentric Irish baronet who roamed the area for two years in the 1800s with a 40-strong entourage slaughtering game on a massive scale. The town itself gets its name from Charles Vail, the head of the Colorado State Highway department in the 1940s whose gang blasted a pass into the valley.

Traditionally it is the tribal summer home of the Ute Indians who were banished from most of Colorado after broken treaties and intermittent bloodshed led to the Meeker Massacre in 1879. According to legend the Utes retaliated by starting 'spite fires' which cleared the famous Back Bowls ready for an influx of the world's most devoted powder hounds 100 years later. But there is no real evidence for this.

The development of Vail was an indirect result of the Second World War.

The authorities at Vail believe that the future of uphill travel lies in high-speed detachable quad-chairs and have installed seven so far.

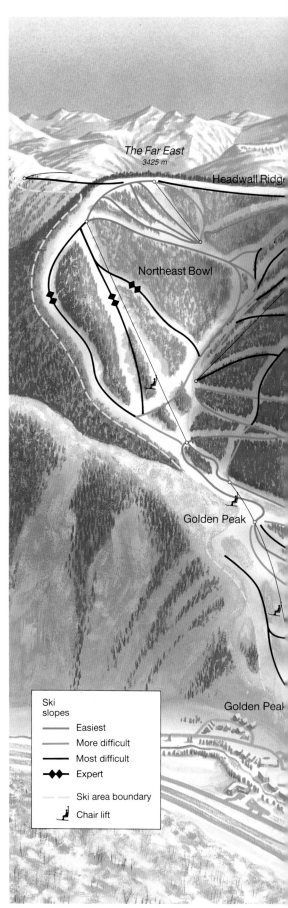

The Far East
3425 m

Headwall Ridge

Northeast Bowl

Golden Peak

Golden Peak

Ski slopes

——	Easiest
——	More difficult
——	Most difficult
◆◆	Expert
- - -	Ski area boundary
🚡	Chair lift

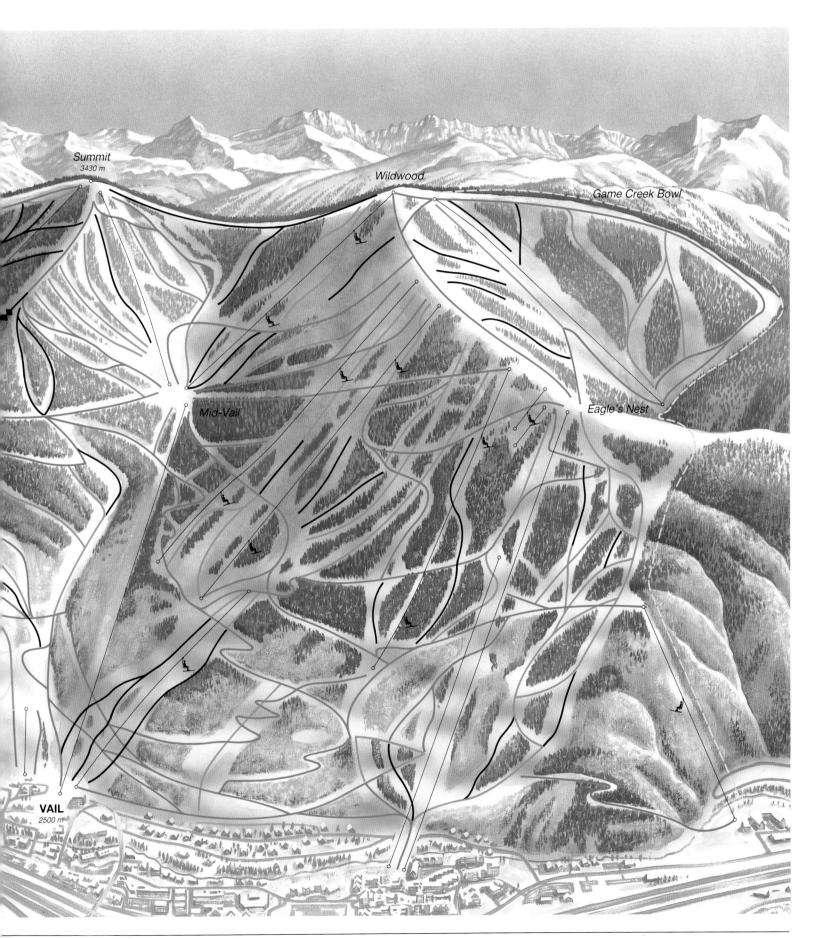

Summit
3430 m

Wildwood

Game Creek Bowl

Mid-Vail

Eagle's Nest

VAIL
2500 m

The Americans saw a need for alpine troops in the invasion of Nazi Europe and the 10th Mountain Division went into training at nearby Camp Hale. Ski trooper Peter Seibert was so impressed with the area that he came back after the war. Together with his friend Earl Eaton he climbed on skins to the top of Vail mountain and saw the wide open slopes invisible from the valley floor. Construction work began in 1962.

Today Vail sprawls over a large area through three exits from Interstate 70 and it is important when booking your holiday to establish clearly where you are staying. The smartest and the most convenient district is Vail Village with its traffic-free streets, designer shops and five-star hotels. Much of the package tour accommodation is at least a mile away to the west in Lionshead. Equally comfortable it may be, but apart from the fact that you have access to the same wonderful mountain, you are to all intents staying in a separate resort.

Luxury hotels like the Westin, situated even further west in Cascade Village, have been built as resorts within a resort, complete with their own ski-lift just outside the door which links into the main area. You return each night to your hotel by a trail inevitably named Westin Ho! The Westin has its own complimentary shuttle service into Lionshead and Vail, but after a day on the slopes few guests can be bothered to stray from its outdoor heated swimming pool, hot tub and adjoining health centre.

Back in Vail Village, The Lodge is the premier hotel and the place in which to see and be seen. Most of the designer ski suits which take their places at the bar after skiing are far too expensive for their beautiful inhabitants to allow them any contact with that cold wet white stuff. The Lodge is right in the centre and ideally placed for the Vista Bahn Express Lift, a detachable four-man chair which whisks you straight up to Mid-Vail. It is also beside the ski school which justly claims to be one of the best in America. There are also ski school meeting places in Golden Peak, Lionshead and Cascade Village.

The school enrolment system is excellent and is sure to be copied one day by a

European resort. The hardest part about joining ski school as an intermediate or potential expert is assessing your standard. People are either too modest — or the opposite! At Vail and at neighbouring Beaver Creek you are invited to watch a series of video clips of classes 1–9 and you can then decide which class is for you. (Remember that ski lessons in America are not cheap.)

Ski rental is generally excellent and you will find none of the ageing rental stock seen in some European shops. This is to obviate the possibility of enormous damages claims over accidents caused by worn or faulty equipment.

American resorts — Vail is among the biggest — are considerably smaller than European ski areas. For example, Vail has

20 lifts against Val d'Isere's 120, if you include Tignes. But the efficiency of the American lift system is beyond comparison. In Vail they believe the future of uphill travel lies in high-speed detachable quadruple chair-lifts and they have built seven of them. Coupled with eight other chairs, a gondola, and two drags the combined lift system has a superb capacity of 35 820 skiers an hour.

It is not true to say that queues never form here, but they do move swiftly and in an orderly and good-humoured fashion which amazes first time American skiers. You form up in groups of four for the quads and are marshalled aboard with a smile and a friendly comment — all too often sadly lacking in many French resorts. Skin-deep these good manners may

Left: Tamara McKinney took the gold medal for the USA in the women's combined event at Beaver Creek in the 1989 World Championships, to the delight of her compatriots.

Right: Ole Furseth won the men's slalom in the 1989 Championships. With the Alps starved of snow, European TV viewers watched enviously as racers competed in perfect conditions.

be, but skiing is meant to be about having a good time.

During the 1989 World Alpine Ski Championships which were held at Vail and Beaver Creek the locals confessed to being deeply shocked by the lack of courtesy Europeans showed to each other on the mountain. However, they were deeply impressed by the European skiers who took the snowbound Rockies by storm. The World Championships confirmed the re-emergence of the Austrians after several years of Swiss domination — but the Swiss still took the biggest haul of medals. Tamara McKinney sparked local interest by winning the women's combined gold for the U.S.A. Also defying the Swiss and Austrian domination, Norway's Ole Christian Furseth won the slalom

ahead of Marc Giradelli, the Austrian who races for Luxembourg. Giradelli bounced back to snatch the men's combined gold.

Vail Mountain is over 11km (7 miles) wide. The front or northern face offers an extraordinary variety of thoroughbred Colorado skiing. The tree line here is at around 3600m (12 000ft) as opposed to 2100m (7000ft) in Europe. This means that in bad weather the skier has a wealth of tree-lined trails offering good visibility. They are so laid out as to allow a group or family of different abilities to ski together. Every black diamond run (difficult) has a blue or green alternative which takes you down to the same lift. On the minus side, many of the trails through the trees do look rather similar.

The lift system fans out from Mid-Vail, a large mountain restaurant and lift station reached by the Vista Bahn Express Lift. The best skiing for near-novices and those seeking to gain a little high mountain confidence is unquestionably to be found on Lost Boy in Game Creek Bowl, reached from Mid-Vail by the Avanti Express Lift. Here, you can cruise all day down the easiest of long green runs until you feel up to facing the next challenge. The Meadows takes you serenely back to Mid-Vail, making sure you follow the signs and don't turn off for the black delights of Kangaroo Cornice, Look Ma or Challenge.

The Far East, at the other end of the mountain, is also good for beginners and all the runs off the Sourdough Lift are easy. You return to the village at the end of the day via Flapjack, Skid Road and Rudi's Run. Intermediates can tackle any of the runs around Mid-Vail without any possibility of running into something tougher than they had bargained for.

A preliminary word here about the quality of Colorado snow. Gather together any two wizened old powderhounds in any bar from Chamonix to Verbier and the talk will turn to the quality of Colorado snow: so light and dry that to ski it is a mystical, almost religious experience. The quality of the snow on the pistes is also excellent and the standard of grooming far exceeds any you will find in Europe.

If the snow is better, it is also gratifyingly easier. Because of the lack of humidity in the flakes the intermediate should find the skiing in the Rockies to be flattering. The truth is that such is the quality of conditions here that, unlike in Europe, you really don't need to apply great technique to get round the corners on a blue or even a red run. As a result you will find the vast majority of American skiers are locked on to the 'intermediate plateau' from which there is no way off unless they go back to the basics. But if you have been taught correctly to angulate and use your edges, you are in for a lot of fun here.

Northwoods and Northstar are ideal runs for the confident intermediate as well as some of what is on the other side of the mountain. Just what is on 'the other side of the mountain' is what draws good skiers from all over the world to Vail in the middle of the winter.

The Back Bowls, as they say around here, are 'where Vail is at'. Until 1989 the larger part of this extraordinary powder wilderness was only accessible to those who had the money to hire snowcats or the energy to do it the hard way on skins. But a $15 million expansion by George Gillet, the owner of Vail and Beaver Creek, virtually doubled the resort's skiable terrain and the Orient Express Lift whisks skiers back up again at high speed.

Sun Up Bowl, Tea Cup Bowl, Siberia Bowl, and both Inner and Outer Mongolia are all variations on a theme of open, often steep, powder skiing. And what a theme! Rasputin's Revenge, Wow and

Dragon's Teeth are among the best, but the choice is yours—1012 hectares (2500 acres) of some of the best powder in America. But the beauty is you really don't have to be an expert to master them.

Family skiing is the market to which Vail always, and with great success, aspires. A recent innovation is Slow Skiing Only areas where mother and father accompanied by small children can cruise together without danger of being cut up by out-of-control piste louts. The ski patrol monitors the areas carefully and anyone consistently infringing the rules will risk having their ski pass taken away and an escort off the mountain. Fort Whippersnapper on Golden Peak is a special children's ski play area in a forest of aspen trees with forts, mines and cabins remembering the Wild West.

Beaver Creek, Vail's smart, even exclusive neighbour is only 16km (10 miles) away but completely different in atmosphere. A large amount of money is now being injected by Vail Associates into this delightful little upscale resort which has the promise of becoming one of America's finest. Former United States President Gerald Ford has a home here and has done much to promote the resort both in America and around the world.

Above: *Both Vail and Beaver Creek have introduced Slow Skiing Only areas to accommodate family parties; there are also several quiet trails away from the centre.*

Right: *Vail is a pseudo-Austrian village set in Colorado's Rocky Mountains. Vail represents the best of American efficiency and hospitality.*

If Vail is the place in which to see and be seen, then Beaver is where you can safely hide yourself away on a traditional family holiday. If you are looking for nightlife, then look elsewhere. The resort is approached through a security gate 1.6km (1 mile) from town. Unless you have a special pass you have to park at the mouth of the canyon and take a shuttle bus into Beaver Creek itself.

The new Hyatt Hotel which opened for Christmas 1989 is definitely the smartest and ranks as one of the chain's greatest flagships. Some might prefer the less American atmosphere of the Inn at Beaver Creek, situated at the foot of the slopes. Both offer every luxury to be expected of top quality hotels including swimming pools and hot tubs as well as valet parking.

If you seek privacy and isolation from

your fellow man, try Trapper's Cabin which is situated two miles up the mountain in a stand of aspen trees, reached only on skis or by snowcat. Trapper's looks like an authentic turn-of-the-century trapper's cabin. In reality it was built in 1987 to sleep 10, with three bedrooms having en suite bathrooms. Your host 'R.G.' greets you with a magnum of champagne and some tasty rattlesnake *pâté* nibbles at the start of what will prove to be a memorable stay.

There is no telephone up here (well, actually there is, but only for emergen-

cies) and this is the place where the weary business mogul can genuinely take time off from the hectic pace of life, relax before a raging log fire, float in an outdoor hot tub or wander on snow-shoes around the mountainside. Guests are served exquisite gourmet meals by R.G. and few guests leave dissatisfied with this unique experience.

Beano's is also one of the great mountain restaurants of the world. Another 'authentic' cabin, it takes its name from settler Frank Bienkowksi who emigrated from Chicago around the turn of the

century, built his cabin and cleared a few fields to grow lettuce and rhubarb. One of the great line of old-timers who tamed Indian territory, Frank never got to eat the kind of gourmet fare dished up in his cabin these days. Beano's is, in fact, a private club for residents of the valley but arrangements can be made to dine there as a temporary member.

As for the skiing, it is reminiscent of many an Italian resort with plenty of interesting intermediate terrain with a few steep mogul runs like the Birds of Prey to tire out the experts.

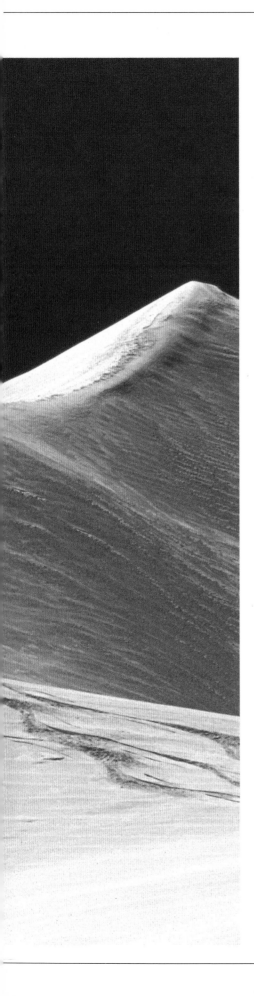

THE REST OF THE WORLD

Where there is snow, there is skiing – all over the world. The Alps and the Rockies are home to the world's best-known resorts but the fast development of ski slopes and attendant facilities in Australia has seen the introduction of Thredbo to the World Cup circuit. Similarly, Les Lenas in Argentina regularly hosts early-season World Cup races while speed skiers drop stone-like on the Flying Kilometre run above Portillo in Chile.

Gulmarg, set in the foothills of the Himalayas, provides the opportunity to sample a combination of heli-skiing and the Indian way of life while resorts have sprouted all over Japan as the result of the skiing having achieved cult status among the locals. New Zealand's snow fields offer both challenge and tranquillity.

With skiing available on every continent, the sport has achieved world-wide status. Televised World Cup races promote skiing's glamour but, for most, the enjoyment is simply being in the mountains with their friends.

THREDBO

Thredbo is to Australia what Aspen is to the U.S.A., Megeve to France and Cortina d'Ampezzo to Italy. It's upmarket, efficient, friendly and fun, though not exclusive in the European sense. Thredbo serves as a lesson to ski area developers worldwide. Due to the vision of its founders and sympathetic management, it has grown from very modest beginnings in 1957 to the slick World Cup venue that it is today.

In the mid-fifties the Snowy Mountains Authority constructed a road through the Thredbo Valley to Dead Horse Gap, known as the Alpine Way. Tony Sponar, a Czech ex-ski instructor working as a hydrographer with the Authority, saw the potential and together with four others formed a company which started the development. The resort has taken the best of North American ideas and style and superimposed them on the flanks of Australia's highest mountain (Mount Kosciusko, 2228m/7308ft) with a real village which, despite its youth, enjoys a truly alpine atmosphere and ambience.

In 1985, a ski area consultancy was commissioned to prepare a redevelopment feasibility study, and concluded that Thredbo had the potential to become the most outstanding ski area in the South Pacific region. Now that potential is being realized. The five-stage plan, now all but complete, includes extensive snowmaking facilities covering 55 hectares (136 acres), supertrails (top to bottom runs), quad

chairs and a purpose-built beginner area at roadside level.

Although the weather is often fickle and conditions can vary from boiler-plate ice to slush, in the main conditions are good and the skiing is remarkably extensive and interesting. Piste machines and snow cannons work all night to provide the best conditions possible and an excellent ski patrol is mindful of your safety. Mountain food is excellent and served in generous Aussie portions. Smiling staff, wood chips by the bottom stations to protect your skis and free plastic slipovers when it is wet are touches which mark Thredbo as a resort which tries hard.

The chair-lifts whisk you up through exquisitely coloured snowgum trees, endlessly creaking a counterpoint to the raucous calls of the currawongs (a sort of mountain crow) and the brightly coloured parakeets. If you are lucky you may catch sight of a wombat rooting, squint-eyed against the glare, for a tasty morsel amongst the trees (an international race at Thredbo was held up for 10 minutes on one occasion while one of these brown teddy-bear-like creatures made its leisurely way across the course).

Then you rise clear of the gums and are suddenly aware that the wide intermediate pistes are beautifully groomed, promising flattering turns. If you have taken the Crackenback chair you will pass Kareela Hut (book your lunch table early in bad weather) and arrive at Eagles Nest whence the flare run departs every Saturday evening at six. Good skiers can volunteer to join in this exciting experience; the view down the valley at night is wonderful.

Kurt's Downhill is Australia's longest and most challenging black run. Designed by the indefatigable Kurt Lance for the World Cup after many years of harassing the establishment, this is a worthy testimony to his tenacity. There is some

Above: *Thredbo has recently become a part of the World Cup circuit, it has extensive artificial snowmaking facilities and an excellent lift system.*

Opposite: *Designed to be the South Pacific's outstanding ski area, Thredbo's skiing is ranged around Australia's highest mountain, Mount Kosciusko.*

interesting skiing to be had in the trees, especially if the 'viz' is bad. Not to be missed is the off-piste run over to Dead Horse Gap. The ski school (multinational and professional) organizes a trip most days with champagne and chicken at the Gap and transport back to the village.

Accommodation varies from a four-star hotel and self-catering apartments to private lodges. All are expensive by European standards, as is the lift pass, but Australians are captive customers and they don't seem to mind too much.

Après-ski in Thredbo has something for everyone, but be warned—the Aussies play hard and it's difficult to have an early night! A sauna or outdoor Jacuzzi to start perhaps? Welcoming bars and excellent restaurants abound and there's lots of live music: piano bars to country and western to heavy metal. The choice is yours.

SAPPORO AND MORIOKA

Although skiing was first introduced to Japan by an Austrian army officer in 1911, it was not until the 1972 Winter Olympic Games in Sapporo that it really began to capture the attention of the Japanese people as a recreational sport. Today skiing is a booming business in Japan with an estimated 15 million skiers flocking to over 600 resorts during the winter months.

The Japanese have been strongly influenced by western ski culture and many resorts have tried to emulate the style of North American ski areas in particular. Western hotels, food and nightlife are synonymous with wealth and sophistication and skiing has become a status sport, attracting a fashion-conscious generation with more time and money to spend on leisure. Competition between resorts is rife and investment in state-of-the-art lift technology, night-time skiing and snow-making equipment has radically improved the quality of skiing in recent years.

While it is easy to opt for the familiarity of western accommodation, sampling the traditional customs of a *Ryokan*, a Japanese inn, makes skiing in the Far East a unique experience. You are provided with kimonos and slippers and sit on cushions on 'tatami' floors, drinking green tea. At the end of the day you can ease your aching muscles in a spacious communal bath — a Japanese ritual essential to *après-ski* — before falling asleep on a futon.

Meals at a *Ryokan* are often served in the room and are typically Japanese with fish, rice, soup and salads for both breakfast and dinner. Cheaper alternatives to *Ryokans* are *Minshukus*, family-run guest houses, while western-style 'pensions' are popular with younger people.

Après-ski varies from sophisticated nightclubs, bars and restaurants in the trendier resorts to more traditional forms of relaxation in quieter villages. Hot spring resorts known as *Onsen* are dotted throughout Japan's mountainous regions and you can experience the special pleasure of bathing outdoors in natural hot water even in the middle of winter.

The most popular and easily accessible

Above: *Skiing has become a status sport in Japan, attracting a fashion-conscious generation with time and money to spend on Western-influenced leisure activities.*

Right: *Not all lifts in Japan have attained state-of-the-art quality, but stiff competition among resorts means that the older systems are being replaced.*

skiing is found in central Honshu (the largest island) in the Nagano Prefecture, about three hours by express train north-west of Tokyo. Known as the Japan Alps, there are some 50 peaks which tower well over 2500m (8200ft), enjoying an abundance of fairly wet snow. To the north the string of resorts around Bakuba offer excellent alpine and cross-country skiing as well as floodlit slopes for night excursions.

East of Nagano lie Japan's two most fashionable resorts, Naeba — the St Moritz of the Far East — and Shiga Heights, Japan's largest ski area, both internationally renowned for their modern facilities and lively nightlife. There is a multitude of smaller resorts in the area, making this winter playground extremely popular with those who live in Tokyo, who flock here on weekends and during the holidays.

In the north-eastern part of the main island, known as Tohoku, unspoilt national parks offer some excellent skiing in beautiful surroundings. In the Yamagata and Iwate prefectures the trees are covered in thick layers of glittering frost, giving the landscape a surreal look. In Yamagata the famous resorts of Zao and Tengendai provide challenging skiing and unbeatable relaxation in natural hot springs. Summer skiing is available on Mount Gassan until late July. The city of Morioka in Iwate is host to the 1993 Alpine World Championships and the skiing facilities are of internationally high standards.

Sapporo, on the northern island of Hokkaido, is no stranger to international competition and serves as a gateway to the ski areas of Furano and Niseko, about two hours by express train from Sapporo. Both areas have night-time skiing and usually enjoy excellent powder snow.

The mixture of modern ski facilities, eastern cuisine and traditional culture make a ski trip to Japan an attractive, if somewhat expensive, alternative for those in search of new ski grounds to conquer. Finally a few words of advice: reserve your accommodation well in advance, be sure to take a good phrase book with you and hire your ski boots at home if you have large feet — the Japanese are not known for that particular attribute!

MOUNT HUTT

Left: *Mount Hutt's car park is a popular lunchtime rendezvous on sunny days – beware of the keas, parrot-like birds who like to join in picnics, uninvited!*

Below: *The phrase 'ski field' is appropriate at Mount Hutt where the skiing is set in a treeless bowl on the edge of the Southern Alps. It is one of the world's most dramatic locations.*

Mount Hutt in New Zealand's South Island is a high, sunny ski field set in one of the world's most dramatic locations. Itt lies in a treeless bowl on the edge of the Southern Alps which rise abruptly from the plains 2000m (6000ft) below. Every run has a spectacular view of chequerboard fields and the distant blue of the Pacific.

Although the proximity of the sea has a warming effect on New Zealand's climate, Mount Hutt has one of the best snow records in the region. The average depth of the snow base is more than 2.5m (8ft) and there is a long season lasting from early June until mid-November. Snow conditions change rapidly because of the strong sunshine and warm air flows from the Pacific, so it is not unusual to ski fresh powder and spring snow on the same day, even on the same run.

The lift system consists of four T-bars, 2 pomas and a triple chair with a vertical drop of 600m (1969ft), the longest in the Southern Hemisphere. There are also several learner tows. This is not the biggest ski area in New Zealand, but its top station at 2075m (6808ft) and its steep runs including a Federation Internationale de Ski (F.I.S.) approved course have made it a favourite training ground for names like Ingmar Stenmark, Cindy Nelson and the Mahre twins. Good skiers will particularly enjoy the Towers and South Basis runs, and they can also take advantage of the excellent heliskiing. Mount Hutt Air operates daily from the car park at the foot of the lifts and opens up exciting terrain in the Arrowsmith and Ragged Ranges. Non skiers and beginners can try what the New Zealanders call 'flight-seeing' by helicopter.

Costs are generally lower in New Zealand than in Europe or the United States and some services offer good value for money. The Mount Hutt ski school, which was founded by Austrians, has very reasonable rates for private lessons. Its group classes—a mix of Arlberg instruction and Kiwi good humour—are also fun, and there's a kindergarten for three- to five-year-olds. The mountain restaurant, on the other hand, is a disappointment with a menu limited to the ubiquitous meat pie and chips. Even worse in a country famous for its fine wines, the pie has to be washed down with a milk shake because Mount Hutt is a teetotal ski field. Gourmets can of course bring their own picnics, and in fine weather this accounts for the popularity of the car park as a meeting place for lunch. The car park is also popular with keas, high mountain parrots which amuse visitors with their comical appearance and droll way of hopping around the picnickers begging for scraps. The amusement lasts, that is, until the visitors discover the birds' mischievous habit of pecking to bits anything made of plastic or canvas—including expensive ski bags.

The reason for the ban on booze becomes all too clear at the end of the day when drivers have to negotiate 13km (8 miles) of hairpin bends to get back to the tollgate at the bottom of the mountain.

The resort management wanted to put in a cable-car for access to the ski field when it was built in the early 1970s, but restrictions on imports forced them to have a road instead. This is not the ideal solution, but the road is well built and well run so it is seldom closed even in heavy snowfalls. There is also a shuttle bus for skiers without chains on their cars, and coach services from nearby towns.

The best place to stay is the small town of Methven 11km (nearly 7 miles) from the tollgate. It's a typical New Zealand country town where Kiwi hospitality more than makes up for the 'dry' café on the mountain. The choice of accommodation ranges from an old-fashioned hotel or a modern ski lodge down to cut-price bed and breakfasts or a youth hostel. Methven can get booked up in the high season between mid-July and mid-September, but it is also possible to stay in Christchurch, the capital of the South Island. Christchurch has an international airport and is only an hour's drive from the base of Mount Hutt, which makes the ski field one of the easiest to reach in the Southern Hemisphere.

GULMARG

Sylvain Saudan's heli-ski operation is in sharp contrast to Gulmarg's relaxed atmosphere and the potential for powder addicts in the surrounding mountains is enormous.

Sometime before breakfast a Kashmiri hill man comes softly to your room with tea and fresh wood for the sweet-smelling stove. Without the renewed warmth of the stove it would take great resolve to get out of bed. Morning in Gulmarg is far removed from the centrally-heated comfort of the Alps. It is not the only difference. Where else would you get a personal bearer to carry your skis to the lifts?

The Himalayan resort of Gulmarg is about 90 minutes' drive from Srinagar, capital of the north-west Indian state of Jammu and Kashmir. Though its piste skiing is limited, the potential for powder addicts in the surrounding mountains is enormous. The Swiss-born adventure skier Sylvain Saudan, who has been running a heliskiing operation in the area, believes there could be as many as 2000 descents within helicopter range.

Gulmarg itself is a former hill station used during the British Raj as an escape from the heat of summer. The old club house with its trophy boards is still there. So is the golf course, where you land if

you use the helicopter link with Srinagar airport. Before India's independence the last leg of the journey was by pony along a forest trail, and though there is now a road all the way, the place still feels very remote.

The resort, with its view of distant Nanga Parbat, is at 2550m (8366ft). Snow falls between November and the end of May. Temperatures are reckoned to be broadly similar to Europe's and, as in Europe, the lower slopes sometimes suffer from poor conditions. At the last count there were seven lifts—up-to-date information is difficult to pin down—of which most are gentle drags on slopes strictly for beginners, and one a chair which also serves a woodland trail of very moderate pitch.

On the slopes of Apharwat, however, where members of the Ski Club of India would walk up between the wars, a new gondola lift has been built. This was planned to reach an eventual altitude of 4134m (13 563ft), giving a fine descent of about 10km (6 miles), with fairly steep possibilities close to the top.

Do not expect sophisticated medical facilities in the resort. There is a hospital in Srinagar. When last seen, there appeared to be little or no downhill ski equipment for hire worth considering.

For accommodation the best choice is the Highland Park Hotel, where rooms are in chalet terraces away from the main building. The hotel has a pleasant bar and lounge, where you may settle down by a fire with a dish of hot cashew nuts and a Kingfisher beer, and a restaurant where, even if the meat may sometimes be a touch scrawny, the parathas are wonderful.

Aside from those tacking a few days in Gulmarg on to a wider-ranging tour of India, it is to off-piste skiers that the Kashmir Himalayas are most likely to appeal. Some experts rate the powder skiing even better than that in the Canadian Rockies, though it is essential to bear in mind the risks on slopes which have seen few, if any, skiers, and on no account should you ski without an avalanche transceiver.

If you were heliskiing you might stay in Srinagar, which is 55 minutes by air from Delhi. Saudan has lodged his clients at the Centaur hotel on Dal Lake, for example. It would be tempting to stay on the lake's famous houseboats but though a few days on the water are strongly recommended, the houseboats are too difficult of access to be practical for skiers.

Sadly, Jammu and Kashmir has seen separatist violence in recent times. Muslims and Hindus in this long disputed and volatile border area were at each others' throats, Srinagar was under curfew, and the medium-term future of skiing there looked, to say the least, very uncertain. But at least the raw material—that wonderful terrain and powder snow—is there for development, one day.

GUDAURI

Skiing, Soviet style, is going through a period of dramatic change. *Glasnost* has been well and truly marked with the creation of a brand new ski resort in Georgia which not only sparked off a good deal of media interest but gained an instant international clientele.

Opened in 1988, Gudauri is undoubtedly a product of the new climate in the Soviet Union, having been co-planned, co-built and co-financed as a result of a unique, *sans frontières* agreement between the forward-thinking Georgian Ministry for Tourism and an Austrian tourist consultancy.

Situated at 2000m (6560ft) in the Soviet republic of Georgia and originally a postal station, Gudauri's southern location (on the same latitude as Naples) gives it an enviable winter climate. Blessed with open, gently sloping snowfields, the resort has been created to use the natural terrain to its best advantage. It lies high above the Aragva River Canyon amid some breathtaking mountain scenery, in a wind-protected valley. It enjoys plentiful sunshine and abundant snowfall, giving an average depth of 1.5m (nearly 5ft). The snow remains good throughout the long season from November until May.

This purpose-built centre is now the most modern and well-equipped winter resort in the Soviet Union. Its main accommodation is the Austrian-built four-star Sport Hotel Gudauri. The ski-lifts are modern, high-speed Dopplemayr chairs and the pistes are manicured to top European standards. The skiing possibilities from this flagship of Soviet resorts are seemingly endless.

The immediate ski area extends across a wide, go-anywhere snowfield, served by four chair-lifts (three triples and a quad) that rise from the very back door of the Sport Hotel, taking skiers up to 3000m (9840ft). Here, the skyline boasts peaks equal to Gudauri's own summit station and above, including Kazbek as well as Europe's highest mountain, Elbrus at 5642m (18 511ft).

The main ski area lies above the tree line and provides splendid beginner and

Cross-country skiing is a feature of a Gudauri's winter sports scenario. A combination of plentiful snow and sunshine provides good skiing from November to May.

intermediate slopes. The resort has already hosted the first ever international downhill ski race in the Soviet Union, the women's downhill, forming part of the women's Europa Cup circuit, and is shortlisted to host the next World Junior Championships.

At the top of the second-stage chair is a mountain restaurant, run as an offshoot of the Sport Hotel. From the top station there are numerous flattering slopes, ideal for improving technique, all feeding back to a lift or right down to the door of the hotel. Alternatively, better skiers can explore the large, varied 'back area' with a choice of descents eventually linking with a road where the hotel bus waits to take skiers back to base. In addition, the hotel ski guides operate a programme of day ski tours which are suitable for people of good intermediate ability upwards.

Almost certainly the most talked-about aspect of Gudauri, other than its unique Austro-Soviet appeal, is the opportunity to ski above and beyond the scope of the ski-lifts on the first-ever Soviet heliski programme. The heliskiing operates directly from the grounds of the hotel and packages are booked in connection with accommodation in the Sport Hotel and must be booked in advance. It is not necessary to be an accomplished off-piste skier to sign up for the Gudauri heliski

itinerary as both expert and introductory packages are featured. The latter includes instruction in basic powder skiing through to the techniques required to cope with the more challenging, unprepared slopes. Two large helicopters, operated by Aeroflot, ferry skiers to the snowy wilderness. All groups are accompanied by qualified Austrian guides, and following a few problems during the last few winters, extra safety measures are being introduced.

Staying in the Sport Hotel Gudauri gives you all the modern creature comforts expected in a top-category hotel. There are three bars, shops, a large elegant dining room, self-service lunchtime restaurant, sun terraces and a very well-run sports centre offering two full-size indoor tennis courts, superb swimming pool, sauna, whirlpool, bowling alley, fitness room and massage. The hotel operates its own ski school and guide programme with English-speaking, Austrian instructors.

The mainly Georgian hotel staff speak English and German and are supported by a team of Austrian and Hungarian consultant staff who, as well as taking care of the more international needs of the hotel's administration, operate a hotel trades training school.

Gudauri is reached by flying to Moscow and onwards by Aeroflot to Tbilisi, the traditional capital of Georgia. The remaining 120km (75 miles) up to Gudauri takes around two hours on what was formerly the Transcaucasian military road.

The Kartvelis, as the Georgians call themselves, are a proud, romantic and artistic people. They have their own language and alphabet and the women are as beautiful as the men are handsome. A visit by a Georgian dance troupe is a not-to-be-missed occasion on the hotel's entertainment calendar. All modern, international communications are available from the hotel. Drinks and all incidental items are paid for in special Gudauri roubles, money vouchers that are purchased from the hotel cash desk.

The Publishers wish to thank the following photographers and organisations for their kind permission to reproduce their photographs in this publication:

AFLO Foto Agency 8–9, 18, 72–3, 80, 82, 88, 101, 104–5, 124, 125, 131, 132, 136t, 144, 150, 152, 157, 169, 171, 172, 180–1, 182–3, 187; AGE Fotostock 22, 44, 46, 62, 70, 75, 83, 110; Alberta Tourist Office 134t; Allsport 28, 37, 74, 95, 102, 103, 116, 133, 136b, 176, 177; Allsport/Vandystadt 1, 2–3, 4, 45, 63, 67, 109; Austrian National Tourist Office 12–13, 16, 23, 27, 29, 33, 34, 36; Colorsport 20–1, 35, 112, 115; Fleet Public Relations 146; French Government Tourist Office 53, 58 60–1, 68, 72; Garmisch Partenkirchen/Kölbl 76; Hardwick Press & Publicity/Vacances Elite 188; Italian State Tourist Office 81; Japan National Tourist Office 184, 185; Kandahar Ski Club 32; Lake Placid Commerce & Visitors Bureau 162; Les Menuires Tourist Office 55; Lillehammer Foto og Bildearkiv/Jarle Kyetil Rolseth 90, 91; Erna Low Consultants 56, 57; Saalbach/Hinterglemm 14, 17; Scottish Tourist Board/Paul Tomkins 92, 93; Ski Club of Great Britain 48; Ski Shoot 24, 26, 31, 38, 39, 40, 42, 43, 49, 51, 52–3, 54, 64, 65, 66, 78, 84, 86–87, 87r, 94, 97,98, 99, 105r, 106, 114, 118, 118–9, 121, 122, 126–7, 134b, 138, 140, 142, 143, 147–7, 148, 150–1, 153, 154, 158, 159, 160, 161, 164, 166, 167, 168, 173, 178, 179, 186; Society of Cultural Relations with Russia 189; Swiss National Tourist Office 108, 123.